WELSH VERSE

Translations by
TONY CONRAN

seren

Seren is the book imprint of
Poetry Wales Press Ltd
Wyndham Street, Bridgend
Wales

British Library Cataloguing in Publication Data

A record for this title is available from the CIP Office
ISBN 1-85411-081-0

*The publisher acknowledges the financial assistance of the
Arts Council of Wales*

Cover Painting: 'Five Stars' by Anthony Evans

Printed by WBC Book Manufacturers Ltd
Bridgend

CONTENTS

CONTENTS

– 6 –

CONTENTS

CONTENTS

CONTENTS

CONTENTS

CONTENTS

CONTENTS

Preface to Third Edition

Most of these translations first appeared as *The Penguin Book of Welsh Verse* in 1967. When Seren Books republished them in 1986, I expanded the historical introduction to cover developments in the twentieth century, added an appendix on the complex metres that are so much a feature of the poetry, and included more translations, such as a selection of folksongs, Ann Griffiths' hymns and some contemporary work. [For this third edition, I have added a few early poems associated with Urien Rheged and mostly attributed to Taliesin.]

I am grateful to Dr Gruffydd Aled Williams for reading the appendix on Welsh metrics, for pointing out my mistakes in this rather complicated field, and for his encouragement. He is not, of course, responsible for any errors that may remain. I am also grateful to Phyllis Kinney for correcting me about the musical side of the Welsh tradition.

Acknowledgements

When these translations first appeared as *The Penguin Book of Welsh Verse*, they were published with my name as translator, in association with J.E. Caerwyn Williams. The translations were evolved through several processes of collaboration between myself and Professor Caerwyn Williams and his former colleagues of the Welsh Department, Bangor. Sometimes they gave me prose cribs of the poems, which I then used as the basis of my work. In other cases, I submitted my own literal versions to them for corrections and comment. When I had completed a translation, in all cases they looked through it, correcting howlers and suggesting alternative reading. Nonetheless, I alone am to be held responsible for the poem that resulted. My purpose was to make poetic sense, in English, of these sometimes very difficult poems; and to that end I have often departed further from the literal meaning than would easily be justifiable were my purpose purely scholarly (though, in all fairness to myself, I should add that I tried hard to be literal). I should add that much the same is true of the opinions expressed in the Introduction: the Welsh Department were most generous in giving me their time and scholarship, but they felt, with me, that I should be allowed to give my own critical impressions of Welsh poetry as a stranger and an outsider. This fact, I think, gives the Introduction such value as it possesses.

While we were finishing the book, Professor Williams left Bangor to become Professor of Irish at Aberystwyth. He joins with me in wishing to thank all the people who have helped with these translations, particularly Mr Brinley Rees, Dr Geraint Gruffydd, Mr Bedwyr Lewis Jones and Dr Gwyn Thomas of the Welsh Department, Bangor, and Mr Gerald Gerald Morgan, Mr Gerallt Jones and Dr Harri Pritchard-Jones. I would also like to thank Mr Anthony East for making suggestions about the phrasing of the English.

For permission to publish poems in this anthology, acknowledgement is made to the following:

For Euros Bowen, to the author and Hugh Evans & Sons; for

ACKNOWLEDGEMENTS

W.J. Gruffydd, to Hughes & Son; for I.D. Hooson to Gee & Son; for D. Gwenallt Jones to the author and J.D. Lewis & Sons; for T. Gwynn Jones, to Hughes & Son; for Saunders Lewis, to the author, Christopher Davies Ltd. and J.D. Lewis & Sons; for A. Llywelyn-Williams, to the author and Gee & Son; for J. Morris-Jones, to the Misses Morris-Jones; for R. Williams Parry, to Gwasg y Bala and Gee & Son; for T.H. Parry-Williams, to the author and to J.D. Lewis & Sons; for Thomas Richards, to Miss Marian Elias; for Waldo Williams, to J.D. Lewis & Sons; for Gwyn Thomas, to the author and Gee & Son; for Nesta Wyn Jones, to the author and J.D. Lewis & Sons.

The editors and publishers of *Welsh Verse* have made every effort to contact with copyright holders of poems included in this anthology, but in some cases this has not been possible. The publishers therefore wish to thank the authors or copyright holders of those poems which are included without acknowledgement above.

Introduction

In the first instance I think it is wiser to treat Welsh poetry as something *sui generis*, a product of a civilization alien to our own. Otherwise, you may find in Old Welsh a somewhat bloodless version of Anglo-Saxon, and in the great classical masters of the fourteenth and fifteenth centuries an interesting but eccentric by-path of the Middle Ages. This approach has some truth in it – after all, no one in Wales could be unaware of either the Anglo-Saxons or the rest of Western Christendom: but it ignores fundamental differences in approach, in purpose and in style. Welsh poetry (as it has come down to us) begins not long after the Romans left Britain; and from then on, at least until the sixteenth century, it develops within a single expanding tradition, metrically, thematically and stylistically distinct from the rest of Europe. There is nothing comparable in Welsh to the great culture-shift, by which both Old German and Anglo-Saxon adapted themselves to Romance standards to become Middle High German and Middle English respectively. Tudur Aled, in the sixteenth century, shares with Taliesin, in the sixth, a common approach to verse composition that would be hard to parallel (except in Ireland) anywhere else. Nor is this continuity the mere conservatism of a backward culture. The tradition developed, both from within and in response to innovations from outside, often with quite startling speed. Like any culture of such age and resilience Welsh sometimes resisted change; but its inertia has surely been grossly over-stressed. One does not rightly accuse Chinese poetry, for instance, of failing to be up-to-date because its basic metrical structure, or even its main subject-matter, did not change for a thousand years. Certainly a poetry which contains in a single century two such mutually opposed and revolutionary poets as Dafydd ap Gwilym and Siôn Cent should not have to be defended on this score. The temptation, of course, is to regard such poets as exceptions which prove the rule, deriving their revolutionary impetus from outside Wales and leaving the whole tradition in much the same state as they found it. But this is not so. Both poets took what suited them from the Mediterranean-centred cultures around them; but both started from a position well within the Welsh tradition, and neither made any attempt to write in Welsh the sort of poem that the Normans, for example, brought to England. There are no Welsh *cansos* or *ballades*. Nor is it true that later Welsh poets rejected Dafydd ap Gwilym's innovations, or with a sigh of relief turned back to their old habits after he had gone. They adopted his metre, the *cywydd*, wholesale; and, I believe, his example was the yeast that worked its way even into formal ode and elegy, and brought about the humanizing classicism of the fifteenth century.

The Welsh tradition started in the sixth century: this was when Welsh, which is a largely analytic and non-inflected language about on the same evolutionary level as French, crystallized out from Brythonic or British Celtic, which was more or less comparable to Latin. But it had its roots much further back, in primitive Indo-European magic concerning the making of kings. The poet was one who, at the coronation of the king and at his funeral, and at sundry important events in between, chanted the praises of the king, invoked ancestral strength and piety, and unified (in a kind of communion-rite of song) the whole tribe around its leader. This *magical* content of Welsh poetry waxed and waned in importance; but it was always there, and it was always acknowledged. Sometimes, as in the lesser poets of the thirteenth century, its demands seem the only interest the writer holds out to us; elsewhere, as in Guto'r Glyn, they are transcended in very large measure, so that friendship rather than king-making is the dominant context of his art. But even in the fifteenth century, Henry Tudor owed a great deal of his support in Wales to the 'prophecies' of the poets, saluting his incursion with the age-old magic of verse.* Much of the intentional obscurity of Welsh poetry springs from this magical origin. The spell, as an art-form, is not usually conducive to sweetness and light. A whole vocabulary, even a whole syntax, derived from archaic Welsh, was later joined by an elaborate heraldic mumbo-jumbo in the spell-binder's box of tricks. In general, one might hazard the judgement that Welsh poetry is at its most civilized and mature

*This is not to ignore the distinction between praise and prophecy, which is always maintained. But the two genres seem to me clearly cognate.

whenever conditions enabled the poets to transcend the magical element most completely.

Transcend, please note, not forget or discard. One goes to Welsh poetry, it is true, not primarily for its anthropological interest but for its unique vision and enactment of the good life; but the dominant theme, the over-riding symbol of that good life, is always the hospitality extended by the great to the small. In this, of course, it agrees with New Testament parables. It is a personal relationship that is at its centre, the relationship of the lord as host to the poet as guest: and in its origin, this was a relationship of tribal king to tribal bard, or poet-priest. By itself, therefore, the magical side of Welsh poetry may be very largely a reactionary and de-humanizing bore, tending to appear naked only at moments of stress, something to fall back on in time of trouble. But as part of the Welsh poet's background, as a rich undercurrent to his career and work, it was invaluable. It gave him a traditional status in society, a place in the councils of the great; and, through him, it gave that society a dignity and an aesthetic ideal. This was his 'office' in the world – to praise the great lords. But a full understanding of what a complex and civilized poet like Guto'r Glyn meant by this 'office' is not won so easily. We live in an anti-aristocratic age. It is hard for us to imagine praise of a lord without it being also downright flattery. We distort the image of the dignified *prifardd*, the chief poet, into a toadying sycophant, parasitic for his bread upon the favours of petty lordlings. This distortion is not peculiar to us: we find Siôn Cent, in the early fifteenth century, at a high peak of Welsh literary history, echoing our distaste to the letter; and somewhat later, the Renaissance humanists had some hard things to say about the poets who flattered their patrons. Even so, it is a distortion. The *prifardd* keeps his mystery still, too proud to beg, too traditional to flatter. For consider: if you want to flatter someone, you play upon his weaknesses, you learn what are his private daydreams, what he would like to be good at. You tell Nero how well he plays the fiddle. The flatterer has to engage his would-be patron's interest by the originality of his fawning. Flattery, by its very nature, is a competitive business. But when a president of a cricket club retires, a good eulogy of him, expressed perhaps as a vote of thanks, will not materially differ from every other good eulogy of every other retiring president of cricket clubs. What makes a eulogy uniquely applicable is much less important than what makes it a eulogy at all. The Welsh poets pass this test with flying colours. If they are good poets, of course, their eulogies have individuality enough: but what is involved is artistic individuality, belonging to themselves and their art, not a piece of special pleading designed to curry favour with idiosyncratic patrons. Not that the particular is forgotten, any more than a highly successful season is forgotten in the vote of thanks to the cricketer. But the relevance of the particular to the general praise is determined almost entirely on publicly admitted or purely artistic criteria, not by private insinuation or subterfuge.

This reference to votes of thanks, however, brings into the open another source of our distaste. The ritual act of praise is suspect in our culture, or at least in the more literate reaches of it. We feel embarrassed by it, we want to laugh, we are bored, we don't trust its sincerity. Frank O'Connor (who ought to know better – one of his most brilliant translations is of an Irish court-poem to Hugh Maguire) comments that "Court poetry is a peculiar and unattractive form, and to me always reminiscent of an illuminated address or a song for Reverend Mother's feast day."* English readers are more likely to be reminded of Theseus's good-humoured indulgence of Bottom and his 'rude mechanicals'. This intellectual snobbery (for the whole tone of voice in which we mock betrays its deep-seated class-roots) is a product of the bourgeoisie's distrust of ritual as being, *par excellence*, the art of community living – consider the spontaneous rituals on a football pitch – and as therefore conflicting with its own cult of individual fulfilment and sincerity. It is significant that in modern psychoanalysis, *ritualistic* is a term describing the symptoms of anxiety-neurosis. But if we are honest with ourselves, we find a great many social situations are (or would be) richer and more satisfying for a touch of ritual; and that there arises in us some kind of need for eulogy, even for formal eulogy, on a number of occasions where, in our culture, such a need is likely to go unsatisfied. For praise is a difficult art: it is usually done badly, or not done at all. It is the frustration that it is not done well, not the thing itself, that is embarrassing. Formal praise, if it is well executed and right for

Kings, Lords, and Commons, p.41. Try meditating on the *Wreck of the Deutschland* with this infamous judgement in mind.

the occasion, can be a most deeply satisfying thing. I was no particular lover of Churchill, but when President Kennedy spoke making him a citizen of the United States I confess I was moved to the depths. Nor was this a sentimental response to rhetoric: for once in a way, the art of praise was being well done, and rightly done. And it was the art that moved one, and the focus it gave to sentiments demanding to be expressed: just as an actor's art is not merely to delineate but also to channel our feelings. These are public matters, and public arts: in private life the need for praise also arises, but perhaps it is there less formal eulogy than warmth of commendation. In most cultures, however, the distinction between private and public is less firmly drawn than in our own; and this was certainly the case in medieval Wales.

The surprising thing about the Welsh poets is not, in fact, that they composed formal eulogies of their patrons – that is a world-wide occurrence, from Peru to Bangkok. Their uniqueness consists in the centrality they gave to this function, in a culture of such high sophistication and over so long a period of time. The proof of the pudding is in the eating: we can now see, because the Welsh poets are there to prove it, that the poetry of the Good Life can as well rise out of the formal eulogy as anywhere else.

Most of the earliest Welsh poetry that is extant was written on the borders of Scotland and England during the time of troubles following the withdrawal of the Roman legions from Britain. It was roughly contemporary with the great Celtic saints and with the denunciations of Gildas against the wickedness of the British kings. The Anglo-Saxons had already conquered large tracts of South and East Britain, and there the British were, quarrelling among themselves and listening to the vanities of their poets, instead of keeping to the narrow path of Christian unity and obedience. The Anglo-Saxons, said Gildas, were a judgement on such vicious frivolity.

To call these sixth-century poets 'Welsh' is really an anachronism. They were Britons – and might even have still thought of themselves as Romans. King Arthur was no more than a generation or two away from Aneirin and Taliesin; and many of the names mentioned by those poets are Welsh in form, certainly, but Latin by derivation. But the chief areas of Romanization had been the lowlands of the south and east, the very areas now overrun by the Germans. The hilly lands of the north and west remained frontier provinces ruled from military garrisons. Their populations had been left very much to their own devices during the Roman occupation, provided they kept the peace and paid their taxes. The local chieftains continued as petty lords, conscious of the power and attraction of Rome, yet largely Celtic in language and culture.

Now, however, these local chiefs had been separated from Christian Rome by a solid wedge of German paganism, alien to them and preying upon their lands. From Northumbria to the gates of Rome barbarism was triumphant. The Celts were no longer a savage fringe to the Empire; they were now the only surviving representatives of Roman civilization for thousands of miles. In this extreme danger, the local chieftains, so long reliant on the legions, proved incapable of unity among themselves. Various attempts seem to have been made to make Britain an empire on its own. All of them failed: as always in such a situation, the backwoods misunderstood the nature of metropolitan power. The conversion of Ireland to Christianity, which took place during these same centuries of stress, only intensified the problem: for Ireland, now a centre of this beleaguered piece of Christendom, had never been Roman at all. The tendency to look back on the Roman Empire as the only model of civilization was henceforth increasingly counter-balanced by new centres of growth along the former frontiers. The Rhine and Rhône valleys were to become the new axis of Western Europe; but that had not yet happened, and in the meanwhile Ireland and Northumbria – at first British, then English – were dominant on the cultural scene.

And particularly, of course, the newly Christianized Ireland. Irish poetry of these early centuries, both in Latin and Irish, is without parallel in the Dark Ages. It combines the naïve urbanity of a saint caught indulging himself with the song of a blackbird with a sense of history so erudite that it sometimes seems drenched with the sadness of the past:

> The fort over against the oakwood, it was Bruidge's, it was
> Cathal's, it was Áed's, it was Ailill's, it was Conaing's, it was
> Cuilíne's, and it was Máel Dúin's. The fort remains after
> each king in turn, and the hosts sleep in the ground.
> (*trans. Meyer, amended Gerard Murphy*)

INTRODUCTION

Christianity and Paganism were struggling for the soul of Ireland; yet Irish poetry everywhere reflects a cultural security that had known neither Roman conquest nor Roman withdrawal. The poets are free to let their imaginations wander over the struggle for the conversion of Ireland in a way that was not possible elsewhere. Oisin and Patrick taunt each other with what they have done; the spouse of God rejoices that the kings have perished and the Church remains –

> Ailill the king is vanished,
>   Vanished Croghan's fort,
> Kings to Clonmacnois
>   Come to pay their court.
> In quiet Clonmacnois
>   About Saint Kieran's feet
> Everlasting quires
>   Raise a concert sweet.
> (*trans. Frank O'Connor*)

In other parts of Europe, Christianity degraded the old gods and heroes to the level of shadows and things that go bump in the night. Only in Ireland were the heroes and poets permitted to have their say in the green light of day, with the woods and the seashores around them, and their scorn and their doom equally upon their own lips.

Perhaps the most startling feature of old Irish poetry is its tenderness. A blackbird sings, and a hermit writes in the margin of his book,

> The little bird which has whistled from the end of a bright-yellow bill: it utters a note above Belfast Loch – a blackbird from a yellow-heaped branch.

Or Colum Cille (it was fabled) says of the town he loved,

> This is why I love Derry, it is so calm and bright; for it is all full of white angels from one end to the other.

Or again, leaving Ireland, Colum Cille is supposed to have spoken:

INTRODUCTION

> There is a blue eye which will look back at Ireland; never
> more shall it see the men of Ireland nor her women.
> (*All trans. Gerard Murphy*)

When we return to Welsh poetry the difference is marked. It is
rare that either Taliesin or Aneirin, the two poets of the sixth
century whose works have come down to us, refer to anything
except the immediate past. They seem to inhabit an immensely
important present, which, with its troubles, has completely
overwhelmed their memories. There are no meditations on the
fall of Roman Britain; there is only one vague and possibly
corrupt reference to Arthur. Taliesin says, in the poem on 'The
Battle of Argoed Llwyfain', that for a whole year he will sing to
the triumph of Urien and his host: I am sure that an Irish poet
would have regarded this as niggardly in the extreme! It cannot
be entirely that this utter preoccupation with the present is due to
the selectiveness of the texts that have survived. A thousand lines
or so of Irish poetry of this period (or for that matter of Welsh
poetry of a later time) would have revealed twenty times more
historical or legendary preoccupations than this poetry exhibits,
no matter how randomly the selection was made.

In Welsh, Christianity seems to have been taken for granted
right from the start. But, compared with Irish, what a joyless
religion it is! Aneirin says of the young men who died at Catraeth
that

> Although they might go to shrines to do penance,
> This much was certain, death would transfix them.

In one lyric (admittedly much later) the anonymous poet seems
to equate Christ with the sorrows of life:

> In the fine treetops when cuckoos sing,
>   My sadness is greater:
> Smoke smart, manifest sleep-lack
> For my kinsfolk gone to rest.
>
> In hill, in dale, in isles of the sea,
>   Wheresoever one may go,
> From blest Christ there's no escaping.

And though the religious poems do redress the balance a little, still there is nothing like the happy awareness of God's immanence in nature and solitude that one constantly finds in the lyrics of the hermits of ninth-century Ireland. The earliest expression of anything like it in Welsh (that I know of) is the twelfth-century poet Meilyr's lovely request to be buried on Bardsey.

Tenderness, also, is exceedingly rare in old Welsh poetry. There is tragic grief, there is pride in people you love, there is fierce affection for the dead. But not the Irishman's loving concern for blackbirds, for places or for people; not that tenderness towards the living which is in part a fruit of Christian charity, but also in part a sublimation of the exile's homesickness for his community, a fruit of the mellowing of time and the organic relationship of man with the countryside. The tenderness towards the living, the imaginative freedom and the lyrical romanticization of the past set the scene for many centuries of Irish poetry; and despite the fact that Irish civilization was almost totally devastated by successive invasions, so that the promise was blighted and the freedom fossilized, Irish poetry still remained lyrical, humane on the whole, and (of course) obsessed with old glory.

The Welsh, on the other hand, when we first meet them in the sixth century, are in process of undergoing the traumatic experience of Roman withdrawal, re-emergence of total tribalism, failure to keep their lands, mass migration and constant war. A people does not change its language for nothing: suddenly to adopt a whole new pattern of syntax – or rather, to let the old formalities of speech lapse into linguistic chaos – this is tantamount to cultural amnesia. The same phenomenon can be witnessed in Anglo-Saxon England in the centuries following the Norman conquest. We do not know what Brythonic poetry was like; but my guess is that it was far closer to early Irish than it was to most of what survives of early Welsh. The delightful 'Song to the Child Dinogad', which was accidentally incorporated in the text of 'The Gododdin', and slavishly copied there by successive scribes, may in fact be a relic of this old tradition. Tribal poets, of course, always praise their chiefs for bravery in battle and generosity in peace. But that is not usually all they are interested in. They notice the other things of life, the seasons, the women, the satisfactions of hunting and parenthood. It is quite wrong, I believe, to regard Taliesin and Aneirin as typically primitive, or even typically heroic. Their sole emphasis is on the dual role of the chief – to be a brave leader in war, and to give generously to his warriors in time of peace. Aneirin makes the connexion between the two perfectly explicit: he praises Gwlylged, the steward of the Gododdin tribe, because he served meat and wine so well –

> He made famous and costly Mynyddawg's feast
> In order to buy back the country of Catraeth.

In other words, the giving of gifts will guarantee a loyal fighting force in wartime. Expecting poets like Aneirin to be typically tribal and primitive is like saying that the Red Indians, when their hunting grounds were being stolen by cowboys, were still in a state of nature! Aneirin, in particular, shows us a people with its back to the wall. Everything must be subordinated to preserving the morale and survival value of the tribe; and in particular, of the leaders of the tribe. Aneirin's poem is an elegy on three hundred warriors who fell in a vain attempt to recapture Catraeth from the English. It is clearly a political poem, that tries to mitigate the futility of the exploit (and the more general defeatism of the times) by stressing its heroic glory. That was what the poet was for; not indeed to deny the failure – he says that the mead Mynyddawg gave his men proved poison – but to make it tolerable to men's imaginations.

The achievement of these early poets was considerable. They created a heroic age, a new legendary past for ages to come. As long as the Welsh tradition lasted, that is to say, to the sixteenth century and beyond, their patrons were taken as models of generosity and courage. Welsh legend, though it does preserve traces of Brythonic and Roman times, really starts with the fifth and sixth centuries. And not only Welsh legend, of course; for this heroic age was metamorphosed in succeeding centuries into the Matter of Britain, the Arthurian Romance, that had such a profound effect on European culture everywhere. This was the most important Welsh contribution to the literature of the world; but I shall not speak of it here, except to mention the fact that it provided a channel through which other Celtic motifs, often Irish in provenance, could enter the mainstream. Arthurian Romance, while it remained Welsh, stayed very much on the level of folk-tale: the strange thing is, it had to pass through the distorting mirror of Norman French chivalry before it really affected Welsh poetry of the more responsible sort.

It is quite rare for us to have poetry actually composed during the miseries of a heroic age: usually all we have are epics and sagas composed centuries after the folk-wandering that is the heroic age's *raison d'être* has taken place. But in Taliesin and Aneirin we can see operating the forces that make people remember such ages as legendary times. On the positive side we can see the political and economic causes that made heroism an absolute necessity; and on the negative, we can assess the cost in terms of human continuity, one generation to the next, that such ages exact. Heroic ages have no history, no past. Because of this, they have a glamour in retrospect that they share with only one other human experience: the being born in Eden. It is this glamour that carries them across the world. Irish legends are more numerous and reach back into a more organized antiquity than Welsh: but Welsh legends conquered Europe, continually changing their shape as they went, whereas Irish saga has remained as a sort of historical make-believe only really vital to the Irish themselves.

It seems to me that there is a distinct layering of Welsh fables corresponding to the periods where they originated. First there is the level of the Four Branches of the *Mabinogi*, which is Brythonic myth euhemerized into legend. Secondly, there is what became the Matter of Britain, folk-tales about Arthur and his court, and their strange adventures. This level shows us Christianity as the overt religion, with paganism very much alive as magic and as divination. It corresponds in time to the end of the Roman occupation and the early attempts to keep the province of Britain intact. As history it was driven into the subconscious by the trauma of the sixth century, by the Anglo-Saxon conquest, and the other factors in what I have called the cultural amnesia of the times. When it re-emerged as folk-tale, it did so as a vehicle for all manner of superstition and wish-fulfilments. It was intimately connected with the whole prophetic tradition, which kept up its messianic rumblings right through to the Wars of the Roses.

And thirdly, overlapping with this, there was the saga-literature proper, composed in the ninth and tenth centuries about events that took place in the sixth and early seventh – that is, during the heroic age itself. The Welsh were cut off from their countrymen in the North of England and in Cornwall. To the rest of the Island of Britain, they were indeed 'Welsh' – that is, strangers or foreigners in their own country. Only in a few pockets of rugged landscape, like Wales or Cumberland, could they find themselves 'Cymry', that is, compatriots. The sense of exile must have been still further aggravated by the reappearance of Rome, in the shape of St. Augustine of Canterbury, telling them that their traditional Christianity was out of step with the rest of Christendom, and demanding that they should forget their hatred of the Anglo-Saxons and join with him in converting them to Christ. One gathers that the Welsh preferred the idea of the English roasting in hell for evermore! Henceforth the centre of gravity of Britain moved steadily southwards: first Northumbria, then Mercia, then Wessex, and finally Normandy. And with it went the decline of Celtic influence upon it. The pressure from the rival Rhine-Rhône pattern of culture, as it was beginning to be formulated during these centuries, drove the Celts more and more into odd corners. This meant they were more and more in a state of siege, less and less able to move freely towards imaginative creation. Freedom in a culture is one and indivisible: the Welsh failure to respond to England as a missionary opportunity was both a symptom and a cause of their suffering defeat.

By the ninth century, the Welsh were almost completely shut up behind Offa's Dyke. Not unnaturally, in their exile, they turned to the stories of their old homes, in Rheged, Elfed, Gododdin and the rich lands of Eastern Powys – roughly Cumberland, Yorkshire, south-east Scotland and Shropshire respectively. Sir Ifor Williams has shown that many poems that used to be attributed to Llywarch Hen, a near-contemporary of Taliesin, are really fragments of sagas belonging to the ninth and tenth centuries. The prose and narrative parts of these sagas are lost: all we have are the sections in verse, when the story-teller used poetry (and probably song) to stress the dramatic or emotional speech of his characters. Nevertheless, enough remains for us to be able to assess the quality and pitch of these stories.

These sagas, then, were clearly quite different from any Welsh narratives that still survive. Stark in texture, tragic in conception, they seem to have concentrated on the human situations involved

in the Welsh heroic age to the exclusion of magic and super-
natural agents. In the first extract I have translated, for example,
Llywarch Hen, the proud old man of these stories, urges Gwên,
the last of his sons, to sound the horn that Urien gave him if he is
hard-pressed in the forthcoming battle. This horn may or may not
have had magical properties: the way Llywarch mentions it
suggests that it had. But the poet by-passes them completely. All
he is interested in is Gwên's contemptuous reply – 'No, don't
worry, I'm not going to wake your maids!' It is the mutual anger
between father and son, each insulting the other's honour, that
makes any genuine precautions against tragedy impossible. Magic
is quite irrelevant. All that matters is human folly and human
pride. But if there is no supernatural tampering within the tragic
situation, there is at any rate an over-riding Fate or destiny, a
supernatural context in which such situations are allowed, or even
willed, to take place. As in all tragic art, the protagonist is pitted
not only against his own pride and folly, but also against hostile
destiny – *tynged* in Welsh – whose design is revealed to him only
gradually as his downfall proceeds.

The second thing one may notice about this saga-literature is
that, unlike Aneirin or Taliesin's poetry, it is saturated with
feeling for the past. A good deal of it is lamentation of one kind or
another. Sometimes it is personal lamentation, either for the
death of a loved one or, as in Llywarch's famous complaint of old
age, for the speaker's own changed state. Perhaps even more
typical, however, is the lament for a ruined house that the loved
one has died defending. Here the loss is by no means merely
personal. Cynddylan's hall and the hearth of Urien of Rheged
were tribal centres; their overthrow is the ruin of an entire society.
Of course, the idea that the community are involved in the
downfall of the tragic hero is not peculiar to Wales. It seems to be
common to tragedy everywhere. The Greek chorus continually
reminds us of the public nature of the tragic action; and in
Shakespeare also, the protagonists are kings or princes, whose evil
and mistaken deeds have to be purged by blood from the body
politic. But in Wales the tragic hero does not seem to separate
himself from his tribe to nearly the same extent as he normally
does in Greece or England. The saga-poetry, indeed, seems only
half-tragic, half-elegiac by comparison. The lamentation is raised,
seemingly, not so much for one man's death as for the ending of a

way of life. This emphasis is not absent from Greek Tragedy, of course, as *The Women of Troy* shows; but it is not typical, as I think it is of Welsh.

Something of this elegiac quality may be due to the saga-form. Theatrical presentation is not usually convenient at a chieftain's court. Theatre, in the Middle Ages, was almost always a religious expression, originating from the Church. But the art of the story-teller, with its dramatic gestures, its use of song and poetry,and its high degree of professionalism, was far nearer to good theatre than we tend to think. In principle, there seems no reason why it should not be an adequate vehicle of tragic art. However, the simple fact that there is one person telling the story, and not several enacting it, will tend always to rob it of immediacy and displace present tragedy by elegy for remembered woe.

But there is a more fundamental reason than mere formal bias why these poems are elegiac. Just as Aneirin's function was not to deny the failure of the tribal expedition but to render it imaginably tolerable, so also with the anonymous poets of the sagas. Only this time the catastrophe did not happen yesterday, but two or three hundred years ago. The poets are confronting the past, realizing it in flesh and blood terms: perhaps we could call their work therapeutic in its ultimate social function. A comparison may help us to appreciate their value to their own times. The industrial and agrarian revolution was a sociological trauma in eighteenth- and early nineteenth-century England comparable to that suffered by the Welsh in the sixth century. The poetry that was the immediate product of this nightmare was the Methodist hymn and the violent vision of Blake. Very much later, in the novels of such writers as Thomas Hardy, we find English sensibility still wounded to the quick by the disaster, but sufficiently recovered to acknowledge it and confront its past. Hardy's theme is the Napoleonic period in English rural life – nearly a century before he was actually writing. But this does not make him a 'historical novelist', like Scott or the Dickens of *A Tale of Two Cities*. On the contrary, the fact that his subject lies so wholly in the past is, in his case, an integral part of his claim to be a realist writer, not a romantic. Elegy is the keynote of his work, and tragedy its chief mode; and, as with the Welsh ninth-century poets, his characters are at one and the same time wholly autonomous agents that will their own destruction, and (just as important to the psychological effect of his novels) mere helpless playthings of Destiny. The psychological need to reconcile these two mutually opposed views of human responsibility was dissipated finally by the renewed trauma of world war. Hardy's novels have suffered in critical esteem ever since, because of the vague, 'period' flavour it gave them; but his manner, especially that of his poems, has been a constant source of strength to modern English poets, even though the 'tragic' vision that inspired it is now felt to be largely bogus. Something like this may well have happened in Wales. As far as we know, Welsh saga ceased to be a creative form of literature sometime round the tenth century, when it seems to have been superseded by the more romantic styles of story-telling found in the *Mabinogion*. But the *manner*, as opposed to the vision, of the saga-poets remained sufficiently alive to influence Cynddelw's early work in the eleven-fifties.

Comparisons are dangerous: and I would not wish to leave you with the idea that these early Welsh poems are at all Hardyesque in feeling or range. To dispel it, let us return to Sir Ifor Williams' model for them, as the nearest thing to great tragedy Wales has ever produced. Let us remember the dramatic figure of Llywarch as he taunts and goads his sons to a heroic death; and the burning hall of Cynddylan; and Heledd, his sister, watching in terror as the eagle feasts upon Cynddylan's dead body in the woods. She does not dare to go near, in case the birds turn upon her. She has seen them before, these eagles, fishing in the estuaries; now they swim in blood. She thinks of her victorious enemy, the one that slew Cynddylan: the eagles are pampered by him, and he prospers. Then she looks up, hearing another eagle scream and hover in the sky, talons down for the swoop; it is jealous of the flesh she loves (and would so like to save), and jealous of its rival's feast. Her splintered mind remembers Trenn, the "luckless", the "glittering" town that Cynddylan died defending; and the eyes of the eagles watch on the blood. These are superb, tragic images. The poems that enshrine them are high dramatic utterance, not the merely ruminative mode of elegy.

The next two and a half centuries are almost without any surviving poetry. They were dominated by a few great kings, like the traditional Welsh lawgiver, Hywel Dda; and were punctuated by long periods of chaos and Viking raids. On the eve of the

Norman conquest Harold defeated Gruffudd ap Llywelyn, the king of Gwynedd, and for the last forty years of the eleventh century Welsh independence grew more and more precarious. The Norman barons conducted a piece-meal invasion of the country. Unlike the Saxons or the Vikings, their method was not simply to destroy Welsh houses: they marched to a point well inside Welsh territory and built a fortress, from which they proceeded to reduce the surrounding countryside to submission, including any local chiefs who might object.

The recovery of Gwynedd under Gruffudd ap Cynan and his son Owain Gwynedd is the central fact about Wales in the first half of the twelfth century. Gruffudd was half-Viking himself, and lived during his early life in Dublin. He tried to recover his Welsh inheritance several times before he actually did so; and the tradition is that he brought with him Irish minstrels, and that he tried to revive and revise Welsh bardic custom, almost as Hywel Dda is reputed to have done in the case of Welsh law.

Certainly, there was a great flowering of poetry during the last part of his reign and the reign of his son, Owain Gwynedd. Unlike most of the earlier poetry which is anonymous, this is usually by named authors, who often have a very personal style and who assume that they are themselves important people: these poets have a status in society, a position to keep up. They are members of what may loosely be described as a bardic order, professional men with work to do. The school of court-poetry that they founded lasted more or less intact until the Edwardian conquest of Wales in 1282; and in a somewhat changed form well into the fourteenth century. The earlier poets are traditionally called the *Cynfeirdd* – the poets who came first; this second school is called the *Gogynfeirdd* – the poets who came next to the first. Unlike the *Cynfeirdd*, they were a definite movement, all sharing the same general idea of what great poetry was supposed to do. They certainly regarded themselves as inheriting this tradition from older models, and particularly from Taliesin; but in certain important respects they differ from any older poetry that we know of.

For one thing, their diction is characteristically archaic, their syntax elliptical in the extreme. They are difficult, indeed very difficult, to construe; and this is due to their own deliberate policy. Earlier poetry is certainly difficult, because many of the words have either disappeared from the language or changed their meaning, as must inevitably happen in thirteen or fourteen hundred years. By the same token, Chaucer is difficult to modern teenagers. But the *Gogynfeirdd* must have been difficult even at the time they wrote. It is true that this can be exaggerated: the amount of difficulty certainly varies from poem to poem and from poet to poet. But no one who has tried to read them will deny that it exists. What is more, the greatest among them are frequently the hardest to make sense of.

Secondly, they differ in form from their predecessors. The earliest Welsh court-poetry had been written in mono-rhymed sections of usually under a dozen lines apiece. The *Gogynfeirdd* enormously increased the length of these sections: Gruffudd ab yr Ynad Coch's great 'Lament for Llywelyn the Last' has only one rhyme from beginning to end of its hundred odd lines. This is exceptional, but sections of twenty, thirty, forty or fifty lines are by no means uncommon. Earlier poets had used what can roughly be described as variation-technique. Aneirin's 'Gododdin' is a good example: every section is more or less complete in itself, and says more or less the same kind of thing as every other section. It hardly matters in what order we read the different sections, therefore. Whichever order we take, the poem remains itself. The sections are often bound together by what can be called 'epic formulae', typical of oral poetry: the same phrase, sometimes slightly varied, begins each one. Thus, in 'The Gododdin', many of the sections begin with the words, 'Men went to Catraeth': and (apart from the couplets of invocation to God at the beginning and end) every section of the anonymous 'Praise of Tenby' begins with the phrase, "There is a fine fortress". Presumably this device had mnemonic as well as formal utility; but it cannot have been used solely as a guide to memory because we sometimes find the repeated phrase at the end of a section, in the manner of a refrain, not only at the beginning.

It is not really possible to say whether these variations were normal in court-poetry — as they certainly were in saga-poetry — in the period preceding that of the *Gogynfeirdd*. There is so little of it surviving. But there is one significant exception to their likely dominance over the early centuries: the poetry of Taliesin himself. Taliesin must be regarded as one of the greatest masters of form in the Welsh language. He integrates his short poems into wholes, making his points one by one, briefly and often with fine imaginative power. Aneirin undoubtedly appeals more to the modern reader than does his more austere contemporary: this is because of his single lines, which conjure up the tragedy of the times so movingly, and because he does not involve us in prejudice about praising the aristocracy. A war memorial is more moving to us than a statue of a civic benefactor. But Taliesin is the more important poet. He *makes*, he *fashions*. He does not simply comment and record. And it was to Taliesin that the poets of the newly self-confident twelfth-century Wales now turned, as to a master. Aneirin they refer to; but Taliesin they revere and imitate.

Not that the *Gogynfeirdd* copied his forms exactly. He was too simple for them, too concentrated on the heroic issues of his time. The problems of the twelfth century were not those of the sixth. Their poems stand in much the same relation to his as does an ode of Pindar to a Homeric Hymn. They took his basic structures – the *marwnad* or elegy for a lord, the *dadolwch* or poem reconciling a poet to his estranged lord, the battle piece, the poems of praise – and used them as the skeletons of their much longer, much more ornate and 'literary' works. The poems of the *Gogynfeirdd*, as much as the *Mabinogion* or the laws of Hywel Dda, represent a synthesizing and refining attitude of mind at work in the culture of the time. Reading them is like listening to the music of the *organum*: the plain-song notes are held as a kind of drone, while over them a rich embroidery of sounds holds the attention.

The basic sequence of ideas in these odes is usually very simple. Cynddelw's 'Elegy for Madog ap Maredudd', for example, can be summarized as follows:

> I pray God, as I have prayed a hundred times before, that I may compose for my lord a song with all the richness of my art, to mourn for Madog,
>
> Who was a mighty leader in war and generous to poets, whom he loved and protected.
>
> Now that he is dead, may his sins be forgiven, and he go to heaven.

The first paragraph paraphrases six lines of the original; the second thirty-two lines; and the third four lines. Apart from the rather typical reference to his own status as a poet in the introduction, this structure, as far as I can see, is in nowise original or peculiar to this poem. It could serve, almost word for word, for dozens of other elegies. The only differences there might be would be a slight change in the introductory lines, and the name of the lord who is dead. If this structure is compared with that of Taliesin's 'Elegy for Owain ab Urien', the similarities can hardly be missed; though Taliesin contrives to tell us a good deal more about Owain's history in twenty-four short lines than Cynddelw tells us about Madog's in forty-two longer ones; and this despite the fact that Madog was his chief patron as a young man and almost certainly a personal friend.

And yet the 'Elegy for Madog ap Maredudd' is a completely original and masterly poem, with a sweep and intellectual power behind it that only Cynddelw was capable of. Take, for example, the first six lines after the introductory passage:

> Door of a fort he was, companion shield,
> Buckler on battlefield, and in brave deeds;
> A tumult like flame blazing through heather,
> Router of enemies, his shield stopped their way;
> Lord sung by a myriad, hope of minstrels,
> Crimson, irresistible, unswerving companion.

The poet begins his praise of the dead man with two common images of the time: he was a door, a gate of a fort, through which men could either find safety or issue forth to attack; and he was a shield. These are images poised between the two aspects of a great leader – the defence of his people and the extension of their power. The next line develops the shield image, but now it seems to refer less to Madog as himself a shield than to Madog's own shield, in the forefront of battle. This prepares us for the magnificent image in the third line, the only certainly original image in the entire poem. The rush and noise of a fire blazing through dry summer heather shows us the full might of Madog's onslaught; and also, I think, its status as a natural force, like a forest fire. The fourth line both completes this idea of overwhelming force, and returns us to square one. Madog indeed routed his enemies – how could he help it? But he was, the poet reiterates, a shield also, and supremely. And the image of a shield has enough resonance in it by now to cover the other side of the king's function in society, his encouragement and patronage of the arts, the minstrels and the poets. To call a lord the "hope of minstrels" was the merest cliché on the level of tribal economy: without his patronage they could not survive. But surely the context demands something other than a merely perfunctory reference to his generosity. Madog was the hope of minstrels, for they loved him, yes; but also their hope because he stood for what they stood for, and his victories in battle were made theirs by their singing of them. The last line begins (in the Welsh also) with three adjectives descriptive of his leadership in war: but the noun they qualify is *cydymdaith*, one who goes with you on a journey. This is one of the key words of the whole poem, and it has already occurred as a rhyme-word in the first six lines, where Cynddelw implored God

> That I may, of my high speech, fashion a gold song
> For my comrade and lord.

Here again is the same connexion being made between poetry, leadership in war and companionship. And so on, through the poem. Analysis could be much more thorough than this, were it not that sometimes translation is a little uncertain. I have tried not to tangle myself with points that are unsure; but even if I am wrong in detail, this is the sort of analysis that Cynddelw, and the greatest of his contemporaries, demand and satisfy.

The odes of Cynddelw are not merely greater than the sum of their parts, they are much, much greater. Every detail in them, every turn of phrase, every metaphor, may be hackneyed and second-hand; but the whole is magnificent. They reflect a way of life in which human relationships formed a complicated pattern, extending outwards through the family circle. For some purposes, it was important in twelfth-century Wales to know who your third or fourth cousins were: it might indeed make the difference between life and death. Duties to your family, to your local lord, to your king, to your church, and your claims upon them in turn – these were far and away more complex in tribal Wales than they ever were under feudalism. Of course, this is not to say that the individual phrase, any more than the individual person, had necessarily to be ordinary and of no account. This is patently not so. For the principles behind Cynddelw's craftsmanship, like those behind the tribal organization of society, could bestow importance upon such individuals, phrases or persons, where otherwise there would be mediocrity and lack of purpose.

The great, experimental period of the *Gogynfeirdd* seems to have begun in Gwynedd (north Wales) round about 1135. The first poem that can be dated, and is wholly in this style, is Meilyr's 'Elegy for Gruffudd ap Cynan', who died in 1137; but it was certainly not the first poem Meilyr had written to that prince, as we learn from Gwalchmai, Meilyr's son, who refers to his father as being Gruffudd's chief poet. So 1135 is probably a bit late, by a decade or two. But from 1137 to the end of the century there is a continuous stream of poems preserved in the manuscripts. These are not only official poems, odes of praise or elegies for princes. Meilyr's other surviving poem of any importance, for example, is the 'Poem on his Death-bed' (included in this book), which is a meditation on his own life as a poet, a request to be buried on Bardsey Island, the graveyard of the saints, and a commendation of his soul to God. It is a beautiful piece of work, justly famous and imitated several times by later poets. His son Gwalchmai was even more experimental, expressing with a confident freedom the excitement and sweetness of being a warrior and a lover of girls in the early years of the reign of Owain Gwynedd. These two are joined by a third, the romantic Hywel, an illegitimate son of Owain Gwynedd himself and an Irish mother, who played an increasingly important part in Welsh politics, until his assassination by his half-brothers near Pentraeth in 1170. Hywel is likely to be more sympathetic to the modern reader than any other Welsh poet before Dafydd ap Gwilym. Here, for almost the first time, is a genuine lyricism informing whole poems: that is to say, the lyrical feeling shapes the form, instead of merely being its servant, as I think it is in Gwalchmai. From a metrical point of view, there is very little difference; but poetic form is not simply a matter of metre. A lyrical poem is essentially organic in the way it grows: poems by the other *Gogynfeirdd* are typically built up like a Byzantine mosaic, and lack Hywel's 'bounding line' and personal commitment to the way his mind is leading him.

Hywel's love-poems are the first of their kind, but perhaps even more revolutionary in feeling is his 'Boast of his Country'. If we turn to Irish classical poetry, we find it is full of kennings, or conventional phrases that stand for Ireland, as "swan's way" in Anglo-Saxon stands for the sea:

> Goirthear Teach Tuathail d'Éirinn,
> Cró Chuinn is Fonn finn Fhéilim,
> Iath Iúghoine is Achadh Airt
> Crioch Cobhthaigh is Clár Chormaic.

(Ireland is called the House of Tuathal, the Fold of Conn, and Land of fair Felim, Meadow of Iughoine and Field of Art, Territory of Cobhthach and Plain of Cormac.)
Aodh O Domhnaill, trans. Eleanor Knott

Ireland is always present in her poetry as a physical entity, a land made one by ties of history and legend. But in Welsh poetry, there is very little sense of Wales as a geographical whole before the twelfth century. Wales, to use an etymological metaphor, is a back-formation from the Welsh. It is the people, the *Cymry*, who are important: their country is essentially the Island of Britain as a whole, and the fact that they now occupy only that fraction of it called Wales is no more than an unfortunate historical accident. This fact is very important at all periods of Welsh history: even Owain Glyndŵr, the nationalist *par excellence*, was not always content to limit his ambitions to the territorial boundaries of Wales. Hywel's lyricism about Gwynedd, or North Wales, seems to me more Irish in provenance than Welsh. It is quite distinct from Gwalchmai's loyalty to Owain, as Gwynedd's king; but also, I think, different from the intense Welsh preoccupation with the *bro*, or district you come from, that is again crucial to their history.

The expansionist feeling found in these early *Gogynfeirdd* is not limited to Gwynedd. In Powys, or mid-Wales, also, in the poetry of Cynddelw and Prince Owain of Cyfeiliog, the new movement was gathering momentum. Even Deheubarth, the other main division of Wales in the south, by the end of the twelfth century was politically and culturally expansive. The poetry of Powys differs slightly in feeling from that of Gwynedd: as befits a border country between Wales and the rest of Britain, it is more involved with the past, less taken with the joys of the present. Even so, until the death of Madog ap Maredudd in 1160, Cynddelw seems to have been content to stay as Madog's house-poet, celebrating (among other things) the beauty of the princess Efa and his own reception by her maidens.

But round about 1160, the mood seems to change. Very little that is really new emerged after that date; after the excitement and freedom of the earlier poets, the later *Gogynfeirdd* are always a bit grim, as if they were anxious about something. It is true that Cynddelw's greatest poems are his poems to Owain Gwynedd; and that they date from the 1160s. But these, with their historical preoccupations, are really only extensions of what he had been doing before. The poetry of the thirteenth century – though it had its masterpieces, like the great 'Lament for the Last Llywelyn' by Gruffudd ab yr Ynad Coch – does not fulfil the promise of the twelfth.

Perhaps we can locate the change of mood in three things that happened in or around 1160. First, the weak king Stephen died, and Henry II was crowned in England. That was in 1154. In 1157, and again in 1165, English armies marched into north Wales; and though Owain Gwynedd survived both invasions, he had to pay homage and put a check on his territorial ambitions. Welsh expansion, it was now clear, had to reckon on England's strength as a limiting factor: the princes, first the Lord Rhys of the south and then the two Llywelyns in Gwynedd, could no longer see themselves as autonomous, purely Welsh rulers, but rather as feudal under-lords of England. Whether this would work as politics remained to be seen: it was certainly a break with the past. Had Wales been left to her own devices, perhaps some form of canton government would have evolved. As it was, centralization within Wales was the only hope of securing relative independence for the Welsh princes from their sovereign liege the English king. Wales remained self-governing for over a century; but there was never any real security. English troops were liable to appear anywhere in the country, and, ultimately, there was nothing to stop them except the politics of brinkmanship and the main chance.

Secondly, as we have said, Madog ap Maredudd, lord of Powys, died in 1160, and his lands, according to the Welsh custom of gavelkind, were divided among his sons. Powys was never again a united country. This throws into relief the central problem of Celtic political life – the question of continuity. The

INTRODUCTION

King in Celtdom was primarily the chief man of a tribe; and just as a man's share in the tribal property was divided equally among his sons, so was a king's. The tribe always resisted attempts to treat its leaders as something separate from it; and this, though admirably just and fair, made havoc of political succession. Even the rather shadowy Irish High Kingship, moreover, had no equivalent in Wales. At a time when a country's very existence depended on its ability to maintain strong dynasties, Welsh tribal law made it almost impossible for a son to succeed his father without incurring the bitterness of civil war. Ten years after Madog, Owain Gwynedd himself died, and the same thing happened again. Hywel ab Owain, the poet, was killed by his half-brothers, who then split up Gwynedd between them.

Third, sometime after the English invasion of 1157, Gwalchmai the poet fell from favour with Owain Gwynedd and his sons. We would dearly love to know why. It may have been something entirely trivial; but, on the other hand, it may have been the first symptom of the tension that was building up between the tribe and the already feudal ambitions of its chief. The poets were committed to the tribe. On the lowest economic level, it would not have paid them for one prince to have had a monopoly of patronage. Poets, anyway, were guardians of custom, and a privileged order within tribalism. If a feudal state had really materialized in Wales, their place would have surely been lower. in the scale – minstrels, entertainers and jongleurs, in fact. And then again, they were men of conscience, who (like most men) resisted change when it seemed to them unjust. Irish poets were not so high-minded – indeed they were often openly cynical with their bardic favours. But Welsh poets, on the whole, seemed to have maintained their integrity and avoided scandal, even at the cost of political expediency.

At all events, though some of the poets were convinced by Llywelyn the Great's attempt to found a Welsh feudal state in the thirteenth century, others were dubious and even hostile. What is more, even when they tried to advocate a united Wales, their verse-forms remained obstinately tribal. The change to a feudal world-picture, had it been accomplished in Wales, would surely have resulted in a completely new kind of poetry, geared to different rhythms and based on a changed view of the poet's function in society. Hywel ab Owain in the middle of the twelfth century, suggests far more than the poet of feudalism, perhaps because of his high birth and closeness to the ideals of the princes of Gwynedd, than do any of the later *Gogynfeirdd*, ardent supporters of the two Llywelyns though many of them were.

After the death of Owain Gwynedd, the clouds seem to gather. The craft remains the same, but the springtime has left it. In the religious poetry, in particular, the underlying unease finds expression in such themes as the fear of hell, the last Judgement and the urge to forsake the world. Elsewhere, patterns tended to become stereotyped, and lost something of the vital relationship to the living issues of the day that had marked the poetry of Meilyr, Gwalchmai, Hywel and the early Cynddelw. And when the storm finally broke, and Edward I invaded Wales and Llywelyn ap Gruffudd was killed (almost by accident) at Irfon Bridge in 1282, one gets the sense of some kind of release, almost as if this was the tragic moment the poets had been waiting for. Certainly it produced the greatest poem, probably, in the Welsh language, a *tour de force* of controlled anguish and dismay that rises to visionary heights – the aforementioned 'Lament' by Gruffudd ab yr Ynad Coch. Step by step, through all the mazes of conventional lamentation, the poet leads us out into a world that is lost for ever, the deep eschatological darkness of the end of all hopes. What is perhaps almost as moving, in its own way, is Bleddyn Fardd's companion elegy, where the tragedy (as D. Myrddin Lloyd has observed) is seen in braver and more human terms. Indeed, it seems as if it was written to discountenance the naked expressionism and almost hysterical despair of Gruffudd's poem. Bleddyn Fardd refuses, in fact, to confuse the loss of independence with the Day of Doom. He more or less says, pull yourself together. Llywelyn was killed, but so was Christ. The two deaths are equally part of the one Providence, God's dealings with mankind. We who are left are responsible for the future. We must calmly and humbly remember our creaturely and human status:

> It concerns a man, that which I speak of.
> Whoever bears grief, let him be most calm.
> Whoever by nature is highest in authority,
>   Let his thought be most lowly.

What happened next was distinctly odd. Wales was an occupied country, divided up into royal shires and Marcher lordships. Edward I built, at enormous expense, those great castles at Conwy, Caernarfon and Beaumaris that so dominate the visitor's view of north Wales; and he rebuilt those at Harlech, Cricieth and Bere. Each of the castles protected its 'borough', where English settlers were encouraged to live and do trade, and where the Welsh were expressly forbidden to go. The Welsh princely class, on whom Welsh culture and aspirations were founded, was practically eradicated as a force in the land. Wales was thus deprived of any overt national life – apart from times of rebellion, such as Owain Glyndŵr's.* She was economically very poor indeed: too poor even to support her conqueror's defence programme. After the Glyndŵr revolt, her poverty was increased by everyone being in debt for reparations. Conditions do seem to have improved in the second half of the fifteenth century; and, as in most poor countries, some of the upper classes were always rich. Wales was ruled partly by Anglo-Norman bosses, partly by the Welsh *uchelwyr* or high men. These latter were, on the one hand, heirs of the princes, men in whom Welsh idealism could be said to inhere; but, on the other, they were a class partaking of many of the features of the Indian *babu* under the British Raj, half-anglicized middlemen, regarded with very mixed feelings by both sides. On the surface, their ambition seemed sometimes to become English as soon as possible; but the psychological tensions of their position made them, when occasion offered, the spearhead of nationalism and fierce haters of their former patrons. Of course, one must not exaggerate. On the whole, the Edwardian settlement was a conservative matter, because Edward lacked the

*It is true that the concept of the 'Principality' went some way towards being a national ideal. Llywelyn the Last was recognized as 'Prince of Wales' in 1267; and Edward I, as is well known, did not see fit to let the title lapse, but conferred it upon his eldest son. Wales was not, in fact, a part of England, but a quite separate possession of the English crown, ruled by statute not by acts of Parliament. The concept may be seen also during the Glyndŵr rising: for one of the first things Owain Glyndŵr did was to have himself proclaimed Prince of Wales. It can perhaps be compared to the adoption of the title of 'The O'Neill' by the Earl of Tyrone, which Elizabeth I rightly construed as an act of defiance.

resources to carry out the full anglicization and centralization he would have liked. Welsh law still obtained over much of the country; Welsh was still the main language, except in the towns. Many of the social processes that had been operative under the Llywelyns continued much the same under English rule. Nor did the Welsh peasantry change its ways. Wales was, and remained until the Tudors, an isolated backwater as far as the central government was concerned, protected from much contact with progressive England by the thick buffer of the turbulent Marcher lordships. Only after the Wars of the Roses had made Wales 'politically aware' – that is, of English politics – could this buffer be dismantled, and Wales be exposed to the full effects of thorough-going anglicization.

It was hardly, one would have thought, a likely situation for a high culture to flower. As we have seen, Welsh poetry had been going down a *cul-de-sac* a long time before the conquest. In the twelfth century it had more or less attained a level we call *archaic* – using the word technically, as Greek art before the fifth century B.C. is called archaic. It had touched, temporarily, the fullness that its sister poetry of Ireland had attained to centuries earlier. But the political worry had frozen it there, as had the somewhat similar political situation in Ireland. There seemed nothing for it but more and more meaningless repetition of the old conventions.

And yet, within sixty years of the conquest, Wales had produced her greatest poet, Dafydd ap Gwilym, and with him a new freedom, a new and splendid imaginative life. For two centuries, she enjoyed an outburst of fine poetry unrivalled for its sophistication, its brilliance and poise, by anything the Celts have ever achieved, before or since. Poet after poet, many of them of a standard one must call great, attained to a classical elegance in their art that English poetry can only match in the later years of Elizabeth and the seventeenth century. Judged on world standards, it is indeed a narrow achievement: no Welsh poet has anything like the sheer size (or the complexity that can only come with size) of Chaucer, let alone Shakespeare. What is more, Chaucer is in contact with far more mental activity – in other countries, other disciplines and other arts – than even Dafydd ap Gwilym, quicksilver mind though he had. And it is an achievement that is limited to poetry and, possibly, music. The visual arts of the Celt, the decorative pattern-work that had produced the masterpieces of La Tène and early Ireland, had long ago ceased to function. I think it is true to say that any new visual art there was in medieval Wales came from outside. Nor were the Welsh remarkable for abstract thought: there is no Welsh philosophy, theology or science, Only poetry, and that of a somewhat specialized kind, flourished in Wales during the period of Dafydd ap Gwilym and his successors.

And yet, it seems to me, one cannot deny that the Welsh achieved something comparatively rare in the history of mankind: high civilization, unique to themselves. It is as though the cultural forces that had first shown themselves in the art of La Tène, and had been fused with Roman and Christian *motifs* in the culture of early Ireland and Northumbria, had now at last, after terrible setbacks all over their field, come to fulfilment in the poverty-stricken uplands of occupied Wales. The Welsh poets expressed and enacted in their poems a civilization essentially Celtic, however influenced by accidentals from outside; and, what is more, within the terms of Celtic evolution, a civilization that deserves to be called *classical*, in the full sense of the word. That is to say, their work defines a way of looking at things, proper to full humanity, in which men could be free to develop as individuals within the context of a way of life they felt to be good. As such, this poetry is of profound interest: not simply because high culture is rather rare, but also because it exemplifies what is possibly the lowest limit of natural endowment that high civilization can have, and yet come to flower.

We have seen how the tensions, first of invasion and exile, and then of the failure of the Welsh feudalism of the two Llywelyns, had created a powerful cultural stalemate in thirteenth-century Wales. Aspiration and desire were being continually aroused, only to be frustrated by the pressure of events. The conquest released this pent-up energy. It did not scotch the political problem, but at least it anaesthetized it. And after the cries of despair were a generation behind them, the Welsh people had a surplus of energy to play with, and no external ambition to fulfil. That, I believe, is the sociological mechanism behind Dafydd ap Gwilym. Obviously, things were not quite so simple as the mechanical model suggests. But at least we can use it to dispense with the magician's cloak and hat, conjuring up high culture out of nothing – not even the centripetal excitements of a metropolis.

INTRODUCTION

The first thing we can note about this poetry is that it does not fit any of our normal literary categories. It is neither tribal nor feudal in origin; and it is not typically accumulative, like a mosaic, nor lyrical, nor organic, like a tree. Neither is it narrative nor dramatic nor argumentative. It may contain elements of all these things; but none of them are essential, and all of them are likely to be absent in any given poem. In any culture, the pre-classical styles are easier than the classical for a foreigner to appreciate, and easier to translate from. This is because they are less differentiated from the pre-classical style of one's own culture. English people, for example, are likelier to enjoy Villon or Ronsard than they are Racine. And this is certainly true of Welsh, because the typical form of Welsh classical poetry – the *cywydd* – is not at all like any other form of poetry used by Western man.* It looks as though it might be like a lyric written in octosyllabic couplets; but this is an illusion. I cannot now enter into a full consideration of the formal aspect. Here I shall merely state that a classical *cywydd* is only accidentally lyrical, and that but rarely; and that Welsh lyrics of any description are scarce before the sixteenth century.

Secondly, we can say about this poetry that it is a product of a social environment peculiar to Wales; and that it keeps thematically very close to the economic facts of life at the time. The Welsh poets did not need Marx to tell them that culture is a superstructure built upon the economics of survival. They could not easily forget it, living as they did in such a poverty-stricken country. They had no capital city, and only Oswestry, among the towns, had any kind of means to support them. The homes of the noble families, the *uchelwyr* or high men, together with a few Cistercian Abbeys, like Strata Florida or Vallę Crucis, which were Welsh in sympathy – these were the only possible basis for civilized existence. The hospitality the poets continually praised was not a polite diversion from the real business of living: it was a brute necessity if Wales was to survive culturally at all. As we have said, the main function that a Welsh poet acknowledged was the praise of the gentry. To this function he dedicated his life; and round it are formed the main clusters of imagery that are

*Even the Irish *deibhidhe*, remarkably like it in outward form, is entirely unlike it in the way it is written.

characteristic of his art. There is the lord himself, of course, the master of the home; there is the house, where culture and gracious living can be found; the hospitality that is dispensed there, and the feast, that is the sacrament or secular communion of the whole community; there is the lord's lineage, since this is the main link between him and the Welsh people he feasts with, and the Welsh culture that he enjoys; there is the journey from one house to another, the continual circulation of the poets and minstrels around the whole area of Wales, a peculiarly Celtic institution (found even today in the peripateticism of the National Eisteddfod) that to some extent made up for the lack of a metropolis.

And, corresponding to these images, one finds also, particularly in the love-poetry, the anti-images. Instead of the lord, there is the outlaw, the thief, the outcast; instead of the house, there is the glade in the birchwood, or sometimes, even more explicit, the hut that the poet has made there, where he hopes his lady-love will tryst with him; instead of the hospitality and feasting of the great house (and, on a religious level, the sacrifice and communion of the Mass) there is the ritual of the birds, the feasts of love; instead of the lineage of a lord, the roots going down to the rich soil, there is Dafydd ap Gwilym's autonomy as a lover and the wantonness of the wind that bloweth where it listeth:

> You're on the world God's favour,
> High oaktops' tired-cracking roar;

and instead of the poets going on their bardic circuits from one welcoming household to the next, there is the lover's exile from his beloved, and his sending a *llatai* or love-messenger, usually a bird or an animal, to plead his case from afar. These are not the only images, or the only anti-images, that are found in this poetry. Satire, as well as love, is rich in anti-images, as one would expect: the town tavern where Dafydd ap Gwilym had such unfortunate experiences will serve to represent these.

And yet, despite this basis in the economic realities of the time, the poetry is a genuine imaginative creation. It is not, most emphatically not, merely functional. The poets never beg; and in this they compare favourably (for example) with medieval and Elizabethan English writers. They praise their patrons for supporting Welsh poetry; but their praise is in itself the central

INTRODUCTION

imaginative experience of that poetry. Modern readers seem able to register this imaginative creation easily enough in a love-poem; but when they come to a *cywydd mawl*, a poem of praise, their imaginations stop working, and all they see is convention and flattery.

Let us face this difficulty at its most taxing. Here, for example, are two stanzas from Dafydd Nanmor's 'Praise of Rhys ap Maredudd':

> He buys the drink from the vineyards – rich
> > Over the South waters,
> > Eighteen loads, and still there's eight,
> > Eighteen ships full with winecasks.
>
> Winecasks there must be, and swords – surely
> > Both for Rhys Amhredudd,
> > Arms and men numbered as trees
> > Swell roads about his journey.

Eighteen shiploads of wine from the south of France is quite a consignment! One is inclined to wonder what H.M. Customs and Excise would have thought of such an import into Tywyn! The point is, 'eighteen' – *deunaw* or twice nine, in the Welsh – is chosen not because it was factually accurate, but partly because nine is a number of fullness – thrice three, the number of the trinity – and therefore twice nine is twice as full as fullness, and partly because of purely metrical considerations which are necessarily lost in translation. Is this therefore a typical case of exaggeration and lying hyperbole to make the stupid patron think to himself, ' 'Yes, I have a great deal of wine in my cellars; Good old Dafydd Nanmor, for reminding me – give him another drink, someone!" Surely not even the most besotted of patrons was quite as besotted as that!

The lines have to be seen in their context. The opening lines of the poem have drawn a picture of men flocking into Tywyn to partake of Rhys ap Maredudd's hospitality. The poet then changes gear, to the mood of the subjunctive, with the wish that Tywyn may never be disgraced by shortage of any kind. As so often in poetry, the subjunctive is the key to imaginative release: the next three stanzas weave together the eternal fecundity and limitless renewal of nature – stars, dust, flowers, birds on a wheatfield, snow, rain and dew, heaven, rock and soil – with the activity of Rhys in Tywyn, giving and receiving blessings. His hospitality is felt as a part of nature, seeming outside our numbered days; or, at least, it is made so to our imaginations. And so our gratitude for it must similarly be "numbered as the dew":

> As flowers of the earth in each kind – as snow,
>> As birds on a wheatfield,
> As the rain comes, and the dew,
> So on one man my blessing.

All through the poem, Dafydd Nanmor is playing with the inadequacy of number: number cannot really express nature's richness, or the richness of feelings he has about Rhys, or the benefits of Rhys' rule in Tywyn. Yet number is the key he uses to unlock our imaginations. Its accumulation, with the paradox of its basic inadequacy, is what articulates the whole poem: and any particular number is no more (but also no less) seriously meant than Marvell's:

> An hundred years should go to praise
> Thine eyes and on thy forehead gaze;
> Two hundred to adore each breast,
> But thirty thousand to the rest;
> An age at least to every part,
> And the last age should show your heart.

As with Marvell, Dafydd Nanmor is taking advantage of fantasy to tell us about something intensely serious: what the poem is about is the 'eternal reciprocity' – not of tears, but of the good life, as it was found and experienced and created around and under and with the patronage of Rhys ap Maredudd, lord of Tywyn. "In the beginning was the Word..." yes, but also, thank God, "There was a man sent from God, whose name was John." And, in this context, there was a man sent from God, whose name was Rhys. Only Rhys was not the Baptist, crying in the wilderness: he was a man, a good man doubtless, who could be amused, enchanted, purified by poetry. But still, by Dafydd Nanmor's judgement, a man sent from God. As Dafydd as Gwilym remarked in another context:

> From heaven came every gladness.
> It is from hell comes sadness.

Or again,

> No one relish or food
> Empties the bounty of God.

But we have fallen into the trap, as critics always do, on one side or the other: we have become too solemn. The element of 'play', of fantasy, even in a serious poem like this, has eluded us. And the 'play' is, finally, a lot more important, more sophisticated and wise, than any solemnities we might have to utter. I do not think any English readers will miss the resemblances in these poets to their own metaphysical school. The means by which the Welsh poets gain their effects are not at all similar; but the 'play', the fantasy, the serious wit, carried always through the imagery and the closely woven rhythms – these are not wholly different.

And now, let us go back to our two stanzas, with their eighteen shiploads of wine and their men numbered as trees. Dafydd Nanmor was a connoisseur of wine – that is clear from his other poems. So we must take care not to allegorize the wine out of existence, even if we cannot altogether accept that there were eighteen shiploads full of it. The two stanzas are introduced by a compound pun, which I have perforce to leave out of my version. He has just said that he hopes blessings will continue to fall on Rhys,

> So long as heaven stays, or rock,
> Or good loam in the hillside –

Na maen neu bridd i mewn bryn, where *bryn* means *hill*. And now he begins "He buys the drink from the vineyards" – *Ef a bryn y llyn o'r gwinllannau*, where *bryn* is a mutated present tense of *prynu*, to buy. What is more, *llyn*, which here means *drink*, can also mean *lake*. Ignoring grammar (as the very existence of the pun shows us that at least one part of Dafydd Nanmor's mind has done) one gets something like "He 'hills' the lake from the vineyards", as a subsidiary ·'nonsensical' connotation. Scholars will probably throw their hands up in despair; but this kind of thing happens in other poetry, so why not in Welsh? In other words, while the surface meaning registers an abrupt change of key at this point, the nonsensical meaning carries on with its metaphorical discourse. Rhys is to be blest while good loam stays in the hillside; and he is now felt (subconsciously) to be himself creating the hillside · as he goes along, with the wine he buys from the vineyards. In what way does wine create the conditions where Rhys is to be blessed? We need not be afraid of the obvious here, provided we do not limit our response. The Welsh poets did not share our puritannical distrust of alcohol as a social blessing. But from the sixth century onwards, poets had been talking of wine and mead as present-day economists might talk of money – as the symbolic material wherewith armies were paid and the safety of the country ensured. And therefore Dafydd Nanmor passes, without any of our modern sense of paradox at the connexion, from winecasks to swords:

> Winecasks there must be, and swords – surely
> Both for Rhys Amhredudd.

The one implies the other. And indeed, if we look at any society before our own, when we ask what the prevalent idea of the good life was, we shall generally find that it was some kind of feast, with everybody joining in, and wine and food plentiful; and also, as a rule, protected by strong defenders. This is certainly the dominant image of the Kingdom of Heaven in the New Testament. True, the food and drink are sometimes (not always) spiritualized in various ways; and the defenders are not men, but the legions of the Heavenly Host. But at least two of the sacraments of the Church – Holy Communion and Confirmation – derive directly from this primitive conception. I am afraid that our modern inclination to seek the good life in some form of sexual union, although it did exist at earlier periods, would have seemed to most men of good sense in the past as distinctly esoteric and odd.

I have spoken of a kind of 'play' or fantasy as characteristic of the classical Welsh poets. The seriousness, in other words, is not a matter of what the poet says – his personal sincerity is in nowise at stake – but of what the poem, as a whole, does. And what the poem does is largely a matter of rhythm and imagery. It is above all the abounding grace of Dafydd Nanmor's rhythm, its sweep and delicacy combined, that weaves its different images together, and makes the whole poem so triumphant an expression of joy. I have in fact cheated by analysing this poem: for the 'Praise of Rhys ap Maredudd' is not a *cywydd*, and therefore not entirely typical of its period. It is much more expansive, and its texture much more open-grained. Nevertheless, while it still preserves the basic 'accumulative' principle of the *Gogynfeirdd* it does show also the workmanship of a man trained in the *cywydd*. It exemplifies the two kinds of technique, in fact, in perfect harmony.

The Welsh classical poets, like Cynddelw before them, are essentially masters of counterpoint. But whereas I compared Cynddelw's poetry to the music of the *organum*, where the plain-song notes are lengthened into a kind of drone and the attention is given to the embroidery of sound that the composer weaves about them, in the *cywydd* the embroidery does without this formal propping-up from below. A *cywydd* relies for its effect on the simultaneous development (in a musical sense) of its several images. It is nearly always constructed upon the dialectical possibilities of the second person singular: so that 'I' and 'thou' and 'he', 'she' or 'it' are as it were the three *axes* on which the poem is built. This may be recognized formally, by the use of dialogue, of which the *cywydd*-writers are especially fond; but more often it is implicit in the structure of the monophonic discourse. The Welsh poets are fond also of slipping from one person into another, as whim or metre takes them; and this change of perspective is itself a form of counterpoint. More frequently, however, they rely on the juxtaposition of metaphors, as in Dafydd ap Gwilym's poem to 'The Thrush' where the two basic images are those of bright light and formal language: the latter bifurcates, soon, into the language of a priest and the language of a poet. Each of these metaphors is then developed at length, all of them (and the original thrush) meeting momentarily in the 'winged angel' five lines from the end; and the poet ends by a brilliantly headlong coda about the birds in the Garden of Eden, which is next to impossible satisfactorily to translate.

This is a particularly neat example; but it can be paralleled in the Dafydd Nanmor poem we have been considering. There the basic subjects for contrapuntal development are more abstract: the inadequacy of number and the reciprocity of blessing, symbolized by the revellers' riding *into* Tywyn and Rhys' fame spreading out *from* it. Poems of this period hardly ever lack at least one central image, or cluster of images, or (because the word 'image' may be being used too widely) let us say, one central poetic idea. A *cywydd* may go on for whole paragraphs accumulating phrases like a poem by Cynddelw; but sooner or later it will usually get down to its proper business. And, more often than not, there is more than one subject for development, and the life of the poem consists in the relationships between them. Typical in this respect is the *llatai*-poem, where a lover sends a bird or animal (or exceptionally something else) as a messenger to his beloved. Here the messenger, the girl and the poet occupy the three *axes* of the second, third and first person singular respectively. Each is developed in turn, and the poem ends when the relationship between them is fully articulated. Except for the love that the poet has for the girl, this relationship is purely arbitrary, of course: but it none the less proved a popular scheme for the *cywydd*, largely, one suspects, because it did provide three *axes* of development, with a different method proper to each. For the second person, the bird or animal, the poet usually uses *dyfalu*, or the heaping of descriptive phrases – often of a somewhat far-fetched and fanciful kind – in the form of a greeting; for the third person, the girl, he falls back upon the 'heraldic' type of description used in the praise-poetry – tells us where she comes from, in what spot his messenger may find her, how beautiful she is, how she is lovelier than the legendary beauties of Britain, and so on; and for the first person, finally, he employs the lyrical conventions of the troubadour to portray himself as a typical courtly lover, pining for his lady. It sounds rather formalistic and rigid: but two things mitigate this impression. First, the poem as a whole moves towards its total resolution. One subject is not necessarily exhausted first, then another, and then the third. Cross-references are frequent, except in the opening *dyfalu* or description of the messenger. The poet's skill is shown as much in the transitional passages as in the play of his fancy within each separate mode. And secondly, at any rate in the fourteenth century, the messenger is often felt as a projection of one aspect of the lover's own personality, as well as being an independent and closely observed creature in its own right. Thus, the 'Wind' of Dafydd ap Gwilym is a fitting symbol of the poet's wanton and anarchic feelings; while Llywelyn Goch's 'Tit' behaves with all the gay civility that a young page of the court ought to have, according to the best medieval patterns of etiquette. This allows the poet to isolate and express two opposed aspects of the courtly code – his own and his messenger's – at one and the same time.

The form in the praise-poetry that corresponds to the *llatai*-poem in the poetry of love is, I suppose, the 'poem of asking', where one man asks another for a gift which is then described. Suppose an uncle had decided to give his nephew a horse for his birthday. Because poetry was an art that gave dignity to social occasions, the poet would be called in to commemorate the gift; and his poem would take this form. Normally the first section would be in praise of the uncle, a greeting and decorated address in the second person; the second section would then briefly introduce and distinguish the nephew in the first person; and the third section would consist of *dyfalu* or description of the horse in the third person. The poem would end with a brief coda, recapitulating the request. The poem of asking is not, to my mind, so successful a form as the *llatai*-poem, even if it did possess considerable social utility. For one thing, the three *axes* are not so clearly differentiated in the manner of their development. The poem falls too much into a sandwich – an opening and closing passage of praise, with a very different section of *dyfalu* in the middle. For another, in any poem addressed to something or someone, the 'I-thou' relation is potentially much more dynamic than any relationships in the third person. The *llatai*-poem exploits this fact to give life to its opening *dyfalu*, which is essentially a greeting. But the poem of asking wastes this natural source of vivacity, and has to rely on pure force of fancy to make up for it in the third person *dyfalu* of the gift. Lastly, the gift cannot very often be integrated with either the giver or the receiver in any way that yields poetic sense. In the example by Gutun Owain I have translated, all that connects the horse with its giver or its receiver is the bare request:

> Lord of Yale, I crave a boon,
> Ask, without fear, this stallion –

and then, in the final recapitulation,

> Your warrior on a warhorse
> I'll be, if I get this horse.

This is a poor substitute for all the richness of counterpoint found in almost any *llatai*-poem between the messenger, the poet and the girl.

So far we have been considering the large-scale counterpointing that shapes entire poems. But there is a constant, smaller counterpoint of ideas, syntax and sound-structures going on within every paragraph, every couplet and every line. Sometimes two sentences are running in alternate phrases within a single couplet. Sometimes one sentence will take a whole paragraph to unfold, a word or two in every line, the rest taken up with extra-syntactical phrases or even other sentences. Sometimes, again, phrases are piled up, one on top of another, without a main verb. The play of sounds – rhymes, alliteration, assonances of various kinds – is regularized into a metrical system as complex as any in the world. This is not the place to describe it in detail.* But two things ought to be said: first, the system leaves the poet considerable freedom in the matter of which particular pattern he chooses to use. In most metrical systems, you can foretell the pattern of any individual line, once you know the pattern as a whole. But a line in a *cywydd* may be one of a quite large number of patterns, and there is no means of telling which the poet will use next. Secondly, it is fairly certain that Welsh poetry was usually meant to be sung; and in all medieval solo-songs, it is the metre's job to decorate the music, not the other way round. This is a broad generalization, I know. But I think it explains the complexity of (say) troubadour songs, as far as their metre goes; and probably the same was true for Welsh. I am not suggesting that a *cywydd* was sung to a tune, like a Provençal *canso*; in fact, I think the reverse is true. I merely suggest that metrical decoration probably had the same function in both.

Welsh classical poetry started with the love-poems of Dafydd ap Gwilym in the middle years of the fourteenth century. It is usual to see the influence of the Provençal troubadours (however

---

*The only important exception to this rule is the internal rhyming found in *cynghanedd lusg* where a final syllable rhymes with a stressed penultimate one.

indirectly) as the originating impulse behind Welsh love-poetry. As we have said, this started in the middle of the twelfth century – so far as we know – with the work of Gwalchmai, Hywel ab Owain and Cynddelw. Now, with all respect, this is fantastically early for troubadour influence to have reached Wales. The troubadours themselves were beginning to sing in the south of France in the late eleventh and early twelfth centuries. Their northern French counterparts, the *trouvères*, were a product of the last third of the twelfth century. Is it likely that love-songs on troubadour lines were sung in Welsh not merely as soon as, but actually before, they were sung in the French of Paris? It is true that Latin love-lyrics are found, albeit somewhat scantily, before those of the troubadours; but the Welsh poets seem to me not much indebted to either; though later on, in the fourteenth century, Dafydd was certainly not above taking hints from other literatures.

There are two main sources of Welsh love-poetry, both of them indigenous, arising out of the specialized function of the Celtic poet in his society. The first was tied up with his relations with the womenfolk of the tribal king. A house-poet, such as Cynddelw was in his youth, could be required to sing songs to the lady of the house in her chamber. This would naturally be an inducement to sing love-songs, since love is usually a topic to interest women. As a poet, also, he had sometimes to praise the noble ladies of the court, and to write their elegies when they died. A separate technique seems to have been devised for this purpose, with its own vocabulary and conventions. The examples in this book by Einion ap Gwalchmai and Gruffudd ap Maredudd are later than the twelfth century, it is true; but they probably conform to a type that was in use at that time. Among the conventions proper to it is the idea that the poet was in love with the women. he praised. This is certainly very like one explanation of the *amor purus* of Provence. But there is a very useful concept in biology, namely that of convergent evolution, which I suggest may reasonably be invoked to cover this similarity.

The second source of love-poetry in Wales was much the more important for its future development. This was the Boasting Poem, first found in Gwalchmai and Hywel ab Owain, where the poet praises himself, says what a fine warrior he is, how pretty the scenery is all round him, and how loyal he is to his king. It was fundamentally an expression of what St. Paul calls the pride of life, full of euphoria with the world. Naturally, women played a part in this, Gwalchmai tells us how many girls have fallen in love with him, what a fine conversation he has had with one or other of them, and how his thoughts go wandering in their direction. Now, if you listen to young men boasting, they will certainly tell you all this; but they will also very often say: 'All the girls are mad about me, except one, who isn't yet, but I'm still playing her. And boy, she's a smasher!' We need not, I think, posit much more than this in Gwalchmai's case either. Hywel is a little more complex, but not much. He does write love-poems pure and simple. But I cannot myself see any trace of the fatal passion of the troubadours in them at all. In one poem, he actually complains of the fatigue that loving all these girls has given him! Constancy, anonymity, unworthiness before the beloved, endless arguments about love – these are the high requisites of the Courtly Love of Provence. And none of them are typical of Hywel ab Owain.

Or, really, of Dafydd ap Gwilym either. The trouble is, critics have tended to compartmentalize Dafydd's poetry into convenient pigeonholes. So many poems about nature, so many about comic adventures, so many high-principled poems to Dyddgu, so many not so high invitations to Morfudd, and so on. This ignores the salient fact about most of them, which is that they form one of the most artfully constructed self-portraits in the history of poetry. Dafydd is his own most constant and fascinating subject-matter, the Charlie Chaplin of the time. His is decidedly the art of a great comic: like Falstaff he is not merely witty himself, but a great cause of wit in others. The girls who mock him at Llanbadarn are as much a part of his self-portraiture as his agonized reflections on them. And, like all great comics, he can be profoundly sad. The end of 'The Ruin' is as harsh in its baffled melancholy as the barest of Welsh landscapes. One thing he is not – or at least, not very often – is tender. Llywelyn Goch, his only rival as a great love-poet, is far tenderer than he, even in such a light poem as 'The Tit'. I think it was Iolo Goch who called Dafydd the "hawk of the women of the South", and somehow the title fits. He is thinking of the falconer's hawk, of course, a gentle, well-groomed, mild-eyed creature, fit to grace a noble lady's wrist; and yet, under all that, the predator, the accomplisher of death.

It was the self-portrait (and how much truth of representation there was to it, we cannot say – but surely some!) that fascinated, enchanted and exasperated Dafydd's contemporaries. Gruffudd Gryg remarked on the glibness with which Dafydd threatened to die for any girl he sang to; and that it was a wonder the poor man hadn't died already, twenty times over. But for half a century afterwards (and, indeed, spasmodically ever since) when it came to writing a love-poem, poet after poet tried to wear Dafydd's mask. Since they were, on the whole, ordinary mortals, and not one of the supreme wizards of poetic sleight-of-hand the world has ever seen, the mask did not always fit them very well. They have the craft all right, but not the impudence, the hawk's authority with intangible air: they are – dare one say it? – more human; and they certainly do have virtues of their own. Their work was confused with Dafydd's in the manuscripts; and has only just recently been rigorously – some critics would say, too rigorously – weeded out, in Principal Thomas Parry's great edition of the master. Now that the apocrypha has been separated from the canon, it is possible for the first time properly to evaluate his uniqueness.

Perhaps Dafydd's greatest weapon is his all-pervasive irony. Take, for example, the celebrated 'Trouble at a Tavern', which at first sight looks like a straightforward medieval rough-and-tumble in the *fabliau* tradition. I suppose few people will fail to see the joke; though I have had one student complain of it as a bad example of race-prejudice. The story of a conceited young man-about-town making a date with a girl at an inn, and failing to keep it because he bumps into the furniture on the way to her room and wakes the whole house – this is glorious farce, and very funny. But if you read it as merely a romp you are in danger of ignoring Dafydd ap Gwilym. Dafydd came of a family that is known to have befriended the Anglo-Norman cause. The towns in Wales, as I have said, were largely Anglo-Norman preserves. Dafydd's playing at being a fine young aristocrat at a tavern in a town was, therefore, an Anglo-Norman kind of behaviour; and his irony is on himself playing the Englishman, right from the start. This gives point to his using the phrase 'may Welshmen love me!' as a sort of swearword when he knocks his shin on the (English) ostler's stool. And at the very peak of his misadventure, with all hell let loose round him, he comes upon the three Englishmen:

INTRODUCTION

> In a foul bed, at the wall,
> Bothered for their packs, and fearful,
> Three English lay in panic –
> Hickin and Jenkin and Jack.

It is surely a judgement on him that the first thing they splutter is, "It's a Welshman" and therefore a thief after their belongings. No wonder the poet exclaims, "O hot ferment of betrayal!" In fact, read properly, the poem is hardly contemptuous about the English at all. There is, I suppose, a certain snobbery in it; but this, again, is shot through and through with ironic undertones. After all, if Dafydd will try and make dates in the middle of the night in a crowded inn, and then gets caught in the act, he cannot expect to be treated as a visiting celebrity!

Any other poet would have been content to leave it there. Not so Dafydd! With a flick of the wrist, his irony extends itself to cover the entire Christian religion. As he shivers there, with the whole tavern up in arms against him, he bethinks himself to pray:

> And such power has prayer for us,
> Such the true grace of Jesus,
> I found my own bed safe and sure...

This, in fact, saves him; but he cannot help counting the cost:

> I found my own bed safe and sure
> Though without sleep or treasure,
> Thank the Saints, freed of distress.

His own bed – his *henwal*, literally his old lair, his place by the wall. Is there not an implied contrast here with the *dinas dethol*, the "chosen city", with which he started?. Is he not saying that, anyway for one night, he will be content to be poor and Welsh, because that at least is safe? I spoke earlier of the town tavern as an 'anti-image', contrasting it with the central 'image' of the house of a Welsh nobleman: the phrase "without treasure" - *heb sâl*, without benefit, profit or gain – points this out. Obviously it refers mainly to the girl Dafydd has tried to seduce; but at a Welsh house, Dafydd would have had his *sâl*, his payment, as a poet. So the ironies cluster; and he ends with the marvellously flat line, "I ask now God's forgiveness." It leaves us gasping at his audacity. Chaucer could use that kind of demureness – yes, when it was merely a matter of agreeing with the enthusiastic, if rather garrulous eagle of *The Hous of Fame*. Surely even Chaucer would not have tried to be demure when it came to the Almighty himself! Is it really possible that Dafydd was the faithful child of Mother Church that his editor makes him out to be? Perhaps it is. One is always being surprised by the blasphemies of the faithful. But, with this sort of irony in the balance, I would not like to bet too heavily on the angelic leanings of Dafydd ap Gwilym.

It is beyond the scope of a book of this kind – even if I had the necessary knowledge, which I do not – to trace the decline of the Welsh tradition after the Act of Union with England in 1536, when the doors of happy Anglicization were flung open to the Welsh gentry queuing up outside, and English was made the sole official language of Wales. There were fierce political, social and economic pressures involved. The act dissolving the monasteries, for example, deprived Welsh poets of one of their chief sources of patronage. Places such as Jesus College, Oxford, which was set up to educate the Welsh in a way that had nothing to do with their native learning, drew the young nobility out of Wales during their most formative years. Welshmen flooded to London to seek their fortunes. As one historian puts it (writing of the reign of Henry VII):

> Hitherto it had been a disadvantage to be a Welshman; now it was the other way about, possibly for the first time since the Saxon invasions. It is true that Henry's absorption in affairs of state gave him little time to attend to Wales. But he opened wide the doors of opportunity to Welshmen in the period of greatest expansion in English history. Henceforth the destinies of Wales were inextricably mingled with those of England.
>
> (David Williams in a broadcast talk: *The Rise of the House of Tudor*)

After the Act of Union, the Welsh M.P.s were so delighted with its effects that they wanted to extend it to Scotland; and bored the House of Commons with their enthusiasm.

It is important, however, to remember (even as an act of faith) that civilizations do not decline solely because of outside factors. Welsh culture of the old, Celtic kind declined primarily because of Welsh sins against it. Welshmen were too solemn about it; or too apathetic; or they did not think clearly enough, letting opportunism rule their souls. Even in the fifteenth century, Siôn Cent was a puritan; that is, one who is too solemnly anti-cultural. Then, of course, the poets could afford to make fun of him. Rhys Goch Eryri says of him:

> Mere copper you are, you scab,
> Siôn Cent, for all your hubbub.

During the sixteenth and seventeenth centuries, however, the poets lost confidence in their own imaginative freedom. Humanists, puritans and Englishmen all said their praise was mere flattery. Their patrons were no longer vitally interested in what they were doing. They had, to be sure, a trade to keep up, lineages to trace, lords to compliment: why not leave it at that, and ignore the imaginative scope of their predecessors? The old tradition of Taliesin became more and more a matter of *vers de société*, lacking any significance wider than that of the events it commemmorated. Even the craft declined, the poet's control over his medium often falling below the barest minimum that art requires. It was a gradual business, of course: there are still quite good poems written to patrons as late as the eighteenth century. But, even in Elizabethan Wales, the rot was inexorably taking possession. It is important to notice the difference between Wales and Ireland in this matter. In Ireland, the Celtic aristocracy were either killed off or driven into exile. A Munster poet like Egan O'Rahilly, therefore, even as he laments their passing, can maintain his own pride in them intact. His splendid poems, however unreal they may sound to the economic historian, are humanly a fine expression of cultural defiance near the end of its tether. But the Welsh aristocracy were not so conveniently disposed of: they turned into complete Englishmen, squires of the shires. Welsh culture was betrayed to a more wasting sickness even than Irish; for the English (*pace* Shakespeare's Fluellen) wanted so badly that the Welsh – who had given them their most splendid dynasty to date – should be their friends, and partake to the full in the prosperity of Great Britain. We can see the results of this benevolence in the pathetic poem by Owen Gruffydd, written when the tradition was almost dead on its feet. Owen Gruffydd and Egan O'Rahilly were contemporaries of each other. The contrast between them is almost unbearably poignant; as, too, is Owen Gruffydd's plight as an old man compared with that of Guto'r Glyn at Valle Crucis, looked after by the kindly abbot until he honourably died in his bed.

There were two allied attempts in the sixteenth century to find a substitute for the declining tradition of Taliesin. The humanists tried to foist an alien learning on to the bards that were left. Renaissance values, brought to Wales from Oxford and from Catholic exiles on the continent, can be traced right through to the eighteenth-century school of Lewis Morris, the most important poet of which was Goronwy Owen, an Anglesey man who spent most of his life in exile in England and America. Goronwy Owen's work can perhaps be best seen as an attempt to reconcile Welsh classicism with English middle-class Augustanism. He is the first great poet of the Welsh middle class, in his best work achieving a remarkable synthesis between the Welsh great-house tradition and the social ease and equality with which one townsman greets another. Horace and Dafydd Nanmor mingle in his poems; and there is also found there the great Romantic nostalgia of the exile for his homeland that has, more than any other single factor, made him the symbolic figure of the time. But the whole attempt was doomed from the start: the Welsh middle class were in no position to take over the patronage of the poets from the defecting nobility; and, in any case, whenever they were able to, they defected also. A Welsh Renaissance could not help being provincial, because the Renaissance was a culture entirely preoccupied with urban values. It needed a capital city to make sense at all; and the only capital Wales had was London, to which it was a province as remote as Britain was from Rome. The greatest contribution that the Renaissance made to Wales was the translation of the Bible into Welsh. This has been one of the decisive factors in preserving Welsh as a living language down to the present day.

The other Welsh attempt to find a substitute for the tradition of Taliesin lay in the field of the so-called 'free' metres. During the Middle Ages there had been no Welsh equivalent of the Anglo-Irish nobility – men like Gearóid Iarla, Gerald Fitzgerald (called the Rhymer), fourth Earl of Desmond, Lord Chief Justice of Ireland – who had combined a knowledge of Irish as their first language with a cultural heritage partly derived from Normandy and (ultimately) Provence. These Anglo-Irishmen, as early as the fourteenth century, had initiated a school of love-poetry, the *Dánta Grádha*, written in Irish lyric measures (usually in a simplified or looser form known as *óglúchas* – equivalent to the Welsh free-metres) but modelled in style and subject-matter on the *amour courtois* of France. This kind of poetry is not found in Welsh manuscripts until the sixteenth century: it may have been composed before that, but presumably it was not popular with the Welsh nobility, who had their own indigenous love-poetry of the *cywydd*-writers. In the sixteenth century, due to the turning of the Welsh gentry towards London, there occurs for the first time in Wales an elegant school of courtly love-poets, writing in stanzaic free-metres some of which are native, others are borrowed from England. It is not, of course, the high medieval love that finds expression in their work, but the rather decadent pastoralism of the Elizabethan lyricists. The school was essentially a temporary and amateurish affair; it lasted (we might say) to find its ultimate *raison d'être* in the sheer metrical ingenuity of the carols of Huw Morus, the chief poet of the seventeenth century.

After such knowledge, what forgiveness? A high culture in its death throes is surely one of the most unregenerate manifestations of mankind. The eighteenth century found Wales practically a spiritual vacuum, neither one thing nor the other, betrayed by its leaders into a kind of limbo. Culturally, the mass of the people were Celtic still; on the level of folk-culture, I suppose Wales was a lively enough place to live. Village poets, travelling play-actors, music and dancing were common to every part of Wales. Folklore and superstitions of every sort were interestingly varied and widespread. Some of the squires still patronized the local arts. But these things had once been a part of something else, which meant vitality and the power to live the good life. A post-Christian culture which does not include the way to Heaven and the way to Hell (or only includes them as sanctions external to its essence) is hardly a culture at all.

What changed Wales was Methodism. It swept through the country like wildfire, bringing with it a new sense of purpose and a new kind of leadership and intellectual orientation. It completely broke the mystique of hierarchy, the sense of relevance dependent upon a man's place in a scheme of things. To this day, Welsh people are often quite blindly prejudiced against anything they think is snobbery or 'swank' about class-distinctions. They see no point to it; or perhaps it would be truer to say, it morally offends them, and they hit out at it with all their power. In due time, this made them political radicals, and even communists. This was not the intention of the Methodist preachers, of course: they were not interested in merely social attitudes. It arose out of their sense of the unique importance of the individual's salvation, independent of any order of precedence in heaven or on earth.

The price that the Welsh had to pay for this new heroic age was the suppression – at any rate in part – of their cultural heritage as a Celtic nation. Under the stress of the great revivals they emerged as something entirely different, a peculiar people bound together by two things: their language (which was old) and the passionate sincerity with which they looked for salvation in Christ (which was new). Brought to the judgement of this sincerity, dancing, harp-playing, public houses, even long hair, all came under the Methodist indictment, as dangerously profane and irrelevant pleasures. Minstrels and strolling players, last heirs of the tradition, were particularly attacked. It is true that the folk-culture went out by the front door only to come in again at the back; but much was lost, and it is natural for us to regret it. But folk-culture (as much as court-culture) is essentially a product of the principle of hierarchy at work. One would not have folk art in the New Jerusalem. Methodism objected to it, of course, on moral grounds; but one can see that ideologically the two things are really incompatible, however human it may be to try and combine them.

Only two arts escaped the general holocaust; or perhaps it would be truer to say, two new arts emerged from it. First, of course, the sermon, the ministry of the word. The preachers were the new heroes, the new prophets of Israel, leading God's people from their exile. They were men of great ability, with a profoundly intellectual grasp of doctrine. They were also possessed of considerable histrionic ability and fire, who could stimulate in their congregations the wildest surges of emotional release. And secondly, more durable, there was the hymn, the congregation's response to God's grace. English hymns usually

– 63 –

contrive to sound both under-nourished and artificially over-blown at one and the same time. Welsh hymns are quite different. William Williams of Pantycelyn, usually known simply as Pantycelyn, the greatest of all the hymn-writers (among his productions being the English 'Lead me, O thou great Jehovah'), was a lyric poet of quite remarkable intensity and range. He is certainly the greatest lyric poet in Welsh; some people would say, notwithstanding Dafydd ap Gwilym, the greatest poet of any kind.

Pantycelyn's hymns reveal very closely the connexions that there were between the social and religious forces that erupted in Methodism and the cultural and literary movement we call the Romantic Revival. To all intents and purposes, Pantycelyn is a great Romantic poet – indeed, as Saunders Lewis has pointed out, there is a strong case for claiming him as the first great Romantic poet of Europe. No other Welsh poet is remotely like him – even his fellow hymn-writers lack his totality of response to the feelings of the moment. He is alone in a desert land, led only by the divine spark in his soul. He uses the imagery of the Bible and of Bunyan to suggest the Romantic aloneness of the individual, and also the individual's salvation in communion with that Other who is all-terrifying and yet all-fascinating. Poetry is no longer a craft, a product of society. It has become a witness to the individual's commitment to the quest for redemption. His style is masculine and colloquial, careless of mere polish and formal graces; he will cheerfully mix metaphors rather than lose the impetus of his sincerity. His output was enormous: he is one of the very few Welsh poets whose sheer bulk is a meaningful factor in any assessment of his art. Despite his concentration on the individual's response, his hymns have become the staple diet of Welsh Nonconformity, and (paradoxically) the greatest expression of its over-riding sense of belonging. Nor did he only write hymns, though these are his best-loved works. Poems in blank verse, epics, elegies for his friends, and so on, all poured from his pen. He used the long poem, as did the later Romantics, as a kind of spiritual biography of his own conversion, a testament to the grace within.

Reviewers of the first edition of this book expressed surprise that I had not included any poems by Ann Griffiths. The omission was due to my incompetence: I made several attempts to translate her and failed dismally. For this present edition, however, I have had a go at three poems and found the

INTRODUCTION

experience intensely rewarding. Ann Griffiths of Dolwar Fach in mid Wales is the greatest of Welsh women poets; she is also, by a long way, the finest Welsh poet of the nineteenth century, though she only just qualifies for this distinction as she died at the age of twenty-nine in 1805. But her greatness is of a very peculiar kind. Her total surviving *oeuvre*, apart from eight precious letters, one in her own handwriting, consists of about two dozen hymns and fragments, which she apparently did not write down herself but gave to her maid Ruth to put tunes to. Ruth could not write but she dictated them to her husband John Hughes who in turn published them after their author's death.

Unlike those of William Williams of Pantycelyn, Ann Griffiths's hymns do not seem to have been originally intended for congregational singing. They were part of her life in a community of Methodists around her home, spontaneous outpourings of love and joy in Christ her lord. But that gives a very misleading impression: not since the liturgical hymns of the Latin middle ages has there been such an intellectual pressure on the doctrines of Christianity coupled with a passionate fervour that is almost brittle in its intensity. She is, I think, the one great Welsh poet since Cynddelw Brydydd Mawr who really means what she says. Even in Pantycelyn there is an element of make-believe; the imagination could not be vouched for in a court of law. This is certainly true of the poets of the nobility and Dafydd ap Gwilym. But with Ann, as with Cynddelw, there is no such leeway. Her metaphors are there simply because they bring her where she has to go. Her imagination flashes out towards the incarnate God like lightning from sky to earth.

It is this combination of intellectual pressure and Christocentric imagination that has made critics and theologians compare her with the great mystics. If one means by mystical a religion that allows man to have union with God now, then Ann is clearly no mystic. Her desire for the Bridegroom is still unfulfilled – as it must be in terms of Protestant theology. Even in Catholicism the claim to enjoy union must be viewed with suspicion. The difference between the orthodoxy of St John of the Cross and damnable heresy is not all that large, in doctrinal terms, however crucial it may be to the covenanted salvation of the mystic. But the contemplative life does not start with mystical union or even necessarily involve it. Intellectually it starts with a totally "inhuman" pressure on the paradoxical tenets of belief, a rejection of images and imagination alike, and a vast desire and courage to go into the darkness of faith. Pantycelyn rejects the "created objects" of the natural world, but he seems to do so mainly because they interfere with his quest for salvation. They are moral impediments to the life of faith. With Ann, the unnaturalness of the Way is of its essence – she begins a poem,

> Though clean contrary to nature
> Is my path in the world...

There is a constant play of paradox in her poems, a holy glee in mixed metaphors –

> A way to win its travellers,
> Way that is husband, way that is head,
> A holy way, I'll go along it
> To rest in it beyond the veil.

Christ is the Way, of course (*John xiv 6*), but *way* is feminine in Welsh so that the very pronouns underline the paradox. The Way *wins* its travellers, like a gambler or a hero, or of course like a wooer; it becomes a husband, which recalls St. Paul's model for marriage, with Christ's headship of the Church symbolized by the husband as the *head* of the family; and perhaps the holy way of matrimony provides the matrix for the other two metamorphoses of the image in the last line: the Way becomes a *rest* as she goes *beyond the veil*. So, by the end of four lines, she has been courted and won, married, accepted a leader and promised to go with him till she finds peace in death. As in Cynddelw Brydydd Mawr, the individual images are often traditional enough. They are the bricks, or the tools of her trade. But the way she builds her visionary poems out of such commonplaces is alert, energetic and convincing. It is the same with the way she mixes registers of speech. In the space of a quatrain she will go from the oriental and erotic floweriness of the biblical Song of Songs through down-to-earth colloquial Welsh into the abstruse and dry-as-dust terms of Calvinist theology, the whole thing transposed into the intensity of the singing voice.

But, as in Cynddelw again, not all the images are commonplace, nor are all the registers given to her by the Bible, the farm or the sermon. Every so often the poetry deepens into vision, the paradoxes quieten into awe. With Cynddelw, this deepening and originality of image usually comes from his contemplation of the ferocity of war; with Ann, from her wonder and astonishment at the Incarnation of God in such a thing as man. In the greatest of her poems, for example, which I have translated as "Full of wonder", she moves through the implications of Christ's life for us, from Bethlehem to Calvary, surrounded even in the tomb by the triumphant symphonies of the angels –

> O my soul, look! Chief of kings, author
> Of peace, he lay in that room,
> The creation in him moving
> And he a dead man in the tomb!

It is at moments like these that Ann Griffiths stands with the greatest poets of the language. She is very difficult to translate, and that for the opposite reason to Pantycelyn. Whereas with him, the difficulty is how to render the tone of a hymn which happens also to be a romantic poem: there are no sufficient models in English verse to follow. With Ann, the problem is to be absolutely literal and yet preserve the energy and form of the original. It is so fatally easy to compromise, to slip into hymnwriter's jargon, to suppose that phrases are interchangeable. Before you know where you are, a great and original poem becomes something that anybody could have written, a nullity. With Pantycelyn, the problem is one of feeling – of finding a suitable vessel for it. With Ann, the problem is one of accepting that she means exactly what she says, and nothing else will do.

Methodism was not, however, the only cultural force at work in eighteenth-century Wales. It might be said that the old Celtic civilization fought back in the work of the antiquaries and scholars, men who first collected and then tried to understand the great legacy of the past. Some of their theories were wild, in key with the romantic notions of the age. Speculation about the Druids, for instance, arose at least partly out of a desire to rehabilitate the past, if not as high culture, then at least as interesting and primitive lore. The positive value these men gave to scholarship varied considerably. One of the greatest of them,

Iolo Morganwg, was so far seduced by his imagination as to fake a whole literature, with poems and documents to match, which he claimed had been written in the Middle Ages in his native Glamorgan. His forgeries were believed for over a century. Other scholarship, however, had more substantial results. Much of the older literature was printed for the first time, and a beginning was made to the laborious task of understanding it.

The most important Celtic come-back, however, was the rise of the Eisteddfod, an annual festival of poetry and music held at a different town in Wales every year. It was associated with a good deal of rather fanciful nonsense, but it did have the great merit of bringing people together from all parts of the country for what were largely cultural reasons. The poetry it stimulated is not usually very readable today – I give one example of it at its best in Eben Fardd's 'Jerusalem Destroyed' – but it did make many Welshmen conscious of both national and aesthetic considerations at a time when there was every temptation to forget them.

English poetry, not always of very high calibre, powerfully influenced nineteenth-century Wales, both in lyric and in philosophical verse like Islwyn's 'The Storm'. But perhaps the purest lyrics of the period were Alun's, in the style of the traditional free-metre poetry that was sung to a harp. On the whole, though, the poetry of Victorian Wales is not very exciting. There is in it a peculiar kind of provincialism, naïve and pompous at the same time, that seems to be sentimental about Wales as a way of apologizing for the fact that the poets are Welsh. It is a great deal too complacent. At a time when the new industries and economy of Wales were changing her people and her landscape almost beyond recognition, a poet like Ceiriog writes as if the changes were no more than might be expected in an isolated Alpine community!

Throughout the nineteenth century the national self-consciousness was growing; and with it the demand for education. Education has always been Janus-faced in Wales. On the one hand it meant a genuine imparting of Welshness, a deepening and widening of the national consciousness; but on the other, it has always implied the desire to escape. Town and country both had a bottleneck of talent. Education was the one way to be free. In order to make use of the gifts God had given you, you had to be able to compete with Englishmen, in their own language and on their own terms. Otherwise you, and your children after you, would be condemned to be quarrymen, or miners, or farm-labourers, for the rest of your days. When the University Colleges of Wales were founded in the late nineteenth century it was largely with this aim in view: the teaching was done in English, to enable the students (most of whom were Welsh-speaking) to leave Wales, if they so desired, and to share in English middle-class prosperity.

Nevertheless, the founding of the Welsh Colleges was an all-important step as far as poetry was concerned. It brought about a much more responsible attitude to the past, and a new and more intellectually respectable approach to literature generally. By precept and example men like John Morris-Jones created a poetry that was European – at least in intention – and yet thoroughly Welsh, rooted in the craftsmanship of the poets of the Middle Ages. They translated vigorously, and not merely from English. Their romantic attitudes should not blind us to their fundamental grappling with contemporary problems. T. Gwynn Jones, for example, cannot be dismissed as only another late Pre-Raphaeliter. His romanticism, unlike Pantycelyn's, is a social affair. It does not pretend that the problem of violent cultural change does not exist, and that Wales carries on much the same as ever despite new industries and rapidly increasing anglicisation.

The underlying factor in twentieth century Welsh literature has been the rise and decline of the south Wales coalfield. During the last quarter of the nineteenth century the demand for steam coal to fuel the railways and steamships of the world was so enormous that south Wales went into overdrive, enjoying forty years of continual boom, radically distinct from the rest of Britain. The immigration into the coalfield was almost comparable, proportionately, to that into the United States. Up to 1900, most of these incomers came from Wales itself. Though anglicisation was already in progress, there was as yet no fundamental danger to Welshness in the industrial revolution that was taking place. On the contrary, industry stopped Welsh people leaving Wales. Farm labourers were leaving the land, and so were other industrial workers: but they went to the valleys of the south, not to America or the colonies. On the whole they took their language with them. What they left in the countryside was a world of small family farms engaged in provisioning the industrial centres. Some of the wealth created in the coal rush did percolate through to the rest of the country; and as the century went on, aided by the holiday resorts of the North and the extraction of other raw materials, such as slate from Gwynedd, the prosperity of the country rose to a level Wales had never known. It was this prosperity which underlay the founding of the colleges of the University of Wales and eventually the National Library. National aspirations and idealisms were at their peak, borne along on the wealth of the new age.

Radical agitation tended to be directed against the English-speaking landlords and their religion, the Established Church. Welsh solidarity, uniting petty bourgeois, small farmer and industrial worker, was Nonconformist, Liberal and (on the whole) Welsh-speaking. It was not separatist. There was a national movement in the eighties – *Cymru Fydd*, Young Wales – but it collapsed into the arms of the Liberal Party in 1896. Even more than those of Northern Ireland, Welsh industries required imperial markets: the coalmines depended on free trade. The economic base for separatism was confined to rural industries and the like, demanding protection against the import of English factory-made commodities that threatened their market at home. They are comparable to the capital-starved peasants and tiny industries of the south of Ireland, that formed the basic economic drive towards Irish nationalism; but unlike their Irish counter-parts, they were in a powerless minority in Wales. Culturally, nevertheless – as is often the way – *Cymru Fydd* and the aspirations it channelled were important in the renaissance of Welsh literature, the Romantic Revival that took place around the turn of the century.

Romanticism in England had been a series of 'strategies' – to use a term from the study of animal behaviour – adopted by writers at a time when a great impulse towards social liberation (the French Revolution) had been blocked or betrayed or otherwise rendered uncongenial. The individual English radical had felt the mighty current and greeted it as his own; but, in the case of Wordsworth, the Terror had disillusioned him. For a long time he was disaffected, feeling that life was pointless. Then, like the Ancient Mariner blessing the water-snakes, he found release in that "serene and blessed mood" where his imagination reached out to the lowly and poor and found a home for itself in 'Nature'.

INTRODUCTION

Each of the great Romantics has a different case-history, a different strategy to offer. Some, like Wordsworth himself, emerged from the Romantic experience into traditional Tory conservatism; others kept their radical fervour. But in all their variety we can say of English Romanticism as a whole that it both allows us to avoid the uncomfortable imperatives of Revolution, and at the same time conserves the energy that the revolutionary situation has generated. It puts the revolutionary situation 'on ice' (as it were) by transposing it into the introvert mode and treating it as aesthetic rather than political experience. The imagination of the poet himself – instead of the revolutionary activist – becomes the heroic agent. I suspect that something like this is true of all vital Romanticism, and is what distinguishes the real thing from its mediaevalist or nature-loving trappings.

It would be absurd to classify *Cymru Fydd* as a revolutionary *débâcle*. Nevertheless, coupled with the enormous expansion and sense of human possibilities in the melting pot of nineteenth century Wales, its inevitable failure marked a limit – and for some a shocking limit – on a great impulse towards social liberation for the Welsh nation. In the Bangor National Eisteddfod of 1902, a North Wales journalist called T. Gwynn Jones won the Chair with an *awdl* called 'Ymadawiad Arthur', 'Arthur's Passing'. It was the first major work of the new Romanticism, and the first of a series of narrative poems that mark T. Gwynn Jones as the great poet of the age. As Derec Llwyd Morgan says:

> For a generation previously, Welsh poets had worked without a symbolic system, indeed without a poetic language. And had it not been for the committee-man who proposed that 'Ymadawiad Arthur' should be the title of the *awdl* at Bangor, it is quite possible that Gwynn Jones would never have developed a poetic language out of Welsh, British and Celtic mythology – and the greater part of contemporary Welsh letters would have been different.

'Ymadawiad Arthur' tells much the same story as Tennyson's 'Morte D'Arthur', but whereas that poem is an exercise in Victorian stoicism, a reflection on evolution and defeat, the Welsh *awdl* is an episode in a continuing battle. For the English, the value of Arthur as a culture-hero is limited. He is an example of civilized behaviour and the necessity of good government; he is a model of a good king and a good husband betrayed. But for the Welsh he represents the central myth of their civilization. As a leader who did not die, who will rise again at some future date to lead his people to victory, he is one of a series of Welsh messiahs – Owain, Hywel, Cadwaladr – to which Owain Glyn Dŵr was the latest recruit. But Arthur is more than that. He fought for the unity of Britain as a continuing Romano-British province. He registers a Welsh claim to be the rightful people of Britain, the inheritors of Roman civilization. Britain not Wales is his proper sphere of operation. Aneirin praises one of the Gododdin as a great warrior, "though Arthur he was not." Cynddelw in his praise of Owain Gwynedd associates the resurgence of the Welsh in his reign with the heroic deeds of Arthur. With Geoffrey of Monmouth, Arthur is seen as a climax to British history, and the English are encouraged to see themselves (by a historical paradox characteristic of them) as Arthur's heirs, a viewpoint enthusiastically taken up by the Tudors. Henry VII named his eldest son Arthur. If he had not died before his father, it would have been King Arthur who passed the Act of Union and so fulfilled Arthur's traditional role of uniting the Welsh and the English under a British king. The continual invocation of Arthur can be seen as a major leit-motif in Welsh history, and one, moreover, which has almost always led to disaster. For the Welsh, Arthur is the major myth of Britishness, a perpetual invitation to look beyond the needs of Wales and to regard Britain as a whole as the promised land of the Welsh people.

T. Gwynn Jones is the only great Welsh poet known for his narratives. His *awdl*, compared with Tennyson's poem, is dramatic and relatively fast-moving. He can tell a story and his characters don't speechify or talk about philosophy. They are believable warriors. When Bedwyr is told to throw Arthur's sword into the water, he is reluctant to do so – what will save the Welsh people now? The gesture has symbolic force: it is not through force of arms that Welsh deliverance will come. The maidens of Afallon enter to take the wounded king away and Bedwyr asks to join him in the boat, united in death as he had been with his master in life. But no, that's not the answer either. The Welsh people – of whom Bedwyr is the representative – are told that they must wait. Bedwyr's role is that of a witness. Arthur is not to die. As he is seated in the boat and already sailing to Afallon, the otherworld, his tone changes. He speaks as an oracle, one of the undead, like one of the severed heads that the ancient Celts used to worship. He tells Bedwyr to endure. The Welsh will suffer betrayal at the hands of their enemies, their life and the truth they have lived will be forgotten; but at last their day will come. They will receive honour among nations and he, Arthur himself, will return from Afallon to lead them. Bedwyr hears the maidens singing about their country of Afallon in a lyric that has become famous.

What then is Afallon? First, it is one of those island Otherworlds so common in Celtic mythology, the home of the ancient gods, the land of eternal youth where old age, sickness or grief never come. Secondly, it is some sort of Platonic country of eternal ideas, where the ideals of the race never die and no one suffers the attrition of lost faith or broken heart. But thirdly, Afallon represents the continued possibility of change. In an extraordinary stanza Gwynn Jones identifies Afallon, the Otherworld, with what really protects Wales, the "breath of life to the nation", the source of energy for those who want reform, and a basis for always wanting to hope. It is from this source, the poem is saying, that Arthur will return.

Notice that Gwynn Jones is re-appropriating Arthur. He is a Welsh leader. Fairly obviously the nation he is talking about (which he generally calls 'bro' – a highly emotive term meaning 'district' or 'region') is Wales, not Britain. Clearly, too, this is hardly a Christian poem, and certainly not a Nonconformist one. That is typical of the Romantic poets. One would hardly think, reading their work, that Welsh nationality during the last half century had increasingly crystallised round Nonconformist irritation at Anglican supremacy. Disestablishmentarianism seems a million miles away from their consciousness. Actually, the disregard (we soon realise) is deliberate. These poets were agnostic in religion, and critical of the social greyness and hypocrisy they saw in Nonconformity. In this they were typical of nineteenth century Romantics everywhere, except that in most of Europe instead of Nonconformists one can read Bourgeois.

'Ymadawiad Arthur' is an 'awdl' not after the old form – a monorhymed sequence – but according to the eisteddfod rubric. The eisteddfod awdl is intended as an exhibition piece to show off its author's mastery of *cynghanedd* and the twenty-four measures, being a poem of some length in as many of the strict metres as the author chooses to use. As a formal recipe for a poem, its requirements are illogical: one would think it is almost bound to encourage a poetry of 'bits'. The monorhyme of the old *awdl* is not pursued beyond a stanza of four to eight lines, and sequences of *englynion* and *cywydd* indiscriminately interrupt the *awdl* measures. Yet to win the Chair with a poem written to this prescription is the quickest and surest way a Welsh poet has of achieving fame and drawing attention to his work. What is more, the fine scholarship of John Morris-Jones had cleared away the misconceptions that had cluttered strict-metre poetry. To write in the strict metres was for the Romantics a way of showing a proper appreciation of the true Welsh tradition. More significant eisteddfod *awdlau* were produced in this period than in any other, before or since. They were the spearhead of the new movement, as the disciples of Morris-Jones challenged and took over from the eisteddfod *ancien regime*. It is also true that T. Gwynn Jones was possibly the greatest master of *cynghanedd* since the fifteenth century. For him, the eisteddfod *awdl* was the starting-place for the metrical innovations of his maturity. In his second example, 'Gwlad y Bryniau' ('Land of the Hills') he started to rationalise the form by using for much of the poem an alternation of only two metres – an innovation followed with complete consistency by R. Williams Parry in his 1910 *awdl*, 'Yr Haf' ('The Summer'), where the whole poem is in one stanza-form. After that Gwynn Jones wrote no more *awdlau* for the eisteddfod, but he started to use one metre all though a poem, with *cynghanedd* but without end-rhyme. It is a sort of strict-metre blank verse. 'Argoed', using ten-syllable lines, is one example which I have translated, though I have not of course kept to the original form. In this way, Gwynn Jones was enabled to write narrative poems using *cynghanedd*. He solved the problem (as old as Goronwy Owen) of writing Welsh strict-metre epic poetry.

These epic idylls will remind an English reader of Tennyson and William Morris; but Gwynn Jones can draw on Welsh myth and make it carry profound social meaning for us; in a way that none of the English Victorians can. Morris was a socialist and an important figure in the history of ideas, yet his narrative poems are generally only picturesque. Most of the major poems of

Gwynn Jones centre round the theme of the earthly – or sometimes otherworldly – paradise. When we first meet it, it suggests romantic self-indulgence and escapism; and indeed many Welsh critics have been content to discuss it in this sort of way, as a feature of Gwynn Jones's psychology to be explained and 'placed' in a context of late romantic neurosis. We want realism and nature-red-in-tooth-and-claw from our poets; if not tragedy, at least social comment and the ironic stance. It is only later that we come to appreciate that Gwynn Jones is not a late Romantic but an early one: he is talking about the way to protect the growing point of his civilization, whether socially, as in 'Ymadawiad Arthur' and 'Argoed', or in more individual terms, as in 'Madog' and 'Broseliawnd'; in the latter poem, the creative imagination itself becomes a temptation and a captivity.

'Ymadawiad Arthur' and the *awdl* by Williams Parry that we have already mentioned, 'Yr Haf', represent the first, hopeful phase of Welsh Romanticism. If Gwynn Jones was the Beethoven of the movement, R. Williams Parry was its Schubert. He was a lyrical poet, not very often given to mythological themes; after the completion of 'Yr Haf', he was a writer of *lieder*, not generally a symphonist like Gwynn Jones. His poems often concern epiphanies or intrusions into the everyday world, messengers, powers; latterly the irruption of Saunders Lewis as an Amos-like prophet and martyr of nationalism. It is significant perhaps that his only major mythological piece is also about a messenger, a meditation on the starling that Branwen, in the *Mabinogion*, trained to fly across the Irish sea to tell of her sufferings, an act which precipitated bloody war and the death of her brother Bendigeidfran. Unlike Gwynn Jones, whose imagery Derec Llwyd Morgan has called "richly unoriginal" (an overstatement, but one sees what he means), Williams Parry is a master of surprising metaphor and epithet. One doesn't always want to be reading Gwynn Jones – mythological tragedy is somehow not everyday fare; but Williams Parry, for all his emphasis on strangeness, is a very companionable poet. With him you have something of the excitement of a personal friendship. He shows you things. Personally rather shy, rather quick to take offence, a painfully sensitive observer of nature, a passionate and perhaps ultimately a defeated man, it has often been said that if you met him in the street you would have taken him for a small-time business man or bank-clerk. Yet it is arguable that he possessed the greatest potential of any twentieth century Welsh poet, but that he never found either the theme or the upbuoying social need to realise it fully. Perhaps it was also an ideological matter: his poetry insists on the detachment of the artist, lonely, agnostic and very much his own master; yet a poet sensitive to the tragedy and fear in things, the "fallings from us, vanishings" of Wordsworth's Ode. He was involved in society, certainly, because he had friends, he was close to his neighbourhood, his *bro*, and he had literary friendships as well. In many ways, far more than Gwynn Jones, he was a typically Welsh poet, a wonderfully accomplished 'country poet' or *bardd gwlad*. He served the needs of his *bro* as a Welsh poet should, writing perfect *englynion* for epitaphs and social verse to entertain them and dignify special occasions. This localness must not be overstressed, of course: Williams Parry was a poet of wide sophistication, part of the British scene, the very opposite of a parish-pump poet. The localness was also part of his strength, part of his genuineness and his concern for the human predicament. But he was uneasy with large-scale social demands, except when society outraged him and he had to fight back. Perhaps this very detachment – at least until 1937, as we shall see in a moment – this element of the 'ivory tower' in his attitude, or more accurately this desire to "kiss the joy as it flies", prevented him responding to the great themes that the churning up of his nation was all the time uncovering.

The work of R. Williams Parry has tempted us to anticipate too much. Let us go back to the buoyancy of the Edwardians. Three things were to undermine and finally topple the optimism of the Romantics and indeed Romanticism itself.

First, coal. Up to about 1900 the growth of the coal industry had aided the Welsh struggle to keep their language and culture alive. Wealth from the mines had percolated through to finance capital investment in Welsh culture; and the vast need for coalminers had meant that Welsh people had not had to emigrate on anything like the scale of the Irish or even of the English or Scots. Anglicisation had certainly started, but it seemed containable. Much of the coalfield was still pretty solidly Welsh-speaking. But as the growth of the industry went its seemingly unstoppable way, the demand for manpower was such that Welsh recruits to the collieries were no longer adequate to meet it. More and more foreigners – English, Irish, Scotsmen, Spaniards, Italians – were sucked into the melting pot. Had the language of education and authority been Welsh, this too could have been contained; but it was not. Inevitably the common language was English, and Welsh was doomed. By 1914, certainly, this process was showing signs of reaching critical proportions.

Second, war. Welshmen – with Lloyd George at their head – responded to the outbreak of war in 1914 with a jingoistic hysteria that saddens and surprises one still. It was not until the last stages of the war, when its brutality and meaningless slaughter was bringing grief to every valley and hillside of the country, that this war-fever abated. It broke Keir Hardie, the pacifist leader of the I.L.P., to which Gwynn Jones belonged. The pacifist tradition of Welsh life was swept aside, leaving the poets dismayed and all but silent. There was nothing like the trench poetry of Sassoon, Rosenberg and Owen. Perhaps the most important poems to come out of the war were, first, the *englynion* that Williams Parry wrote as epitaphs or elegies for the dead, including those for Hedd Wyn, a young poet from Trawsfynydd who was killed in action just before his *awdl* won the Chair at the National Eisteddfod in 1917; and, second, Gwynn Jones's masterpiece, 'Madog', that appeared in the same year and was written, according to the author, "as some sort of escape from the horrors of the period". But the reaction of shame and stunned release from trauma that followed the abatement of the hysteria and the signing of the Armistice had important literary consequences. For one thing, the strongly pacifist strain in modern Welsh writing – for example in Gwenallt and Waldo Williams – dates essentially from this period. For another, nationalism of any kind was suspect. Had it not led to the greatest holocaust in the history of the world? This was the reaction, for instance, of T.H. Parry-Williams, himself a conscientious objector during the fighting. It made the growth of any Welsh nationalism during the inter-war years morally difficult, even when the economic argument against it, based on the imperial nature of the coal industry, had ceased to weigh so heavily.

And third, coal yet again. After the war, the bottom fell out of the coal industry. Cutbacks produced the great strike of 1921, the abortive General Strike and the long-drawn-out miners' strike of 1926. The miners were defeated totally. In the Depression that followed, unemployment soared to something like seventy per cent in the mining communities. About half a million – a fifth of the population – left the country, overwhelmingly from the South. What is more, English people, retired or affluent, poured in, mainly along the coasts. The Welsh language suffered badly. With the drift of population many of its cultural institutions were left derelict. Welsh culture thrives on a network of chapels, societies, eisteddfods, groups in friendly competition with each other. Without their support the language would lose its public viability and become a family patois, as Breton is in large areas today, not to be spoken except within the home or taken out for an airing on a trip to the rural west. This seems to have been what happened in large areas of Glamorgan and Gwent.

It is not necessary here to dwell on the humiliation and poverty of that terrible time, nor to analyse its underlying causes. It has become the main subject of a whole *genre* of Anglo-Welsh novels and short stories; but Welsh poetry is not short of passages that register its impact. It is a complete mistake to see Welsh culture, and Welsh poetry in particular, as almost always rural. If one does a spot check on the major writers of this century contained in the present very brief selection, two (Alun Llywelyn-Williams and Bobi Jones) come from Cardiff; one (Saunders Lewis) from Wallasey in Merseyside; two from the coalfields (Gwenallt and Euros Bowen); no less than four from the slate-quarrying towns and villages of Gwynedd (W.J. Gruffydd, Williams Parry, T.H. Parry-Williams and Gwyn Thomas); and only three (T. Gwynn Jones, Waldo Williams and Nesta Wyn Jones) from farming communities. Kitchener Davies, a major writer unfortunately not included in this book, was born on a farm, but is so much associated with the Rhondda that it is difficult to know where to place him. Of course, if one included more of the strict-metre poets the balance might tip towards the countryside a bit more. But even so, the rural affiliations of Welsh poetry are not all that clear-cut. The trouble is, a mining village in the uplands of Glamorgan is invariably labelled 'industrial', whereas a quarrying village in Gwynedd is called 'rural', though in fact much the same conditions operate in each. The Gwynedd one is slightly more likely to be in a worse state of decay, that's all; and to be more infiltrated with hippies and holiday homes.

There are, as I say, plenty of poems which register directly the demoralising effect of the Depression – in this book, for example, poems by Saunders Lewis and Gwenallt. But right at the beginning of the catastrophic decline, just after the miners had gone back to work after their heroic 1926 strike, T. Gwynn Jones produced 'Argoed'. Its relation to its time is, after his fashion, not made explicit, and like all his poems it has to be seen in the chronological sequence of his work as a whole. When it is so placed, its crucial nature will at once be apparent, and its prophetic quality also. Effectively, in this poem, Gwynn Jones decides that his civilisation is finished, and himself destroys its secret strength. To appreciate the significance of this last of his variations on the theme of the Land of Heart's Desire (which I have translated as a whole), we must sketch in what his work had been doing between 1902 and 1927, the year of its publication.

We have seen how in 'Ymadawiad Arthur' the growing point is presented as a Celtic Otherworld, Afallon, from which Arthur will return once the dangers which afflict Wales are over and her culture can expand once more. I say *her* culture, and certainly it is primarily Welsh civilization that Gwynn Jones is talking about. But his socialism and his relation to William Morris give his Land of Heart's Desire also a Utopian significance, a News from Nowhere. In his next *awdl*, 'Gwlad y Bryniau', 'The Land of the Hills', the relationship of this Land of Heart's Desire to the history of Welsh culture – now coming close, now receding – is symbolically sketched in. The poem is still Utopian, hopeful and nationalist. In 1909 the poet gave up journalism for an academic career. Retirement from any job brings anxiety with it: was he going to abandon what he had gained, and lose himself in the fairyland of learning? Gwynn Jones wrote a short verse play in *cynghanedd* about the Irish story of Osian, 'Tir na'n Og', 'The Land of Youth'. Osian falls in love with Nia, the queen of the Land of Youth. He lives with her there, staying as young as when he first met her. But he still hankers to see his own country again. Nia agrees he should go, but warns him that if his feet touch the ground time will catch up with him. When he gets there his land is in ruins, and the people are dwarfs compared with the heroic folk he knew. Inevitably he breaks the tabu and instantly becomes old and dies. It is a nice use of a legend to illustrate a personal predicament. Will he too lose all contact with his people, so that to return among them is to risk disillusionment and spiritual death? This is the first major poem (though there is a similar story told as part of the previous poem 'Gwlad y Bryniau') in which the Land of Heart's Desire, the growing point, is actually felt to be destructive of real life, not simply at some distance away from it. It is a light piece, however, and the division is clearly not all that serious.

It becomes so in 'Madog', which reflects Gwynn Jones's horror at the Great War and his desire to escape. It is based on the legend of Madog, the son of Owain Gwynedd, who was supposed to have sailed away and discovered America in the twelfth century. In the poem Owain is dead and his sons are fighting for his kingdom. Hywel – the poet Hywel ab Owain Gwynedd – is killed by his brothers, and Madog in disgust leaves Wales in his ship *Gwenan Gorn*, symbolically made explicit in the poem as the cradle of his imagination in which he can escape to freedom. He will seek an island across the sea which is the country of content, the land of youth, the place of peace. (It reads like a roll-call of Gwynn Jones's works!) But Madog and his men are drowned in a storm and their ships are lost. As he goes down, Madog kneels in prayer and the monk who is his mentor blesses him with the sign of the Cross.

In a way the atmosphere is not unlike that of Tennyson's 'Ulysses'. But the pressure on Madog to sail in search of his island is the intolerable nature of war, not the bourgeois staleness and boredom that Ulysses escapes from. What is clear is that in 'Madog' the distance between Afallon and modern Wales at war has widened till it destroys those who would travel it. But in the post-war poem, 'Broseliawnd', he toys with the idea of the imagination creating its own autonomous world, a Land of Heart's Desire that is made and sustained in being by the will of the magician alone. If Afallon, because of a lack of innocence or disillusion, cannot be reached, can it be fabricated?

> Better the enchantment than the frenzied malice
> Of the glittering halls' fretful temper,
> Where there was no heart not restless,
> Nor pleasure's ferment without folly's blush.
> *trans. Joseph Clancy*

But this retreat into the individual's will to create his own Eden leads to sterility and isolation. The end of the poem is profoundly ambivalent: the magician is lost in his calm despair in

> Broseliawnd, where there was crystal purity
> And the beauty of young, untroubled inspiration!
> *ibid.*

But it is a captivity, not a growing point, that he creates there.

One can almost feel Gwynn Jones rejecting this answer. His next poem, 'Anatiomaros', appeared the year before the General Strike. Again it concerns a Land of Heart's Desire set in the remote past, in ancient Gaul. But this time, Afallon is explored as a social organization, a simple one it is true, but performing economic tasks and having an age-old culture related organically to its way of life. Clearly itis a social utopia similar to some of William Morris's mediaeval visions in his prose stories. The reason why one kind of socialist tends to put his *exempla* in the long-ago past is that he wants to portray a world before the viciousness of class oppression started to operate; a world, too, before the uglification that industrialism effected. Though it is clearly dangerous, from a Marxist point of view, to idealise a tribal or peasant world, in a sense the socialist does want to return to the undivided consciousness and simplicity of soul that we can see in those societies, however mixed with less desirable elements. These poems are not simple, however perfect and smooth their textures. Anatiomaros himself, the ancient seer whose death and funeral form the main plot of the poem, seems mysterious. Is he a projection of Gwynn Jones the poet, or in some way the embodiment of the growing point, the Land of Heart's Desire personified? In any case, why is the poem centred on his death? But what is clear is that after the despair with an actual society of 'Madog' and the false recourse to enchantment of 'Broseliawnd', Gwynn Jones was going back to first principles. The archetypal free society of the poem is what his vision had always implied: a society in which the individual imagination is at one with its tradition and its community. 'Anatiomaros' seems to be as complete an exposition of the vision as he ever composed.

What it does not say – as 'Ymadawiad Arthur', for example, did – is that this vision is going to be realised in history. And the next poem, which is 'Argoed', says very definitely that it is not. As

I say, Gwynn Jones was watching the failure of the proletariat – and the working class of south Wales in particular – to fend off the terrible destruction that was being visited upon them. Wales was being demolished before his eyes. He had been a journalist, don't forget. He was a socialist also, and a Welshman. More than most, it is likely that he foresaw what the events of 1926 implied. He certainly felt that anglicisation had already proceeded to a point of no return. That, at least, is clear from 'Argoed'.

Once again we are in ancient Gaul, just before the Roman conquest. The rhythms are circling, heavy, almost trance-like and full of repetitions – quite unlike the dramatic crispness we have in 'Ymadawiad Arthur'. He delineates the life of the tribe, the Children of Arofan, who live out their simple, traditional, virtuous existence in the forests of Argoed, proud of their independence and of their skills. Their culture is highly wrought and part of the wider culture of Gaul as a whole. Then the Romans come, conquering their neighbours and bringing triviality and vice wherever they go. A poet from Argoed goes to the city of Alesia which is in their hands. In the past the Alesian people have honoured him and valued his songs. They do not now. They turn their backs on him, mock him in bad Latin and get on with their depravity. He realises that the culture of Gaul is collapsing and goes out into the night, bitterly disappointed. It is a scene that seems to have been enacted over and over again in modern Welsh history – not always involving the language and not always with this effect. One thinks of Lloyd George trying to sell *Cymru Fydd* to the South Wales Liberals and being shouted down – the only time he ever lost his magic with an audience: never again did he have any truck with Welsh separatism, realising that if he was to have the power he wanted it had to be in an imperial context. Or Keir Hardie howled down by a screaming mob in his own constituency of Aberdare because of his pacifism. Or latterly, the fiasco of Devolution, where a socialist electorate rejected their own prime minister and let in the miseries of Thatcherism.

Three times the Romans demand tribute, and three times the men of Argoed refuse. Rather than become slaves and lackeys of Rome they commit cultural and political suicide. They set fire to the forest and Argoed is destroyed. What happens to them after that is not recorded. Nor need it be, for like all T. Gwynn Jones's later idylls 'Argoed' uses the logic and the suddenness of dreams. All the same, they are not idle dreams: to dream like this carries a heavy responsibility for the artist. If the pitch and direction of his dream is not right, the society and culture that he dreams for will pay heavily for his mistake, and he himself may be destroyed. We must ask ourselves what is implied by the burning of Argoed?

One thing that was not implied was that the Welsh should stop trying to be Welsh. T. Gwynn Jones did not turn into an English poet. The struggle went on. It was seen more and more (by other poets as well) in terms of honour: the past must not be dishonoured, or the language, or the moral teaching. Drama and the passion of elegy or lyric invective are the modes to convey this struggle. In the only major poem Gwynn Jones wrote after the fire in 'Argoed', 'Cynddilig', it is significant that he returned to a much more dramatic presentation of the battle: in fact he went back to the drama of the Llywarch Hen cycle of sagas, inventing a new episode in the relationship between Llywarch and his sons. The last of them, Cynddilig, is a monk, a pacifist and intellectual, whom Llywarch reviles as a coward because he will not fight, as Gwên and the rest had done, to defend the ford against the invading English. "Ah, Cynddilig, you should have been a woman," is the taunt against him, recurring over and over again. But though he will not fight, he dies, his honour vindicated; and not merely his honour, for those caring and compassionate qualities that our society tends to see as feminine are also shown as not incompatible with honour.

What 'Argoed' does announce is the end of Wales as a Land of Heart's Desire. The chief poet, the *prifardd*, was saying that in the conditions of 1927 the preservation of the growing point of his civilization was a burden too great to be borne. And almost all the major poets since that time have agreed with him. Only Euros Bowen (and in some moods perhaps Waldo Williams) still writes as if the woods of Argoed still stood in all their Spring beauty. Mostly the poets have abandoned the Romantic 'strategy' of the free imagination. Most of them are committed to nationalism, most of them have discovered a new strength in their Christian inheritance. From the storms that·sweep over Wales, they have run for cover – or that is how a Romantic might see it. In practical, real-life terms, however, it means that some of them have suffered for their commitment to Wales and to the conscience of Wales as perhaps no other generation of Welsh poets has ever done.

From now on, drama or the passion of elegy or lyrical invective become the preferred weapons. There is a greater immediacy of impact in the poetry. This is certainly true of Gwenallt and Saunders Lewis, the two major writers of the forties and fifties in this book; and it is true of the radio poem, 'Sŵn y Gwynt sy'n Chwythu', 'The Sound of the Wind that is Blowing', by Kitchener Davies, the finest long poem of the time. But before that movement became dominant, there was something of an interregnum. Gwynn Jones having burnt his Argoed was hesitating into a new style and a new subject-matter. Williams Parry was on a sort of poem-strike, for reasons of his own. He was one of the first artists (but by no means the last) to take umbrage at what he considered the wrong priorities of official patronage, in this case the University College at Bangor for whom he worked as a lecturer. It meant that he did not publish any poetry for several years: like Achilles he was sulking in his tent. The third great Romantic, W.J. Gruffydd, whom we have not mentioned yet, more and more appeared as a critic, scholar and editor of genius, rather than as a poet. His poetry had been notable for its variety of styles, some of them naturalising patterns of feeling found in English or American or other foreign literature. His poems vary from the mode of Keats to that of the Spoon River Anthology. They had a liberating effect, certainly, freeing Welsh sensibility from the clichés of its Nonconformist past: but as a poet he lacked the thrust and sense of direction of a major artist.

The one writer who did develop as a major poet in the early thirties was T.H. Parry-Williams, Williams Parry's cousin. Before the war he had already created a record by twice winning the Crown and the Chair at the same eisteddfod; but with one exception these early triumphs were Romantic works which he never re-published. The exception was 'Y Ddinas', 'The City', which was notable for its realism in dealing with life in Paris. It has been called the first modern Welsh poem. Then for many years he published no poetry. When he did, his collections contained only two kinds of verse: sonnets, and what he called *rhigymau*, 'rhymes', usually the loose couplets that previously had only been used for light verse. The sonnets are classic examples of the form, weighty, precise in their notation of experience, bleak in their awareness of ageing and death. The couplet-pieces are more colloquial, but very sure-footed in their modulations of tone and their spareness of verbal effect. The colloquial voice makes its impact all the more after the literary language and rather high-flown diction of much Romantic verse. R. Gerallt Jones says of this poet's work:

> One approaches it almost with a sense of observing a natural phenomenon. One sees in it the huge, inexorable stamina of a glacier. It is awe-inspiring. And yet it is all of a piece. One is struck, as one looks at it, by the rightness of things. This, in a sense, is paradoxical. For much of the content of his art, in both prose and verse, probes deeply into facets of human existence that seem to him anything but right. But the art itself, measured, structured, fashioned in granite, classically restrained to a degree unimagined by his Romantic contemporaries, makes the only kind of sense that is possible.

It is likely that the poetry of Parry-Williams represents an orthodoxy of feeling among respectable, intelligent, middle-class Welsh people. I am always being surprised by the warmth of commendation that it inspires. I suspect this is because he manages to eat his cake and have it too, in a way that answers a deep need in contemporary Wales. The Land of Heart's Desire, which in this poet is equated with his childhood home in Rhyd-ddu in Snowdonia, is gone for ever; yet he is stuck with the feelings that pertained to it. All the rational examination, the play of scepticism, the scientific world-picture, is used to defend the inner certainty that in Rhyd-ddu (and only in Rhyd-ddu) life really did make sense. His poems in no way lead the way to any change. They are deeply conservative. They seem to me to express with consummate art the characteristic desire of the respectable North Walian to sit on the fence for as long as he possibly can.

Parry-Williams's most popular poem, 'Hon', exemplifies his strategy very well – though he has certainly written much better poems. Gerallt Jones says that his art makes the only kind of sense possible, so let me look at 'Hon' and try to make out what kind of sense it is. And first, as a non-Welsh-speaker, I am clearly at more of a disadvantage reading this poem than I am where the language is more literary and the idioms less rich in connotations. The poem opens in a mood of mock impatience – the question is, how mock is it? – something like, "Why the hell should I care about Wales? It's an accident that I live in its backyard." He says Wales is a mere backwater, insignificant on the map, but a bit of a headache to those who believe in order. And who lives there but the dregs, the garbage of society? Stop talking about a unit, a nation or a country – there's enough of those without Wales in the world. He says that from all this noise of Wales and the Welsh, he needs a holiday. He'll go back home for a bit, on fantasy's train. And there he is, in Snowdonia, thank God, away from all the fanatical talk. He sees Yr Wyddfa (Snowdon) and "its crew", the lake and the river and the cliff, and over there the house where he was born. The whole place is haunted by the voices of his past, and he begins to grow faint –

> And I feel the claws of Wales tearing at my heart.
> God help me, I can't get away from it.

Clancy translates the final word "hon" as "this spot", which misses the point: it is Wales he's talking about.

One wants to ask questions. Who exactly does yr Athro Parry-Williams, Professor of Welsh at Aberystwyth, see as the dregs of society? Not very long ago Wales had been one of the most expansive economies in the world. It had been the country of Mabon, of T.E. Ellis, D.A. Thomas and Lloyd George; of the I.L.P., of the Miners' Federation; in his own field it had produced great scholars like Sir John Rhys and Sir John Morris-Jones, and poets of the order of Gwynn Jones and his own cousin, Williams Parry. Now in the Depression, clearly, with Welsh culture in ruins, with the markets of England exercising their attraction and snobbery (as always) pulling people away from any real commitment to Wales, the desire to escape from the 'backwater' was undoubtedly very real – Dylan Thomas's family in Swansea offers a familiar example. And Parry-Williams is certainly being ironic about the attitude he is expressing. But what he posits as a positive is none of the real achievement or tragedy of Wales but his personal attachment to Rhyd-ddu. It is not even to the social benefit and fellowship he has had there, or still has. William Parry's commitment to his *bro*, though it may have stood in the way of greater things, was at least productive in terms of the people who lived there. But Parry Williams's *bro*-worship was a matter of memories, of Welshness getting its claws into him. 'Fern Hill' is often cited as an example of Dylan Thomas's fantasy retreat into childhood as an escape from adult life; but I cannot see that 'Hon' is even as respectable as that, because the issues it raises are more damaging. If this "makes the only kind of sense that is possible" in Wales, then God help us! Buy a holiday cottage in Llanllechid and emigrate to Brighton!

It is a relief to pass from 'Hon' to the *bro*-less Catholicism of Saunders Lewis and Gwenallt's "Utopia that vanished from the top of Gellionnen." John Saunders Lewis was surely one of the most exotic as well as the most powerful personalities ever to appear in Welsh Wales. Although the language of his childhood home in Merseyside was exclusively Welsh, he was given the education of an English provincial bourgeois, and served as an officer in the British army. He caught the nationalist bug from reading Anglo-Irish literature and the French author Maurice Barrès. At first, indeed, he tried to become an Anglo-Welsh writer on the model of Synge. He wrote a short play in which he attempted to use literal translations of Welsh conversation as Synge had used those of Irish. He disliked the English dialects of South Wales which he described as "the horrible jargon of men who have lost one tongue without acquiring another...no feebler stuff is spoken in these islands". His hatred of industrialism and all its works drew him back to the Welsh language as the only source of patriotic culture. The failure to see any good in the industrial South led him later to deny the possibility of an Anglo-Welsh literature at all. Like Yeats he disliked democracy and saw the only salvation for art in a combination of peasantry and aristocracy. But France as well as Ireland claimed his cultural allegiance: there is something wilful, not to say quaint, about his insistence on the mediterranean and European affiliations of Welsh culture. But his eccentricity as a Welshman – Catholic, aristocratic, fond of good wine, admiring the military virtues, a city-dweller and a gentleman – gave him considerable purchase as a literary critic. He revolutionised the way we look at Welsh literature. Always at the storm-centre of controversy, the intellectual brilliance and consistency of his insights have led to their uneasy acceptance in the long term.

INTRODUCTION

He was led to take an active part in politics by his patriotism and his awareness of the spiritual degradation that industrialism had caused. He was a founder-member in 1925 of the Welsh Nationalist Party, and very soon its president. His political ideas included the de-industrialisation of the south, petty capitalism for everyone, no large businesses or monopolies, no mass-production and no socialism. The main industry of Wales should be agriculture. The family, as the basic unit of society, and the community, built up of many families, were to be protected from interference. It is a prescription for a petty-bourgeois utopia, wildly unreal in the circumstances of most of Wales in the twenties and thirties. Saunders Lewis's ideology as a whole has had very little real influence, though one keeps bumping against things that resemble parts of it: a European context for Wales, for example. But the way he has acted on that ideology is a different matter entirely. Twice what he has done has shaken Welsh Wales to its foundations and decisively altered the way Welsh people have resisted anglicisation.

In 1936 the Government decided that the R.A.F. needed a bombing range, and various sites were proposed and considered. Those in England were rejected because of local historical or ecological reasons. The Government fixed on Penyberth in Llŷn, and no amount of opposition from all over Wales to the desecration of a piece of the Welsh heartland pregnant with Welsh history and culture, was even considered. The Prime Minister refused to see any deputations. Saunders Lewis, D.J. Williams and the Rev. Lewis Valentine set fire to the timber that had been put at Penyberth to begin work on the site. It was the first act of civil disobedience done in the name of Wales for centuries. The three men gave themselves up immediately and were committed for trial. The jury at Caernarfon could not agree, in spite of the judge being very hostile; but when the retrial took place in London, where the nationalists refused to plead, they were sentenced to nine months in prison. When they were released, they were given a tumultuous reception but nothing further developed. Saunders Lewis was dismissed from his post as a university lecturer at Swansea.

So began the politics of gestures towards rebellion so typical of modern Wales. Tension builds up, people make an existentialist gesture – burning some timber, destroying a power-cable, sitting down at a busy road-bridge – the law moves in, respectability triumphs and, for a time, the tension is released, the potential is safely earthed. It was not until the sixties and seventies that these gestures became at all frequent or achieved any solid results; but the fire at Penyberth established the pattern. One wonders whether Saunders Lewis and his fellow arsonists were right to give themselves up so meekly. True, they achieved the shocking martyrdom of going to prison – the first patriots to achieve that Victoria Cross of modern Wales. But had they not also reasserted the discontinuity principle in Welsh politics, the idea that nothing done in Wales can rely on its successors to perpetuate it? It was that principle that had destroyed the native princes and it was the relaxing of that rule under the Kings of England that had allowed Welsh culture to flower in the fifteenth century. Right at the beginning of his career, Saunders Lewis had put forward two desiderata for modern Wales: the founding of what amounts to a Citizens' Army, groups meeting together openly, without weapons, to drill and to learn military discipline; and the "great blessing for Wales if some Welshman did something for his nation that caused him to be put in prison." The second "blessing" has certainly been achieved, many times over; but the first – in spite of the tragi-comic episode of the Welsh Republican Army – is as far off as ever. Cunning, fanaticism, strategy – these have been sorely missed.

The trouble is, no issue has emerged (such as Disestablishment in the nineteenth century) which is capable of uniting north and south, Welsh-speakers and English-speakers, country and town, under the same banner, of dislodging the Labour monolith in south Wales, and of allowing clear leadership to put the claims of Wales to the whole nation. We cannot go into this question here. The reader must be referred to the essay, 'His politics' by Dafydd Glyn Jones, from *Presenting Saunders Lewis* (ed. Alun R. Jones and Gwyn Thomas), 1973. The following quotation may be apposite:

> It is a safe conjecture that if Saunders Lewis's nationalism had been of a cruder kind, if it had appealed more often to mass prejudices, if it had offered a means of escape from the responsibility of personal choice. and if it had been less discriminate in its use of violence, it would have gained

support more rapidly... It is perfectly true that Saunders Lewis had made a liberal use of the word 'revolution', and true also that his followers today, the young men and women of the Welsh Language Society, refer to themselves with some pride as 'extremists'. But it is an ironic pride, part of the Society's banter and self-critical leg-pulling. It comes from the knowledge that they have not yet earned the label, and provides a good hint that they will never do so... Moderation is the most important single factor in the psychology of Welsh Wales today. Usually it is carried to ridiculous extremes, and is used as another name for cowardice, indifference or inertia.

It is a just comment, with the proviso that the cowardice or inertia can arise just as well from neurotic tension as it can from real indifference.

To get back to poetry and 1937. The sacking of Saunders Lewis as a lecturer had two important consequences: one, it brought Williams Parry out of his self-imposed silence as the death of his friend brought Achilles out of his tent. In spite of his dislike of the poet turning propagandist, he acknowledged that there were times when Nature herself, the "hag inhuman and unreclaimed" of his sonnet, 'The Propaganda of the Poet', loosened her thunders and showed "the worm in the wood and the creation cracked", driving "brave men to mosque and mascot" as he ironically put it; driving himself to invective against the Welsh authorities for the unbelievably spineless fashion in which they had treated Saunders Lewis. The incident released more than invective in him, though: his later poetry, and particularly the great series of sonnets in the second part of his book, *Cerddi'r Gaeaf*, 'Poems of Winter', have an authority and range beyond anything he had achieved before.

And secondly, the incident deflected Saunders Lewis himself into a creative writer: he began to compose the series of plays that make him Wales's greatest dramatist so far. He also wrote poems, about forty or so over the years. They are not well-represented in this book. Each of his poems is very distinct. Some dramatise the Passion of Christ; some satirise Wales; some present sharp annotations of the natural scene, in the fiercely clear light of his Catholicism. He can handle historical process – as in 'The Deluge

1939', or even more impressively, the elegy for the Welsh historian Sir John Edward Lloyd, which with its echoes of Dante is probably his greatest poem. His technical range is very wide, from the surrealism of 'Scene in a Cafe' to the attempt to modernise the ancient *awdl* of praise in the 'Awdl to his Grace the Archbishop of Cardiff'. The latter presents the dichotomy of Wales then and Wales now (so typical of him) in a form which Bruce Griffiths has seen as contorted, but which in itself acts out the breakdown.

In 'The Deluge 1939' he presents the collapse of South Wales from the viewpoint of a Government in Exile. He has no share in the specifically proletarian experience of the Depression. To him the Welsh working class has lost its manhood. It cringes. It accepts the charity of the masters who have betrayed it. He sees it in ruling-class terms, as a people who have "lost the good of their minds", as Dante put it. They have abdicated from their responsibility to the Welsh nation and to themselves. Saunders Lewis cannot feel how economic defeat makes certain things impossible for a class or a people, even though an individual may escape. To judge a proletariat as just a collection of individuals is to deny its experience and to see it in merely bourgeois terms. It is the old capitalist mistake of regarding the sale of a man's labour as if it were the sale of his property: the mistake of seeing the wages you pay a man as if they affected his individuality as little as they do yours.

But if 'The Deluge' shows Saunders Lewis at his least sympathetic, it also shows what gifts he brought to Welsh poetry in its hour of need: his clarity, his sense of both Wales and Europe, his historical forthrightness, his commitment and serious honour. Other pieces show this hard, intellectual clarity put at the service of religious passion; but 'The Deluge 1939' is one of a group of poems which taught Welsh people how to articulate what had happened to them. They gave Welsh poetry a new realism, an ability to call a spade a spade, and a rhetoric of dismay and horror that was both necessary for its sanity and much more extremist than the Welsh people as a whole could countenance. That is, they established the dimension of guilt as one of the primary co-ordinates of Welsh sensibility.

Clarity is also one of the keynotes of the poetry of Gwenallt – David James Jones as he was christened: his name comes from the village of Alltwen ('White Slope') on the opposite side of the Pontardawe steel-works to the wooded hill of Gellionnen where he said Utopia disappeared. He was brought up there. His father was killed by molten steel. He was a member of Keir Hardie's very left-wing I.L.P. and went to prison for two years for his political pacifism – he had no objection, he said, to fighting enemies of the working class, but he didn't see why he should fight for one capitalist state against another. He went to college in Aberystwyth and became a lecturer in Welsh. His father had originally come from Carmarthenshire, and was a poet of local eminence. Gwenallt combines, therefore, the countryside civilization with the raw realities of the south Wales industrial explosion and collapse. Gwenallt became a nationalist after a visit to Spideal, in Conemara; as with Saunders Lewis Ireland played a significant role in his development. He had left his father's chapel because he felt it compromised with the system, but now he turned to Catholicism, or at least to the Catholic wing of the Anglican Church –

> Like wolves we lift our nostrils, ravenous,
> Howling for the Blood that ransomed us.
> ('Sin', trans. Clancy)

Gwenallt has a big story to tell and he tells it with tragic power. Like that of Saunders Lewis, his poetry re-establishes the praise-satire polarity of Welsh poetry. He too had obeyed the imperatives of revolution: there was no need for either of them to adopt Romantic strategies. But unlike Saunders Lewis he knew the proletarian experience of south Wales from the inside. Inevitably we are reminded of Idris Davies, the Anglo-Welsh poet of the 1926 strike and the Depression. But Gwenallt has a tragic clarity and a massiveness of response that Idris Davies lacks. He has the full Welsh tradition behind him, and his Catholic Christianity gives him a framework, a language of suffering, that Idris Davies never quite achieved. Idris Davies had to concoct a poetic speech from the odds and ends of English literary and sub-literary poetry – Housman, Yeats, popular song, hymnody. Gwenallt is a very original poet; but his originality rests on a civilization that was, so to speak, fitted to what he was feeling.

Gwenallt, for all his power, is a fairly simple writer. Perhaps this selection will serve to introduce him. I do not feel it is all that inadequate, at any rate, though it misses out most of his religious poetry. When you translate him, you become aware of how massive he is, how his language has a physicality even with abstract words that reminds one of Ted Hughes, however different they are in other respects. And above all, there is his clarity of vision. When it lets him down, as sometimes it does in the later poems, it becomes over-simple, too black and white — perhaps it does in his poem on the German passion-play at Oberammergau. But that doesn't happen very often. His clarity is a force to be reckoned with. It embraces subjects as diverse as the proper way to paint pictures or the experience of Holy Communion. What in English would be made into a journalistic Observer profile (for example, in his poem on the German painter F.R. Könekamp who had settled in Wales after the war) is as much grist to his mill as laments for the rural way of life at Rhydcymerau, that was being taken over and destroyed by the Forestry Commission.

The question is, was clarity enough? The 1939-45 war did not affect Welsh poetry very much, with one major exception. As Dafydd Glyn Jones remarks, the Welsh poets had seen it coming, they regarded it more or less as the onset of a barbarism that they had been expecting, and they had simply to sit tight and wait till it was over. Of course, it did affect them, and it affected the post-war generation as well. But it introduced little that was new. The exception was the Cardiff poet, Alun Llywelyn-Williams. He is the only major writer who corresponds to the Auden-MacNeice generation in English. Dafydd Glyn Jones says of him that his poetry

> tells a familiar enough story. It is that of the failure of ideology. Most contemporary Welsh writers differ from him in that their ideology has not yet failed them. And, being existentialist in character, rather than historicist, it is not as likely to do so. What we see in the war poems of Alun Llywelyn-Williams is the floundering of the historicism [that is, the Marxism] implicit in his early work: war is seen now not as a necessary step in the fulfilment of the historical process, but as an aspect of man's eternal penance, of a crisis as old as the second chapter of Genesis.

'*The Poetry of Alun Llywelyn-Williams*', *Poetry Wales*, *Vol.7*, *No.1, p.23*

But since this urbane, grave and cultured poet is only represented here by one not very typical poem, we had better pass over him quickly.

And over Kitchener Davies, who is absent altogether. His long radio poem, 'The Sound of the Wind that is blowing', is the first psychological analysis of Welsh Nationalism, its frustrations, guilt and bitterness, from a personal point of view. It presents a self-criticism of a man reared on a farm and then working himself to the bone (as so many good Welshmen do) for the language and the nation in the Rhondda of the Depression. The terrible Wind that bloweth where it listeth, the whirlwind of modern Wales, receives here its finest expression.

Is clarity enough? After the war a Labour Government was returned to power and there was a brief resuscitation of the miners' Utopia. The coal industry (amongst others) was nationalised. Aneurin Bevan created the National Health Service, on the model (so we were assured by old miners in Rhymney and Merthyr) of the miners' own medical service. For a short time, in the first few years after the war, some degree of real social planning was practised. Wales of course shared in the benefits of the Welfare State, and in the long boom of the fifties and sixties that followed its creation. But there were snags: for a start, the ruling Labour Party was very centralist in its ideology. It was only with extreme reluctance that Bevan agreed to the creation in 1951 of a Minister for Welsh Affairs, and for a long time his powers were minimal. Cardiff was declared the capital of Wales in 1955. The Welsh Office was only established in 1964. Administratively a degree of separatism was being created, and like all administrations it has tended to increase its powers over the years. But the economic base was still lacking for a full separatism to succeed. As the coal industry of south Wales continued to decline, Cardiff operated as a regional extension of the London-Bristol axis rather than a national capital. Even so, its wealth increased as it became a centre for administration and service industries.

The power of the Welsh nation to preserve what it regarded as important was very small indeed. When it was planned to drown the valley of Tryweryn (near Bala, and in the centre of the Welsh-speaking heartland) to make a reservoir to supply Liverpool with water, no amount of Welsh protest could stop it. All legitimate pressure was put on the Government, but to no avail. It was

INTRODUCTION

Tryweryn, more than anything else, which persuaded a large section of young Welsh people (and some of their elders) that it was useless simply to use constitutional methods of protest. Civil disobedience, direct action, even violence, would henceforth be possible. After Tryweryn, Saunders Lewis a second time changed the course of Welsh resistance. He was commissioned to give the B.B.C. Wales Annual Lecture for 1962, 'Tynged yr Iaith', 'The Fate of the Language'. He analysed the way both the English Government and the Welsh people had betrayed the Welsh language since the Act of Union in 1536. He advocated a policy of deliberate confrontation with the law – civil disobedience on the Gandhi model – to win for it official status and to ensure that it was used to administer the Welsh-speaking areas. As a result, the Welsh Language Society, *Cymdeithas yr Iaith Gymraeg*, was formed, and a steady stream of incidents, sit-downs, refusals to obey summonses, daubs on road signs, respectable folk being sent to prison and so on, started to win considerable concessions for the use of Welsh.

Meanwhile *Plaid Cymru* had entered the realm of practical politics. Ever since the war, it has moved further and further to the left, becoming a left-wing alternative to Labour, as well as holding on to a central role in Welsh-speaking Wales. In 1966 its president Gwynfor Evans won a by-election in Carmarthen, its first parliamentary success. Nationalism became a force to be reckoned with, even in the south; while in Gwynedd *Plaid Cymru* has won and held the two constituencies of Caernarfon and Merioneth.

Thus, by the mid-seventies, many factors were operating to preserve and extend the consciousness of Wales as a separate identity. Many others, of course, worked the other way, and the nationalists were wrong-footed badly over the 1969 Investiture of the Prince of Wales and even more disastrously over the Devolution Referendum in 1979. But in general the period 1962-1979, in spite of the huge worry about the decline in the number of speakers, was one of activity, of possibilities opening up, of excitement in being Welsh. Saunders Lewis's lecture was the occasion of their banding together, but he was not the true poet of the young men and women of the Language Society; nor of the new nationalism either. Even Gwenallt, with his characteristic dichotomy between Wales the ancient princess and Wales the modern whore, was too tragic, too clear, too rooted in the sense of Wales as a whole, not just the Welsh-speaking areas. Gwenallt was where they started to become aware. But they needed more than tragic clarity to send them out in droves, painting out road signs, demonstrating, being sent to prison.

They found their laureate in the Quaker poet of the Preseli hills in Dyfed, Waldo Williams. Like Saunders Lewis and Gwenallt, and like so many of them, he went to prison. During the Korean war, he refused to pay taxes. What is more, in order to stop his taxes being stopped at source, he resigned from his job as a teacher and took on temporary employment. He refused to pay taxes until the last conscript was released in 1963; and twice he was sent to prison for it. He was a much-loved, affectionate, rather reserved man, by all accounts, with a great delight in his friends and a marvellous sense of fun. He was also something of a mystic, and something of a saint. His poetry, behind all the sadness in it for the state of the world, for the human condition, for the deaths of friends – and for the state of Wales – is the deepest and fullest expression of joy that I know of in any modern language.

It was a country of brotherhood that he invoked, a field full of folk. God is immanent, the quiet huntsman, the exiled king. The quiet of the field is alive with possibilities, and at the same time it calms our anxieties. Wales is not so much a lost paradise as a world to repossess:

> My Wales, brotherhood's country, my cry, my creed,
> Only balm to the world, its mission, its challenge,
> Pearl of the infinite hour that time gives as pledge,
> Hope of the tedious race on the short winding way.
>
> It was my window, the harvest and the shearing,
> I glimpsed order in my palace there.
> There's a roar, there's a ravening through the windowless
>   forests.
> Keep the wall from the brute, keep the spring clear of filth.
> ('Preseli')

It is the language that he personifies as a woman, not Wales:

INTRODUCTION

She is danger's daughter. The wind whips her path,
Her foot where they failed, where they fell, those of the
    lower air.
Till now she has seen her way more clearly than prophets.
She is as young as ever, as full of mischief.
('*Cymru a Chymraeg*', '*Welsh Land, Welsh Language*', *trans.
Clancy*)

He bids his countrymen –

We who can see her dignity, through the mist of her misfortunes,
Let us raise up, here, the old indestructible stones.
And who are these flying through the cloud and sunshine,
Coming like doves to her windows?
('*Yr Heniaith*', '*The Old Language*', *trans. R.Gerallt Jones*)

What we have in Waldo Williams is a sense of a new beginning, just as we have in Pantycelyn or 'Ymadawiad Arthur'. Once again, Welsh-speaking Wales is re-grouping after catastrophe. Once again, Welsh poets are talking about a future. The shift from nationalism to the ideology of the language revival might seem a small one – smaller, certainly, than that from the Rationalist Nonconformity of nineteenth century Wales to the Romanticism of Gwynn Jones. A great many Welsh idealists were almost not aware that any change had occurred. In Anglo-Welsh Wales, however, it registered as a sudden drop in temperature. Anglo-Welsh writers were turning back to a Welsh market, trying to establish a relevance for themselves in their own country after their brief whoredom in London – "Land of my fathers – my fathers can keep it!" as Dylan Thomas remarked. For a time we had a sense of being welcomed back: the nation needed a bi-lingual literature, the prodigal was greeted, if not with a fatted calf at least with hot tea and ham sandwiches. We were almost made to feel wanted. But then, suddenly, the idealists excused themselves, we were left in the cold. The English literature of Wales had become a ghost again – an unfortunate episode that had no real right to exist:

Here are the mountains. One language alone can lift them
And set them in their freedom against a sky of song.
('*Cymru a Chymraeg*', '*Welsh Land, Welsh Language*', *trans. Clancy*)

INTRODUCTION

Our literary feelings were echoed at a possibly more mundane level, as the language movement took root and jobs and influence were at stake. For far too many Welsh people, Welsh has become a neurosis accumulating jealousy and resentment.

However, that was a by-product, and one I think English speakers will just have to learn to live with. The ideal of Wales as a nation has not, of course, been abandoned: but it has been relegated to the subjunctive mood, a kind of future-in-the-past. Waldo's poem on the Welsh Catholic martyrs ends –

> Welshmen, were you a nation, great would be the glory
> These would have in your story –

"*Gymry, pe baech chwi'n genedl*". The main job now is to restore the language to her former glory, as the language of Wales as a whole. And it is a change of emphasis, a new direction, that has released an enormous amount of energy, goodwill and determination. And, as befitting its inspiration in Waldo's poetry, a great deal of joy.

The Language Revival had a liberating effect on other poets also, and notably on Bobi Jones who could almost be called one of its earliest products. He learnt Welsh at school in Cardiff, and was inspired to graduate in it and eventually to become a Professor of Welsh. His poetry has all a convert's joy in his new world. He enjoys it like a holiday, its strength and oddity and beauty. He writes of love, of having children, of nature, as though the delight he has found in his new language has liberated him to see everything for the first time. It is like a paradigm of falling in love. He is tender, dogmatic, fanciful and compassionate. As with Waldo, his experience of Welshness is above all an experience of fellowship, with poetry a part of oneness with other poets and speakers of Welsh. Once again, my selection here does him no sort of justice, though in the poem about the poetry clubs, which he wrote while he was working in Canada for a year, I have tried to suggest his commitment. He is a very prolific poet who wears his language and his Calvinism (both of them newly found) like the shining armour of humanity on a fine Spring morning.

The third member of this oddly assorted triad of joy is Euros Bowen. His relation to the language movement is more oblique, but I think it exists. Until his retirement in 1973, he was the rector of Llangywair and Llanuwchllyn near Bala. His poems are often complicated, both in form and meaning. He continued Gwynn Jones's experiments with what he calls 'free' *cynghanedd*, using the *cynganeddion* with both free verse and prose rhythms. His work is more concerned with the aesthetic than the political, with the sacramental nature of poetry and the wonder that wakens man to the divine. But his poems are shaped objects in their own right: he rejects any idea of poetry as 'imagist' or photographic, nor will he allow it to preach doctrine. His poems are icons, perhaps, patterns of words in which insights and feelings inhere. At their best they are very beautiful.

The immensely forceful metaphoric life of Waldo's language, the new-minted fantasy of Bobi Jones and the complications of Euros Bowen are equally divorced from the tragic clarity of Saunders Lewis or Gwenallt. With Gwyn Thomas there is a return (in his mature work, at any rate) to a plainer style. Gwyn Thomas is fully a twentieth-century man, in a fashion that would be as recognisable in San Francisco or Berlin – or Cardiff, for that matter – as it is in Bangor or Blaenau Ffestiniog where he comes from. He concerns himself with the tragedy and pleasure of ordinary life, seeing a road accident, watching children, listening to the news, walking on the beach. Though he is a scholar and an academic, he wears his learning lightly. His early work was more literary in style; but his openness to contemporary living, his interest in the media and communications, and the inevitable exposure to the mechanics of family and community life since the birth of his children, have given his poetry a much more colloquial manner. He takes risks with language, changing from one register to another as the mood takes him. Look for instance at his poem on the dustcart lorry, the 'Goggy', and his son's longing to see it. The basic tension between the academic pedant's way of talking –

> by a linguistic convention
> Peculiarly non-indoeuropean –

and the baby's way of expressing himself, the single, all-important word, "goggy", the squirming, the face of tears and shouting, and the frown of displeasure – this tension calls into question the whole rigmarole of high-flown utterance. Other modulations in the poem are into biblical language and into the pedantry of the law-court – "Behemoth" and "the said owner of the cot". Then, near the end, the high-falutin' tone of the narrative breaks down. There is the use of a dialect form, "ydi" instead of "ydyw" which I have over-translated as "ain't", and the final confession of failure –

> I'd a frown turned on me. I don't find it easy
> To explicate that frown in any way
> Except: "Where's that bloody lorry?"

"Ble mae y blydi lorri"? The use of the English expletive at the climax of the poem tells its own story. Partly, the poet is mocking the verbalism of academics, the need to explicate, but it is also a way of writing a poem about a baby and a corporation dustcart, two subjects that are not often contiguous in poetry. It is more than that: the poem offers a comment on the state of the Welsh language and on the limits of communication generally. The high-flown language is mere guesswork on the poet's part about how the baby actually responds to the "goggy", and the more it tries to comprehend, the less adequate it is. And of course, even more is this the case when the poet tries to explain to his child what is happening in order to mitigate his distress.

This sort of serious play – sometimes high comedy, sometimes, as in his poems about animals, a tender awareness of otherness –is one side of Gwyn Thomas's work. Another is the violence, the horror, the indictment of our irresponsibility and cruelty, particularly to children. A third element is his sense of time, of the 'thisness' of now which is never to be repeatable, no matter how commonplace it seems.

Gwyn Thomas's loyalty to the Welsh language is not in doubt, but it is rarely that he speaks either as a prophet or as a propagandist for it. Indeed one of his funniest poems mocks the automatic knee-jerk that the language occasions:

> Talk of Welsh to some politicians and county councillors
> And they'll instinctively reach for their consciences...

He says that Welsh is a great doer of good – it transforms noisy children into dear little things who haven't got a playground; old

folk are suddenly hoisted into the centre of concern; and hospitals
get bit by bit improved. One would scarcely dream, the poet says,

> That these causes have always been
> With them. They must hide all the time
> In the cellars of their concern and require Welsh
> To make them go look for them there.

And when all the children are catered for, and the old folk, and
the hospitals, still the process cannot stop –

> Talk of Welsh
> And some are sure to discover
> Causes of crises in our land
> Like the desperate need to have a supply
> Of lifebelts for fish in distress and homes for orphaned moles.
> *'Soniwch am y Gymraeg'*, *'Talk of Welsh'*, trans. Clancy

Let me plead ignorance now, and stop the story in the days of
the great dismay, the Referendum of St David's Day 1979. I hope
what I have put together in this introduction won't be too
jarringly misleading. Welsh poetry since 1900 has been very
creative on all levels. There have been at least ten or twelve major
writers, as well as scores of interesting minor ones. The traditional
crafsmanship of the 'country' or 'folk' poets has flourished
mightily. The poems written for eisteddfod competitions have
often been significant works of art and occasionally masterpieces.
Latterly as well the 'pop song' and the modern 'folksong' have
added a demotic element. But for the fact that it has represented a
continuous response to a culture in crisis, one could well describe
it as a golden age.

In the most famous of his lyrics, Waldo Williams remembers
the "forgotten things":

> Like the foam of a wave that breaks on a lonely shore,
> Like the wind's song where there is no ear to hear,
> I know they call in vain upon us –
> The old forgotten things of human kind.
>
> The achievement and art of early generations,
> Small dwellings and great halls,

INTRODUCTION

The fine-wrought legends scattered centuries ago,
The gods that no one knows about by now.

And the little words of transient languages,
They were gay on the lips of men,
And pleasant to hear in the chatter of little children,
But no tongue calls upon them any longer.

('Cofio', 'Remembering', trans. R.Gerallt Jones)

'Remember' – the word haunts contemporary Wales. Remember
Tryweryn, remember our children. Remember Welshness. And if
the unspeakable should happen, and the Welsh language die out
except as a specialist subject for academics, what then? Well,
there are hundreds of languages on the verge of extinction in the
contemporary world. Hundreds more have already died out. Two
sister languages, Cornish and Manx, have perished in modern
times; two more, Irish and Scots Gaelic, continue as faint ghosts
in territory they once lorded over. Breton across the Sleeve is in a
parlous state. Even on the continent of Europe, there are several
tongues that will be lucky to last the century out. The extinction
of Welsh would no doubt be sad, but in the nature of things
minority languages are in danger. Would Welsh be a greater loss
than, say, Lapp or Wendish or the nearest extant relative to
English, Frisian?

The short answer is, yes it would. Though it has never been
spoken by more than a million at any one time, and is now spoken
by about half that number, Welsh is one of the great carriers of
Western civilization. Only Greek and possibly Irish, out of all the
languages of Europe, have a longer continuous tradition. Welsh
cannot compete with French, Spanish, Russian, German, Italian
or English in the quality or importance of its literature; and I
suppose Greek is a special case. But after those seven, is there
another literature in modern Europe with anything like the
wealth of Welsh? The demise of such a member is a catastrophe
that has not happened in Western civilisation before. The collapse
of Provençal as a literary medium in the thirteenth century, and
the breakdown of Anglo-Saxon under the Normans are the most
comparable disasters I can call to mind; and both these survived,
at least as *patois*, and were revived later. But if Welsh goes, it
leaves no successor.

INTRODUCTION

One can only reiterate. The death of Welsh would be a major betrayal of civilization. Welsh is a modern language in the fullness of its creative power. It is a classical tongue, with the first modern literature to arise out of the ruins of the Roman Empire. Far from being the *patois* that many people think it is, it is a sophisticated and urbane speech, that has lived through one industrial revolution and promises to survive another.

But enough of the deeming of doom. Let me finish with my favourite poem by Gwyn Thomas, a good enough palliative, if not remedy, for all apocalyptic bumps in the night:

You've Lived

All through the play, Hamlet's
Looking for some hold in the world.
All through it, he's searching for something in life
To bear the weight of his being.

And neither his father's murder,
The adultery of his mother
Nor Ophelia's love –
Things shattering enough
One would have thought –
Is sufficient to root him
In the rank, unweeded garden
Which was what he called life.
He was here without an anchor
In a fruitless sea of being.
And he never evolved an interest
(As we say) 'to keep him going' –
He, with his wayward life; he, the lost one.

So take comfort –
Even if you only grow onions,
Breed rabbits or put ships in bottles,

INTRODUCTION

If that grips you, you are one of the saved,
The light shines on you, you can fear death,
Go in dread of the end.
That is to say, you've lived.

TALIESIN
Late 6th century

The Battle of Argoed Llwyfain

There was a great battle Saturday morning
From when the sun rose until it grew dark.
The fourfold hosts of Fflamddwyn invaded.
Goddau and Rheged gathered in arms,
Summoned from Argoed as far as Arfynydd –
They might not delay by so much as a day.

With a great swaggering din, Fflamddwyn shouted,
"Are these the hostages come ? Are they ready ?"
To him then Owain, scourge of the eastlands,
"They've not come, no! They're not, nor shall they be ready!
And a whelp of Coel would indeed be afflicted
Did he have to give any man as a hostage!"

And Urien, lord of Erechwydd, shouted,
"If they would meet us now for our kinsfolk,
High on the hilltop let's raise our ramparts,
Carry our faces over the shield rims,
Raise up our spears, men, over our heads
And set upon Fflamddwyn in the midst of his hosts
And slaughter him, ay, and all that go with him!"

There was many a corpse beside Argoed Llwyfain;
    From warriors ravens grew red,
And with their leader a host attacked.
For a whole year I shall sing to their triumph.

And till I die old
    With death's constraint on me
I'll not be happy
    Save to praise Urien.

WAITING FOR URIEN

All the one year
    One man was a wellspring
Of wine, bragget and mead
    To reward the brave.

And the levy of bards
    Swarmed round the spits.
Each diademed
    And seated with honour
Went yearningly eager
    To journey to battle

With a stallion under him
    Riding to Manaw
For the more profit,
    Abundance of booty.

But Oh, eight score the same colour
    Of calves and cattle,
Milch cows and oxen,
    Fine beasts every one of them —
I'd have no pleasure in
    If Urien died of it!

It's dear he went, joining
    In the clatter of javelins —
Is his white hair soaked
    And borne on a bier,
Cheek of him crimson,
    Blood of men wallowing?

That great constant man —
    Oh is his wife widowed
For her true lord,
    True pledge of him,
Share, care, guidance
    In the threat of fierce war?

What's that, boy? Go and look.
    What's that noise? Listen.
Is it an earthquake

Or the sea breaking over us?
It's the song of his soldiers
Swells like a wave –

'If the boar's on the hill
Urien thrusts at it.
If the boar's in the valley
Urien will stab.

'If the boar's on the mountain
Urien overpowers it.
If the boar's on the slope
Urien wounds.
If the boar's in the pit
Urien will strike.

'Boar on the path, boar on the peak,
Round every turning –
One sneeze nor two
Will keep it from death.

'There shan't be hunger
With the herds he's got round him.
Like death was his spear
Killing his foe.'

And till I die old
With death's constraint on me
I'll not be happy
Save praising Urien.

PRAISE OF URIEN

Urien Erechwydd,
Most bounteous in Christendom,
Abundance give
To the men of the land.
As you gather in
So do you scatter.
Bards of Christendom
Joy while you live.

But greater's our pleasure
  That Urien and his children
– Greater our glory –
  Have fame of their wealth.
He is the chieftain,
  The high ruler,
Refuge to wanderers
  And swift companion.

The English of Lloegr
  Know this as they count
Deaths that they've suffered
  And frequent affliction,
Farmsteads burnt
  And the trappings taken,
Many a loss
  And great misfortune
And no escaping
  From Urien Rheged.

Rheged's defender,
  Fame's lord, land's anchor,
I've pleasure in you
  Every report.
Tight order of spearplay
  When you hear battle,
Battle when you seek it
  You wreck your vengeance,
Homes set alight
  By the lord of Erechwydd
Erechwydd most fair
  And its generous men.

No help for the Angles . . .
  Round the bravest of kings
The bravest of progeny –
  Best that are now
Or have been or will be:
  You have no peer.
Though only to see him
  Causes great terror,
Joy's usually round him,
  King who inspires:

Geniality's round him
    And great store of treasure –
Gold king of the North
    And the chieftain of kings.

And till I die old
    With death's constraint on me
I'll not be happy
    Save praising Urien.

THE BATTLE OF GWEN STRAD

Men of Catraeth rise with the day*
Round a ruler, winner of fights, cow-reaver.
This is Urien, statesman of fame,
He that curbs kings, cuts them down.
War's onslaught, leader of Christendom.

Men of Pictland, ill luck on their armies
Gwen Strad the station of the sharpener of war!
Forest nor field gave enemies shelter
(O bulwark of our people!) when they came
Like harsh-yelping waves over the land.

I saw fierce men in war-bands
And after battle at morning, mangled flesh.
I saw, from over the border, companies dead.
Cries, cruel, exulting, were heard.
Saw, in that fight for Gwen Strad,
Narrow pain and the champions broken.
In the way to the ford I saw men, blood-stained,
Surrendering arms to the grey master.
In such straits they sued for peace,
White-faced, hands crossed, on the ford's shingle.

* Presumably before the Anglo-Saxons took Catraeth (Catterick) –
see under Aneirin. Urien was Taliesin's patron, king of Rheged in
Cumbria and S.W. Scotland. The Eden is a river in Cumbria.

O the red wine of the Eden! Their chiefs should
        admire it –
The waves washed their horse-tails!
I saw pillaging men dispirited,
Blood bespattered on their clothes.

With his rapid, passionate ordering for battle,
He, battle-shield, intended no flight.
Lord of Rheged, I marvel they dared him!
I saw the nobles throng round Urien
When he strove with his enemies. At Llech Wen,
Scattering foes, he had joy in the bout.

Let your shields, men, be borne at need –
Who serves Urien has his fill of fights.
And till I die old
        With death's constraint upon me,
I'll not be happy
        Save praising Urien.

TO PROPITIATE URIEN

Fairest of bright lands,
        I'll not leave it.
I'll go to Urien,
        His praise I'll sing.
When I get safeguard
        I'll be welcomed
To the best of regions
        Under its chief.

These princes I see
        Are to me nothing.
I'll not go to them
        Nor with them stay
Neither with half-kings
        I'll leave for the north.
Though much I should wager
        – There's no need to vaunt it –

It's certain that Urien
    Will not refuse me.

Lands of Llwyfenydd –
    Mine are their riches,
Mine the graciousness,
    Mine their bounty.
Mine are the rayments,
    The nourishments of them,
Drink from meadhorns
    And no want of good –
From the best of kings,
    Kindest I've heard of.

Kings of all nations
    Are captive to you.
You're a cause of grief
    They need to escape.
Though I intended
    Jest at an old man,
I loved no one better.
    While, before, I knew it,
Now I can see
    How much I shall have,
And except to the high God
    I'll not surrender him.

Your kingly sons,
    Most generous of men –
Their spear shafts sing
    In enemy lands
And till I die old
    With death's constraint on me,
I'll not be happy
    Save praising Urien.

TALIESIN

Death Song for Owain ab Urien

God, consider the soul's need
  Of Owain son of Urien!
Rheged's prince, secret in loam:
  No shallow work, to praise him!

A strait grave, a man much praised,
  His whetted spear the wings of dawn:
That lord of bright Llwyfenydd,
  Where is his peer?

Reaper of enemies; strong of grip;
  One kind with his fathers;
Owain, to slay Fflamddwyn,
  Thought it no more than sleep.

Sleepeth the wide host of England
  With light in their eyes,
And those that had not fled
  Were braver than were wise.

Owain dealt them doom
  As the wolves devour sheep;
That warrior, bright of harness,
  Gave stallions for the bard.

Though he hoarded wealth like a miser,
  For his soul's sake he gave it.
God, consider the soul's need
  Of Owain son of Urien.

ANEIRIN
Late 6th Century

From *The Gododdin*

The Gododdin (Ptolemy's *Otadenoi*) were a British tribe who lived in S.E. Scotland, roughly between the Forth and the Tyne. Sometime in the late sixth century, their chief, Mynyddawg Mwynfawr, lord of Dineiddyn or Dineidyn (Dunedin, later Edinburgh), collected a band of some three hundred picked warriors. For a year he feasted them on wine and mead; and then they marched southward, in an attempt to recapture from the English the natural stronghold of Catraeth (Catterick, or rather Richmond-Catterick, in Yorkshire). The expedition was a disastrous failure: all but one – or three, in another account – of his men lost their lives in attacking an enemy who were much more numerous than they, but less well equipped. The poem that is called *The Gododdin* is a series of heroic elegies, in no perceptible order as we have it, commemorating the bravery and deaths of the British warriors who 'paid for their mead' with their lives.

Man in might, youth in years,
Courage in battle.
Swift, long-maned stallions
Under the thigh of a fine lad.
Behind him, on the lean, swift flank,
His targe, broad and light,
Swords blue and bright,
And fringes of goldwork.
There'll be not between us now
Reproach or enmity –
Rather shall I make you
Songs in your praise.

Quicker his blood to earth
Than to his wedding,
Quicker the crows were fed
Than we could bury him.
Alas, Owain, that dear friend,

ANEIRIN

Lying under the crows!
Horror for me, that region –
Marro's one son slain!

* * *

Diademed in the forefront, wherever he went;
Breathless before a girl, he paid for his mead.
His shield boss is broken. Hearing the warcry
He gave no quarter to those that he hounded;
Never left battle till blood was streaming;
Cut down like rushes those who'd not fled.
On the floor of great houses the Gododdin shall tell
How before Madog's tent, when he returned,
There came but one man, though a hundred set out.

* * *

Men went to Catraeth, keen was their company.
They were fed on fresh mead, and it proved poison –
Three hundred warriors ordered for warfare,
And after the revelling, there was silence.
Although they might go to shrines to do penance,
This much was certain, death would transfix them.

* * *

Men went to Catraeth with the dawn.
Their fine spirit shortened their lives,
Mead they drank, yellow, sweet and ensnaring:
For that year, many a minstrel was glad.
Red their swords – may the blades not be cleaned! –
White shields, and quadribarbed spearheads,
In front of the host of Mynyddawg Mwynfawr.

* * *

ANEIRIN

Men went to Catraeth, they were famous.
According to dignified custom, that year
Their drink from gold cups was wine and mead.
Three and three score and three hundred, gold-torqued,
And after flowing mead, from those that charged
Only three by valour of battle escaped –
Aeron's two war-hounds and resolute Cynon,
And I from the bloodshed by grace of blest song.

* * *

The men that charged then were nurtured together;
For a year over mead great was their purpose.
Wretched to tell of them, greedy the longing!
Bitter the home they'd found, no mother's son nursed them.
So long to grieve for them, and yearn
For those fiery men, from a land of wine!
Gwlyged of Gododdin served them most readily:
He made famous and costly Mynyddawg's feast
In order to buy back the country of Catraeth.

* * *

Men went to Catraeth with battle-rank and warcry,
Power of horses, blue armour and shields,
Shafts held on high, and spearheads,
And shining coats of mail, and swords.
He led the van, and cut through armies,
Cast down twelve score before his blades –*
Rhufawn Hir, who gave gold to altars,
And to the poet rich presents and gifts.

* * *

*Literally 'There fell five fifties before his blades', where fifty
possibly refers to a customary number in a company; 'blades'
perhaps indicates that Rhufawn the Tall *and his men* killed the five
fifties, and not Rhufawn alone.

– 115 –

ANEIRIN

The warriors rose, they mustered together.
All of the one intent, they charged.
Short their lives. Long their kin miss them.
Seven times their own number of English they slew.
In that contention, they made women widows.
On the lashes of many a mother are tears.

* * *

Savage in war, stubborn in conflict,
In battle he'd not make peace.
In the day of anger he'd not shirk hardship.
A wild boar's fury was Bleiddig ab Eli.
Wine from the brimming glass cups he drank,
And did great deeds in the day of battle
Off a white charger, before he died.
He left behind him bloodstained corpses.

* * *

He, most splendid, thrust beyond three hundred.
At the centre he slew, and on the flanks.
He, most magnanimous, was worthy before a host.
To their horses he'd portioned out oats that winter.
Albeit Arthur he was not, he fed
The black ravens on the walls of the fort.*
He in battle put forth his strength,
In the front rank, Gwawrddur, the rampart.

*This is probably the earliest reference to Arthur in world
literature. The text, as in many of the early poems, is sometimes
obscure, so that the translation can only be regarded as tentative:
but I have tried to follow the best scholarship available.

ANONYMOUS
7th century

Song to a Child

Dinogad's smock is pied, pied –
Made it out of marten hide.
Whit, whit, whistle along,
Eight slaves with you sing the song.

When your dad went to hunt,
Spear on his shoulder, cudgel in hand,
He called his quick dogs, 'Giff, you wretch,
Gaff, catch her, catch her, fetch, fetch!'

From a coracle he'd spear
Fish as a lion strikes a deer.
When your dad went to the crag
He brought down roebuck, boar and stag,
Speckled grouse from the mountain tall,
Fish from Derwent waterfall.

Whatever your dad found with his spear,
Boar or wild cat, fox or deer,
Unless it flew, would never get clear.

ANONYMOUS
*c.*875

Praise of Tenby

This has all the marks of being a *dadolwch*, or poem of reconciliation
between a poet and his patron. The patron is a lord of Dyfed, or
Pembrokeshire, called Bleiddudd; but the poem is remarkable among
those of its type in that Bleiddudd is dead, 'gone to the oaken church',
and the poet is making peace with his heir, the new head of Erbin's line,
master of the 'little fort' – Dinbych or Tenby. If the last line of this
translation is correct, which is open to doubt, it looks as though the poem

ANONYMOUS

was intended for recitation at Bleiddudd's funeral feast, at the November
Calends, the festival of the beginning of winter. It is markedly anti-North
Walian: Dyfed and Gwynedd must at this time have been at one
another's throats. I have omitted the final couplet to God, and also a
stray, fragmentary stanza that follows it in the manuscript.

I ask for God's favour, saviour of the folk,
Master of heaven and earth, greatly prudent and wise.

There is a fine fortress stands on the sea,
The bright headland is gay at the Calends,
And when the ocean puts forth its might
Commonly poets are loud over mead-cups.
The hurrying wave surges against it,
They abandon the green flood to the Picts.
And through my prayer, O God, may I find
As I keep faith, atonement with you.

There is a fine fortress on the broad ocean,
Unyielding stronghold, sea round its edge.
Enquire, O Britain, who rightly owns it –
Yours, head of Erbin's line, yours be it now!
In this palisade were war-band and throng,
Eagle in cloud on the track of pale faces:
Before that lord and router of enemies,
Prince of wide fame, they drew up their ranks.

There is a fine fortress on the ninth wave.
Finely its populace take their ease.
They do not make merry with taunts and sneers,
It is not their custom to be hard,
Nor shall I traduce their welcome –
Better a slave in Dyfed than yeoman in Deudraeth!*
Their throng of free men, keeping a feast,
Would include, two by two, the best men alive!

*In Merionethshire, North Wales.

ANONYMOUS

There is a fine fortress of revel and tumult
A multitude makes, and crying of birds.
Gay was that company met at the Calends
Round a generous lord, splendid and brave.
Before he had gone to the oaken church
From a bowl of glass gave me mead and wine.

There is a fine fortress on the foreshore,
Finely to each is given his share.
I know at Tenby – pure white the seagull –
Companions of Bleiddudd, lord of the court.
The night of the Calends it was my custom
To lie by my king, brilliant in war,
With a cloak coloured purple, having such cheer
I were the tongue to the poets of Britain!

There is a fine fortress resounds with song,
Where every concession I wished for was mine –
I say nothing of rights! I kept good order:
Whoever knows otherwise deserves no feast-gift!
The writings of Britain were my chief care
Where the loud waves broke in tumult.
Let it long remain, that cell I visited!

There is a fine fortress on the height,
Its feasting lavish, its revelry loud.
Lovely about it, that camp of heroes,
Is the wandering spray, long are its wings.
Hoarse sea-birds haunt the crest of the crag.
Let all anger be banished over the hills!
I wish for Bleiddudd the best bliss that may be –
Let these words of remembrance be weighed at his wake!

ANONYMOUS
9th century

Poetry from Lost Sagas

These poems and sequences of *englynion* (stanzas of three and four lines) were for long considered the genuine work of Llywarch Hen, or Llywarch the Old, a sixth-century prince. Sir Ifor Williams has shown, however, that they are not *by* that almost legendary figure, but merely *about* him. They belong to ninth-century sagas, on the Irish model, in which verse was used for dramatic effects – such as dialogue, or the expression of personal feeling – while the narrative was told in prose. The Welsh saga-literature that has survived is very fragmentary; almost all the prose links have been lost, and the verse has been jumbled together and left without a context to explain it. Much of it, indeed, is highly impressive as it stands – perhaps for that very reason, naked and challenging and bleak. Sir Ifor says of these *englynion* that they are the nearest thing to great drama that Wales has ever produced. In what follows, I have tried to paraphrase, between the square brackets, his reconstruction of the sagas that were their original context.

i. *Gwên ap Llywarch and his Father*

[The first sequence tells of the death of Gwên, the son of Llywarch Hen. Llywarch had twenty-three other sons, of whom he was intensely proud. His honour rested in their prowess in battle, and he was for ever taunting them, daring them to great feats of courage. One by one he drove them to a warrior's death. Gwên, meanwhile, had been away on his travels, visiting his uncle, Urien Of Rheged. When he came back, he found his brothers all dead, and the enemy once more attacking his father's kingdom. There is no one left to defend the Gorlas Ford on the river Llawen. Llywarch himself, old as he is, is arming himself for battle, saying:]

Llywarch

Over my heart the shield's worn thin.
Though I am old, I'll do it.
I shall stand guard on Gorlas Ford.

ANONYMOUS

[Gwên comes up to his father, who does not immediately recognise him. The following dialogue then takes place.]

Gwên

After a meal you should not arm. Take heart.
  Wind is keen, poison bitter.
My mother tells me I'm your son.

Llywarch

Now am I inspired to know
That the one stock bore us both.
A dear long time you've been, O Gwên!

Gwên

Keen my spear, it glitters in battle.
I will indeed watch on the Ford.
If I am not back, God be with you!

Llywarch

If you survive it, I shall see you.
If you are killed, then I'll mourn you.
Lose not in hardship warrior's honour!

Gwên

I shall not shame you, giver of battles,
  When the brave man arms for the border,
  Though hardship beset me, I'll stay my ground.

Llywarch

A wave shifting over the shore.
By and by strong purpose breaks.
Boasters commonly flee in a fight.

Gwên

This, only this, shall I say:
Where I am, spears will shatter.
I am not saying I'll not flee.

ANONYMOUS

Llywarch

Soft the quagmire, hard the slope.
By the horse's hoof the stream bank's broken.
A promise not compassed is less than nought.

Gwên

Streams divert round the fortress dyke;
And it is I that purpose
Before I flee, my shield stained and broken.

Llywarch

The horn that Urien gave you
With a gold baldric round its neck –
Sound that, if you're sorely pressed.

Gwên

Though terror press round me, and the fierce thieves
of England,
I'll not shame my pride.
I shall not wake your maidens.

Llywarch

When I was as young as that young man
Who now puts on his spurs of gold,
How I would hurl myself on the spears!

Gwên

There, indeed, is a safe assertion
With you alive, and your witness dead.
Never an old man was faint as a lad.

[Bitterly Gwên rides off to the Ford. He fights the invaders, and is killed.
The news is brought to Old Llywarch, and this is how the father mourns
the last of his sons, as he said he would, and repents in despair of his own
arrogant pride:]

ANONYMOUS

Llywarch

Gwên by the Llawen stood watch last night,
 He did not flee in the murk of war –
 Dire the tale on Gorlas Dyke!

Gwên by the Llawen kept watch last night,
 His shield on his shoulder.
 Since he was my son, he was ready.

Gwên by the Llawen kept guard last night,
 His shield to his cheek.
 Since he was my son, he did not escape.

The great thighs of Gwên stood watch last night
 On the border-ford Gorlas.
 Since he was my son, he did not flee.

Gwên, I know your nature:
Yours the eagle's swoop upon estuaries.
Were I born blest, you'd have escaped.

Wave thunders, roofs over the surf.
When warriors go to battle, Gwên,
Woe to the old man that wants you!

Wave thunders, roofs over flood.
When warriors go on foray, Gwên,
Woe to the old man that's lost you.

A man was my son, stubborn for his rights,
 And he was Urien's nephew.
 On Gorlas Ford, Gwên was killed.

Four and twenty sons I got.
A gold-torqued prince of a host
Was Gwên, the best of them.

Four and twenty sons I had.
A gold-torqued prince of battle
Was Gwên, best son of his father.

Four and twenty sons were mine –
Gold-torqued and princely chieftains.
Mere striplings they were, to Gwên.

Four and twenty in Llywarch's household
Of brave and fierce men.
Too much praise came to trick me.

Four and twenty sons, fruit of my body –
My tongue has killed them.
Small fame were good! They have been lost.

ii. Llywarch the Old

[In the second sequence from the Llywarch Hen cycle, Llywarch is left
alone, his sons – even Llawr and Gwên, the last of them – are all dead
because of his proud taunting of them, and the old man, bent over a
crooked stick, mourns his isolation and despair.]

Ere my back was bent, I was ready with words:
My prowess was praised.
Men of Argoed ever upheld me.

Ere my back was bent, I was bold,
Was welcomed in the beer-hall
Of Powys, paradise of Welshmen.

Ere my back was bent, I was brilliant.
My spear was the first to strike.
A hunchback now, I am heavy and wretched.

ANONYMOUS

Wooden crook, it is autumn.
Bracken red, stubble sere.
I've surrendered all I love.

Wooden crook, it is winter.
Men shout gaily over the drink.
At my bedside, no one greets me.

Wooden crook, it is springtime.
Cuckoos hid, clear their grieving.
I'm disregarded by a girl.

Wooden crook, it is maytime.
Red the furrow, shoots are curled.
For me to gaze at your beak is woe!

Wooden crook, familiar branch,
Prop an old man full of longing –
Llywarch, the steadfast talker!

Wooden crook, hard branch,
God my help will welcome me –
Good stick, my true companion!

Wooden crook, be kind –
Even better prop me up,
Llywarch, the long loquacious!

Old age is mocking me
From my hair to my teeth
And the knob that youth loves.

Old age is mocking me
From my hair to my teeth
And the knob women love.

Boisterous wind. White skirts
To the trees. Stag brave, bleak hill.
The old man frail. Slow he rises.

This leaf, chased here and there by the wind,
    Its destiny's drear.
  It is old; it was born this year.

What I loved as a lad is hateful to me –
    A girl, a stranger, a spry horse.
  No indeed, they do not suit me.

The four chief things I hated
Have come now all at once:
Coughing and old age, sickness and sorrow.

I am old, and alone, and shapeless with cold.
    My bed was once splendid.
  I'm doubled in three, and wretched.

I am old, bent in three, I am fickle and reckless,
    I'm a fool, and uncouth.
  They that once loved me, do not now.

Not a girl loves me, no one comes near me,
    I cannot seek them.
  O for death, to end me!

There comes to me neither sleep nor mirth
Now that Llawr and Gwên are dead.
I'm but a querulous corpse, being old.

Wretched the fortune doled out to Llywarch
    The night he was born:
  Tired grief, and an age to mourn.

ANONYMOUS

iii. Cynddylan's Hall

[For this third sequence, we leave the cycle of Llywarch Hen, and turn to the saga of Heledd, the sister of Cynddylan, lord of Pengwern or Shrewsbury. Here too the English are invading the good land of Powys. By the time this sequence starts, they have killed Cynddylan and destroyed his home. Heledd is lamenting over the ruins. Elfan, Caeawg (if that is indeed a proper name, and not some epithet describing Cynddylan), Cynon, Gwiawn and Gwyn, whom she mentions, are presumably her brothers, the sons of Cyndrwyn.]

> Dark is Cynddylan's hall tonight
>   With no fire, no bed.
>   I weep awhile, then am silent.
>
> Dark is Cynddylan's hall tonight
>   With no fire, no candle.
>   Save for God, who'll keep me sane?
>
> Dark is Cynddylan's hall tonight
>   With no fire, no light.
>   Grieving for you overcomes me.
>
> Dark of roof is Cynddylan's hall
>   After that blest assembly.
>   Woe who neglects the good that offers!
>
> Cynddylan's hall you've gone uncomely,
>   Your shield is in the grave.
>   While he lived, doors needed no bar.
>
> Forlorn is Cynddylan's hall tonight
>   For the man that owned it.
>   O for death, why did it leave me?
>
> No ease in Cynddylan's hall tonight
>   On the top of hard rock
>   With no lord, or retinue, or prowess!

ANONYMOUS

Dark is Cynddylan's hall tonight
    With no fire, no songs.
   My cheek's worn out with tears.

It wounds me to see Cynddylan's hall
    With no roof, no fire,
   Dead is my lord; I yet live.

Waste is Cynddylan's hall tonight
    After strong warriors,
   Elfan, Cynddylan, Caeawg.

Desolate is Cynddylan's hall tonight
    After the respect I had,
   With no men, no women to care for it.

Quiet is Cynddylan's hall tonight,
    Now it has lost its lord.
   Merciful God, what shall I do?

Dark of roof is Cynddylan's hall
    After the English destroyed
   Cynddylan and Elfan of Powys.

Dark is Cynddylan's hall tonight
    For the seed of Cyndrwyn,
   Cynon and Gwiawn and Gwyn.

Hour upon hour, Cynddylan's hall wounds me
    After the great conversing
   That I watched on your hearth.

ANONYMOUS

iv. The Eagle of Eli

[The next sequence evokes the eagles as they feast on the dead bodies of Cynddylan and his host. Here, as elsewhere in Old Welsh poetry, the birds in question are white-tailed or sea eagles, not the larger golden eagles. Sea eagles are now extremely rare birds of passage in Britain, but they were once common. They have a steel-grey head, which looks almost like a wig, and their legs are much barer of feathers than those of the golden eagle, which emphasizes their great claws. Their call is a loud, shrill yelping, not the characteristic scream and bark of the bigger bird. They live on the coasts and larger rivers, mainly on fish, though they do hunt birds and small animals, and also delight in carrion. When fishing, they drop from a great height, alighting on the sea and catching the fish in their claws. Unlike the golden eagle, which in the Old World normally nests on crags, sea eagles build conspicuous nests in the tops of pinetrees or oaks. In the poem, Eli is probably the name of the river where they live – Sir Ifor Williams compares it with the River Meheli in Montgomeryshire, which I would guess is a later name for the same river. Pengwern is Shrewsbury.]

Eagle of Eli, loud was its cry tonight –
    Had drunk of a pool of blood,
  The heart's blood of Cynddylan Wyn.

Eagle of Eli, it cried out tonight,
    It swam in men's blood.
  There in the trees! And I've misery on me.

Eagle of Eli, I hear it tonight.
    Bloodstained it is. I dare not go near it –
  There in the trees! I've misery on me.

Eagle of Eli that watches the seas,
In the estuaries fishes no longer.
In the blood of men it calls its feast.

Eagle of Eli walks in the wood tonight:
    Too soon has it supped.
  Who pampers it, his arrogance prospers.

[The eagle of Pengwern answers it from the environs of Trenn, that Cynddylan died defending.]

Grey-capped eagle of Pengwern, tonight
Its yelp is shrill,
Jealous for the flesh I loved.

Grey-capped eagle of Pengwern, tonight
Its cry is shrill,
Jealous of Cynddylan's flesh.

Grey-capped eagle of Pengwern, tonight
Is its claw aloft,
Greedy for the flesh I love.

Far calls the eagle of Pengwern tonight,
It watches on men's blood.
Trenn will be called a luckless town.

Far calls the eagle of Pengwern tonight,
It watches men's blood.
Trenn will be called a glittering town.

v. The Ruined Hearth of Rheged

[The fall of Urien of Rheged, with his sons Owain and Elphin, formed a companion saga to that of Llywarch the Old. The real Urien had been praised in the sixth century by Taliesin: but now the Welsh, remembering their ancient kingdom of Rheged, that is Cumberland and S.W. Scotland, made a legend out of him. This fifth sequence laments his ruined home.]

Quiet the breeze, side of long slope.
The man worthy of praise is rare.
For Urien, grief is vain.

ANONYMOUS

Many a lively dog and spirited hawk
    Was fed on this floor
  Before it was heaped with rubble.

This hearth, that the grass covers –
Its floor was more accustomed
To carousers calling for mead.

This hearth, that bugloss covers,
While Owain and Elphin lived,
Had boiled its cauldron of plunder.

This hearth, that grey lichen covers,
Was more accustomed round its food
To fierce, intrepid swordplay.

This hearth, that fine briars cover,
Had courtesies upon it:
To give was Rheged's custom.

This hearth, that the thorns cover –
Its warriors were more accustomed
To the warmth of Owain's friendship.

This hearth, that ant-hills cover –
It was more accustomed to the bright
Rushlights and true feast-comrades.

This hearth, that a sow roots in –
It was more accustomed to laughter
And revelry round the mead-horns.

This hearth, that pullets scratch in –
Want did not injure it
While Owain and Urien lived.

This upright post, and that —
They were more accustomed round them
To thronging mirth and the paths of bounty.

ANONYMOUS
9th century or later

The Spoils of Annwn

Many poems attributed to Taliesin refer to ancient Celtic myth or story. Some are included in the sixteenth century *Tale of Taliesin* which Lady Guest translated for her *Mabinogion*; others are much older, some apparently pre-Norman. Their mystery has attracted speculation, so that scholarship has tended to avoid them. Probably they were once part of tales, and the obscurity is partly due to our ignorance of their context. But the minstrel also seems, as one of the tricks of his trade, to be teasing his audience with a show of erudition; and perhaps he himself has not always the key to what he is singing about. More work needs to be done on the Taliesin story: the cycle of poems might turn out to be comparable to the Osian cycle in Irish, as expressing a confrontation of pagan and Christian traditions. How much actual Druidic or pre-Christian lore is buried in these strange fragments is doubtful, but it is difficult to ignore the possibility entirely.

The Spoils of Annwn is quite early, and one of the earliest references to Arthur as a hero of tales. It concerns a variant of the Raid-on-the-Underworld motif which in the Second Branch of the *Mabinogion* is euphemerised into an expedition to rescue Branwen from Ireland. In both, an army crosses the sea but only seven men return. In the *Mabinogion* the leader is Brân the Blessed; here it is Arthur who sails in his ship 'Prydwen'. In the *Mabinogion* the cauldron plays a decisive role but is not the object of the expedition; here it is, and it is connected with Ceridwen's cauldron from which Taliesin got his inspiration. But note that in the *Mabinogion* also, Taliesin is named as one of the seven survivors. The Otherworld, Annwn, the home of the ancient gods, is a tricksy place that changes name and shape: Caer Siddi, fairy fortress; Caer Pedryfan, four-cornered fortress; Caer Feddwid, fortress of the mead-feast; Caer Rigor, intractable fortress; and later in the poem, Caer Wydr, glass fortress. I have translated three of the eight stanzas: the rest of the poem is more fragmentary, but includes an attack on monks, who it says throng together like a wolf-pack.

ANONYMOUS

I praise a prince, lord of king's country,
Over shores of the world widens his sovereignty.
Impeccable prison had Gweir in Caer Siddi,
As the story relates of Pwyll and Pryderi.
Prior to him, there went to it nobody,
To the heavy grey chain that trussed a true laddie.
Because of the spoils of Annwn he sang bitterly.
It shall last till Doomsday, our own prayer and poetry.
Three shiploads of Prydwen we went on that journey.
Seven alone returned from Caer Siddi.

I make splendid fame, my song they heard it
In the rotating fortress, four-turreted.
It was of the cauldron my first word was uttered.
With breath of nine maidens its fire was lighted.
Head of Annwn owned the cauldron. What nature has it?
Dark round the rim, and pearl-encrusted,
Its destiny is, no coward's food cooks in it.
The flashing sword of Lleawg was thrust in it.
In the hand of Lleminawg they left it
And before Hell's gate a lamp was lighted.
When we went with Arthur, bright and ill-fated,
Seven alone came back from Caer Feddwid.

I make splendid fame, my song is heard more
In the four-turreted fort, isle of the radiant door,
Where jet black and noonday are mingled together.
Bright wine with their retinue they had for liquor.
Three shiploads in Prydwen we put off from shore.
Seven alone returned from Caer Rigor

ANONYMOUS

10th-11th century

Winter

Wind sharp, hillside bleak, hard to win shelter;
    Ford is impassable, lake is frozen;
  A man may near stand on one stalk of grass.

  Wave upon wave roofs over land-edge;
Shouts loud against breast of peak and brae;
    Outside, a man may barely stand.

Lake-haunts cold, with the storm winds of winter;
    Withered the reeds, stalks all broken;
  Wind-gusts angry, stripping of woods.

Cold bed of fish in the gloom of ice;
    Stag lean, bearded reeds;
  Evening brief, slant of bent wood.

Snow falls, covers with white;
Warriors go not forth on foray;
Lakes cold, their tint without sunlight.

Snow falls, hoarfrost white;
Idle shield on an old shoulder;
A monstrous wind freezes the grass.

Snow falls, high on the ice;
Sweeps the wind atop the thick trees;
A stout shield that, on a bold shoulder.

Snow falls, covers the vale;
Warriors hurry to battle;
I'll not go, wound does not let me.

ANONYMOUS

Snow falls, over the slope;
Prisoned the steed, the cattle thin;
Here's no question of a summer's day.

Snow falls, white border of mountains;
On the sea, ship's timbers bare;
The coward nurses many a scheme.

ANONYMOUS
Before 1100

THE MABINOGION

The Four Branches of the Mabinogion (as they are usually called) form a
collection of stories based on ancient Celtic myths and folktales. They
were probably put together in their present form in the eleventh century,
but from material much older. It is likely that the small amount of verse
they contain is older than the prose, and could well be the remnant of
much more extensive verse passages. The sequence translated here comes
from the Fourth Branch, *Math vab Mathonwy*, and is one of the few
examples of an englyn sequence still in place within a tale. Blodeuwedd,
the woman made from flowers, and her lover Gronw have killed Lleu
Llaw Gyffes, Lleu of the nimble hands. His soul has flown off in the shape
of a wounded eagle. His uncle Gwydion finds him by following a
rampaging sow to where she feeds on maggots and rotten flesh dropping
out of a tree in Nantlleu.

And when he looked, he saw an eagle in the top of the tree. And when
the eagle stirred, the worms and rotten flesh fell off it, and the sow was
eating them. And he realised that the eagle was Lleu, and sang an englyn –

> Oak grows between lake and lake.
> Sky and glen one darkness make.
> Unless false is what I say,
> Flowers did my Lleu unmake.

And when he had done so, the eagle let himself down until it was in the
middle of the tree. And Gwydion sang another englyn –

MABINOGION

Oak in upland meadow stands.
Not rain, but carrion on it lands.
Twenty crafts the tree commands –
In its top Lleu Nimble-hands.

And then it let itself down until it was on the lowest branch of the tree.
And he sang this englyn to it then –

Oak under scarp grows high
For a lord to hide him by.
Unless false is what I say,
Into my lap Lleu will fly.

And it lighted on Gwydion's knee. And Gwydion struck it with his magic
wand, so that Lleu was in his own shape. No one had ever seen a more
miserable sight on a man than was on him then. He was nothing but skin
and bone.

ANONYMOUS
12th century

Never Tell

The saplings of the green-tipped birch
Draw my foot from bondage:
Let no boy know your secret!

Oak saplings in the grove
Draw my foot from its chain:
Tell no secret to a maid!

The leafy saplings of the oak
Draw my foot from prison:
Tell no babbler a secret!

Briar shoots with berries on –
Neither a blackbird on her nest,
Nor a liar, are ever still.

ANONYMOUS
12th Century

Gnomic Stanzas

Mountain snow, everywhere white;
A raven's custom is to sing;
No good comes of too much sleep.

Mountain snow, white the ravine;
By rushing wind trees are bent;
Many a couple love one another
Though they never come together.

Mountain snow, tossed by the wind;
Broad full moon, dockleaves green;
Rarely a knave's without litigation.

Mountain snow, swift the stag;
Usual in Britain are brave chiefs;
There's need of prudence in an exile.

Mountain snow, hunted stag;
Wind whistles above the eaves of a tower;
Heavy, O man, is sin.

Mountain snow, leaping stag:
Wind whistles above a high white wall;
Usually the calm are comely.

Mountain snow, stag in the vale;
Wind whistles above the rooftop;
There's no hiding evil, no matter where.

Mountain snow, stag on the shore;
Old man must feel his loss of youth;
Bad eyesight puts a man in prison.

ANONYMOUS

Mountain snow, stag in the ditch;
Bees are asleep and snug;
Thieves and a long night suit each other.

Mountain snow, deer are nimble;
Waves wetten the brink of the shore;
Let the skilful hide his purpose.

Mountain snow, speckled breast of a goose;
Strong are my arm and shoulder;
I hope I shall not live to a hundred.

Mountain snow, bare tops of reeds;
Bent tips of branches, fish in the deep;
Where there's no learning, cannot be talent.

Mountain snow; red feet of hens;
Where it chatters, water's but shallow;
Big words add to any disgrace.

Mountain snow, swift the stag;
Rarely a thing in the world concerns me;
To warn the unlucky does not save them.

Mountain snow, fleece of white;
It's rare that a relative's face is friendly
If you visit him too often.

Mountain snow, white house-roofs;
If tongue were to tell what the heart may know
Nobody would be neighbours.

Mountain snow, day has come;
Every sad man sick, half-naked the poor;
Every time, a fool gets hurt.

ANONYMOUS
12th century

Sadness in Springtime

Month of May, loveliest season,
The birds loud, the growth green,
Plough in furrow, ox in yoke,
Green sea, land cut dapple.

In the fine treetops when cuckoos sing,
    My sadness is greater:*
Smoke smart, manifest sleep-lack
For my kinsfolk gone to rest.

In hill, in dale, in isles of the sea,
    Wheresoever one may go,
    From blest Christ there's no escaping.

MEILYR
fl. 1100-37

On his Death-bed

Rex regum, prince, easy of eulogy,
I ask my highest Lord this bounty:
    King ruling the region,
    The high Wheel of Heaven,
    Make reconciliation
        Between you and me.
That I've offended you, mind's sorely
Troubled, feckless and sorry.
      In the sight of the Lord God
      Sin I've committed
    And left unattended
      All godly duty.

*The cuckoo's song – cw cw – means 'Where? where?' in old Welsh.

MEILYR

But to my lord king I'll attend me
Before in earth helpless they lay me.
   A true prediction
   To Adam and all men
   Prophets have spoken,
     Foretelling truly
Jesus in the womb – ah, happy
To bear him! – of the martyr-queen, Mary.
   A load of raging
   Sin I've been gathering
   And now its brawling
     I tremble to see.
Lord of all worlds, so fair of entreaty,
Make me pure, before hell torments me.
   King of all princes,
   In that you know me,
   Because of my vices
     Don't refuse mercy!
   Many times gold and silks in plenty
   For my praise of them, frail princes gave me.
   But after the Muse, a power more mighty –
   My tongue, now it's silent, does but poorly.
As for me, Meilyr the poet, pilgrim to Peter,
   Guard at your gate who judges right quality,
   When the time for all in the grave is ready
   For us to be raised, O then support me!
     Waiting that trumpet,
     May I lie quiet
     In a cloister, and on it
       The beating sea,
   Deathless its fame, and it so lonely,
   Round its graves the breast of the salt sea –
     Fair Mary's island,
     Pure isle of her pure ones,
     To wait resurrection
       Within it, were lovely.

MEILYR

Foretold of the cross,
Christ knows me, guides me across
From the lodging of loss,
    Hell, and its agony.
The Creator who made me, he'll receive me
Among true folk of the parish of Enlli.*

GWALCHMAI AP MEILYR

fl. 1130-80

From *Gwalchmai's Boast*

The sun early rising, summer comes fast,
Blithe speech of birds, weather fine and bright.
It is splendid I am, fearless in battle.
Before the host I'm a lion, like lightning my onset.
Guarding the border I've watched this night out.
Murmuring fords, water of Dygen Freiddin,
Bright green the virgin grass, lovely the water,
Loud the nightingale's familiar song.
The seagulls sport on the bed of the flood,
Their plumage gleams, their factions are turbulent.
Because I love a young girl of Caerwys
In early summer my memory wanders...
I've listened to lips in true contentment
And the gentle sounding speech of a girl.
But for noble Owain's sake, fetter of foes,*
The English scatter before my blade.

Sword flashing, the bold one parries like lightning,
Gold upon my round shield gleams.
Waters all turbulent, brisk is the day
With the loud tune of birds busily rhyming.
In a far land, today, my mind is anxious,

*Bardsey Island, where there was an ancient Celtic monastery, in whose graveyard many saints were said to be buried.
*Owain Gwynedd

Traversing the country beside Efyrnwy.
Appletrees are topped with white clusters of blossom,
Trees gaily covered, every heart seeks its love.
A girl of Caerwys I love, a gentle person,
And all who do not acclaim her, I hate.
Genilles the fair – though she kill me with a word
And my visit be short – yet floods me with gifts...
My sword flashes like lightning in battle,
Gold gleams upon my shield.
Many praise me that never yet saw me,
The girls of Gwent mention me with passion.
I saw before Owain the English in their ruin
And round about Rhibyll that lord in his wrath.
Gwalchmai they call me, enemy of Saxons:
For Anglesey's king I have lunged out in battle,
And to please a girl, bright as snow on the trees,
When Chester was fought for, I have shed blood.

The Battle of Tal y Moelfre
To Owain Gwynedd – 1157

I exalt the generous descendant of Rhodri,
Ward of the Marches, his quality kingly,
Right master of Britain, doom-buoyant Owain,
His princes nor grovel, nor hoard their wealth.

Three legions came, ships of the deep sea,
Three prime stout fleets, avid to spoil him:
One was of Ireland, another was war-manned
With Norsemen of Lochlyn, lank steeds of the flood;

A third over seas sailed here from Normandy,
And, for their pains, vast trouble it cost them –
The dragon of Môn, how fierce he bore battle,
Desperate riot, their trial of war!

GWALCHMAI AP MEILYR

And before him ran a miserable confusion,
    Ruin and battle and a grievous end –
On struggle, blood and struggle; on terror, dire terror;
    And a thousand war-shouts about Tal y Moelfre.

On spear flashed spear, shaft upon shafts,
    On panic woe and panic, drowned with the drowning,
And Menai without ebb from the tide of their bleeding,
    And colour of warriors' blood in the brine.

And the blue chain-mail, and the ache of disaster,
    And the wounded heaped from that lord's red spear,
And the musters of England, and combat against them,
    And their destruction in wild disarray.

And the raising to fame of that bitter sword
    In seven score languages, long in his praise.

To Owain Gwynedd

Gwalchmai's relations with his patrons seem to have soured as he grew
older. In this poem he asks Owain Gwynedd to restore him to favour. His
own father, Meilyr, had been poet to Gruffudd ap Cynan, Owan's father;
and he himself had been befriended by Owain as a young man. We do
not know if his plea was successful; but it is perhaps significant that, out
of all the elegies to Owain Gwynedd that survive, that of Gwalchmai, his
chief poet, is conspicuous by its absence. After Owain's death, moreover,
the poet had difficulty in keeping the friendship and patronage of his two
sons, Dafydd and Rhodri. Cemais, in the poem, was one of Owain's royal
seats, in the Cantref of Talybolion, in Anglesey.

    I exalt the generous descendant of Aeneas,
    I exalt a brave lion, a nature like lightning,
    I exalt the fairest of the princes of Britain,
        Most kingly and fine, Owain, gold youth.

GWALCHMAI AP MEILYR

My father exalted the great king his father
  With a skilled muse, rich blessings were his;
And I too will exalt a high leader of battle,
  Voicing sweet song and record of lineage.

Whom I hear speak ill of him, true scion of Idwal,
  Will not go without vengeance, as payment for blood,
But by the company's giftmaster, at Cadwallon's court
  He that speaks fair of him shall merit a gift.

 I favoured a hero, buttress of heroes,
 I spoke of Cemais, stronghold of Wales.
 Owain loved me as a lad beside him –
 Too much love, usually, turns into hate.
 Out of his gains he gave me ungrudgingly
 Firm-fleshed horses, honourable grace,
And he knew me as eager to fight in the forefront –
  His many blades, armed, champion wolf of the pack!

 Scarcely he greets me now, angry like Goliath,
 Massive is his wrath on a grey and white horse.
The anguish of estrangement hurts me like prison,
  With a wild violence, like an oaktree in flames.

 God created him best of mortals –
 Before I angered him, would I'd been slain!
And though the blame's mine, however much at fault,
  Make peace with your poet, his song's sincere!

 Son of Gruffudd, valour in battle,
 Your violence long, dragon of Ewias,*
 For your fullness of rank, I praise you,
 Everyone praises you, kingdom's head!

*_Ewias_ – between Brecon and Hereford. In _Culhwch and Olwen_ it was
where Arthur checked the murderous course of Twrch Trwyth the
wild boar. So 'dragon of Ewias' is probably a kenning for Arthur.

HYWEL AB OWAIN GWYNEDD

d. 1170

Hywel's Boast of his Country

As J. Lloyd-Jones suggests, the poem known as *Hywel's Boast (Gorhoffedd)* is really two separate pieces, one about his country, the other about women. The first piece, given below, is divided into two sections. In the first, as I interpret it, Hywel is away from home on an expedition. Beleaguered, and afraid he cannot hold out until help comes, he dreams of a wave washing the tomb of Rhufawn Befr, an early Welsh king who died young; and he takes this as a bad omen, and thinks longingly of his homeland in North Wales.

The second section is more confident, and the wave is now a symbol of Hywel's own energy. He talks of his conquests, both military and amorous, the one perhaps standing for the other. He won Meirionnydd in 1143. Maelienydd is a cantref in mid-Wales, and Ceri just north of it. Since the English recaptured it in 1144, Hywel probably refers to an expedition just before that. Gwalchmai says that Owain Gwynedd, his father, had pledges from Dumbarton. Perhaps this diplomatic mission was what Hywel left Ceri for, riding night and day to Carlisle and Rheged – S.W. Scotland. Finally, Hywel says he now desires a girl of Tegeingl, or Flintshire, which was the scene of Owain's conflict with Powys in the late 1140s, culminating in his victory at Coleshill in 1150. Gwynedd retained Tegeingl until the English invasion of 1157.

I

A wave white with foam washes a grave,
Tomb of Rhufawn Befr, chief of kings.

I love, today, England's hatred – open ground
    Of the North, and edging the Lliw, thick woods.
I love him who gave me my share of mead
    Where the seas reach, long in contention.
I love its retinue, its thick-set dwellings,
    And at the king's will, its hosting to war.
I love its sea-coast and its mountains,
    Its castle by the wood, and the fine lands,

The meads of its waters, and the valleys,
　　Its white gulls and lovely women.
I love its soldiers, its managed stallions,
　　Woods and strong men and homesteads.
I love its fields, their wealth of small clover,
　　Where honour could for sure rejoice.
I love its vales, privilege of valour,
　　Both its wild wilderness and its riches.
By God's one son, how great a wonder!
　　How splendid the stags, how abundant the wealth!
Between warriors of Powys and pleasant Gwynedd
　　I did, with a spear's thrust, excellent work;
And now, on a white steed, in the pride of battle,
　　Yet may I win release from exile!
No, there's no saving me, none, till my folk come –
　　A dream has said it – God has spoken –
Waves, white with foam, wash on the grave!

II

A white foaming wave rounds fiercely on homesteads,
Coloured like frost, when it breaks on shore.

I love the sea-coast of Meirionnydd
　　Where a white arm was my pillow.
I love the nightingale in the green wood
　　In the sweet vale where two waters meet.

Lord of heaven and earth, a hero of Gwynedd,
　　(How far Ceri is from Carlisle!)
I mounted a bay from Maelienydd –
　　At last came to Rheged, rode day and night.

A new gift may I have, before I die,
　　Tegeingl's land, fairest in its region!

HYWEL AB OWAIN GWYNEDD

Though I be a lover walking with Ovid,
　　Let God in his mercy consider my end –

A white foaming wave, fierce upon homesteads!

From *Hywel's Boast of Women*

II

A duress that much worries me, has come my way
And longing, alas, can't be avoided,
For Nest, fair as apple in blossom,
For Perweur, heart of my sin;
For Generys the virgin, who'd not calm my lust –
　　May she not achieve chastity!
For Hunydd, matter till doomsday,
For Hawis, the custom I'd choose.

I had a girl of the same mind one day;
I had two, their praise is greater;
I had three, and four, and fortune;
I'd five of them, their white flesh lovely;
I had six, and sin not avoided –
Clear white they sought me on top of a fort;
I had seven and the toil persisted;
I'd eight, to pay for the praise I sang them –
　　To keep tongue quiet, teeth do well!

Hywel's Choice

My choosing, a lovely girl, graceful and slender,
　　White and tall in her cloak, the colour of heather;
And my chosen wisdom, to wonder at her womanly,
　　When she barely but speaks the grace of her mind;
And my chosen partnership, to contend with a sweetheart,
　　And be privy to a charm, to a gift.

HYWEL AP OWAIN GWYNEDD

I have my choice, beauty bright as a wave,
Wise in your riches, your graceful Welsh.
I have chosen you. What would you with me?
What are you silent for, quiet so lovely?
I've chosen such a darling I'll never repent it.
Surely to choose such a fine choice is right!

PERYF AP CEDIFOR

c. 1170

The Killing of Hywel

Hywel ab Owain Gwynedd was killed at Pentraeth in Anglesey by his
half-brothers, Dafydd and Rhodri, the sons of his father's second wife,
Cristin. Peryf, his foster-brother, survived the battle, and composed two
elegies to him, of which this is the second. Concerning the fate of the
other five sons of Cedifor, who together with Hywel and Peryf made up
the seven, there is a discrepancy between the two poems as we have
them. In the first, it appears as though all five were killed fighting beside
Hywel; but in the second, three of the seven – of whom one was Peryf –
remain to mourn the rest. In the first elegy, five sons of Cedifor are
named; in the last stanza of the second elegy, the remaining son,
Caradawg, is named, and in a different metre to the rest of the poem,
which is about Hywel and his foster-brothers collectively. It seems to me
that there is a *prima facie* case for considering this stanza misplaced, and
in this translation I have omitted it.

> While we were seven men alive, not three sevens
>   Challenged or routed us;
>   Now, alas, dauntless in battle,
>   Of that seven, three are left.
>
> We were seven without fault, without fear,
>   Our charge unimpeded;
>   To flee the seven of us was vain;
>   Seven, once, brooked no insult.

PERYF AP CEDIFOR

Before Hywel suffered the fight, and was gone,
     One man we stood by him;
  We are all admitting loss –
  Heaven's household is the fairer!

In a coomb above Pentraeth, sons of Cedifor,
     Full league of his children,
  Fellow of feast and purpose,
  With their brother were struck down.

Because of the treachery brewed, unchristian Briton,
     By Cristin and her sons,
  Let there be left live in Môn
  Not one of her blotched kindred!

Despite what good comes from holding land,
     World's a treacherous dwelling:
  Woe to you, cruel Dafydd,
  To stab tall Hywel, hawk of war!

OWAIN CYFEILIOG
d.1197

From *The Hirlas of Owain*

Owain, prince of Cyfeiliog in Powys, ruled from 1149 until he retired to a
monastery in 1195. He was thus not a professional poet, nor had he to
praise patrons. On the contrary, like Hywel ab Owain he was a patron
himself; and in his poem called *Hirlas*, though its core is still the guest-
host relationship, he himself takes the part of the host, thus exactly
reversing the usual pattern. His war-band has just returned from an
expedition, and they are feasting together. Owain commands his
cupbearer to serve each warrior in turn with drink from the *hirlas*
(literally 'the long-blue') or richly decorated and ceremonious mead
horn. The poet as host naturally plays a more dramatic role than he
would as the more conventional guest; and it is this sense of drama that
distinguishes his poem from those of his contemporaries, and challenges

comparison with the heroic odes of Taliesin and *The Gododdin* – which moreover, Owain Cyfeiliog refers to and consciously imitates in more than one detail.

There was a shout as dawn was breaking –
Enemies sending us noisy bad-fortune.
Our men red-speared, after the wearisome
March to the township wall of Maelor.
I sent out warriors for vengeance,
Intrepid in battle, weapons of red.
Let him beware, he that angers a brave one –
To provoke such a man will lead to grief.

Take the horn, cupbearer, and please to give it
To the hand of Rhys, at this gift-giver's court!
Owain's court has been fed with a feast,
With open gates a thousand have succour.
What quiets me, cupbearer, let it not leave me!
For carousal's sake, you come with the horn
Full of longing, many-hued, bright as the ninth wave,
With a long blue banner, and cased in gold,
And carry a lavish measure of bragget
Into Gwgawn's hand, mighty in exploits –
These whelps of Goronwy's, fierce fury's onset,
Supple whelps of valiant deeds,
Men that merit reward of each hardship,
Men worthy in war, strong to deliver,
Shepherds of the Severn, how proud to hear of them
With clatter of meadhorns, great liberality!

Take you the horn, give it Cynfelyn,
Honourably drunk with the foaming mead –
If you want for another year to live
Don't let his due respect be denied him!
And bring to Gruffudd, red-speared enemy,
Wine with a crystal glass about it –
Warriors of Aewystli, warrant of borders,

OWAIN CYFEILIOG

Good Owain's warriors, of Cynfyn's race,
Warriors who give battle, and are not afraid of it,
   Terror of slaughter, rout of war.
   To merit fame they went as heroes,
   Armed as comrades, their weapons keen.
Like the long-ago warriors of Belyn, they paid for their mead:
   While one man is left, fair will they fight...

Take you the horn, for the thought is with me
   How they defend their mead and our country,
   To Selyf, that fearless rampart of Gwygyr –
   Beware his anger, the eagle-hearted!
And to Madog's one son, famous Tudur the generous,
   Surely a killer-wolf, lightning on spears:
   Two heroes, in their contention two lions,
   Two savage energies, two sons of Ynyr,
   Two in the freedom of blows in the battle,
   Unbroken their onset, indomitable deeds,
   Lunging of lions, fierce thrust of warriors,
   Battle dogs shapely, red are their spears,
   A scourge feared by traitors, and swiftly famed,
   Their shields both shattered, two with one purpose –
   Loud winds vanquish the shore of blue seas,
   Swift fury of waves on famous Talgarth!

CYNDDELW BRYDYDD MAWR

fl. 1155-1200

Maiden Song
for Efa, daughter of Madog ap Maredudd
(Extract)

The poet addresses a horse, which he is sending to a girl he says he loves. But the poem is not quite a love-song, and may be celebrating the girl's marriage to someone else, the horse being sent to fetch her to her new home.

Lusty and passionate steed, it's jealous I am
    For her I praise, have praised for long.
    Peer of the foam, water that wind breaks,
    Fine fluent Welsh from the court in the vale;
    As bright as the dawning day when it rises,
    Brilliant as snow on the wood-slopes of Epynt;
    Virtue of bright eyes half-lowered in shyness –
    The maid puts no store on me, though I am praised
    By her maidens that speak to her of me
    And make much of my Maid Song to Efa.
    I journeyed to visit where they kept home,
    Land of the lord of Powys, to see if they'd have me,
    And when I had come to the place where they were,
    Through glass windows they had seen me,
There they were, watching me, brilliant seagulls –
    A costly answer did they send me!
    Gladly I loved them, though they loved me not,
    Innocent virgins were those handmaids.
    Prudent of purpose, they considered afar –
    They were concerned for the poet Cynddelw.

For a Girl

I have seen a gentle, magnanimous girl
Look sullen with the pride of honour,
Colour of light on the waves' wide seething,

CYNDDELW BRYDYDD MAWR

Estuary tiderace, no lodge or stillness.
Often she sends me harsh reminders of her scorn –
   She, that is pride's frost candle –
Such that the heart within me is bruised.
It's ill luck Gwen's going to Jealousy's bed!

Elegy
For Madog ap Maredudd, Prince of Powys, d. 1160

I implore my King, the hope of grace,
I implore him, as I've done this hundred times,
That I may, of my high speech, fashion a gold song
   For my comrade and lord,
To mourn for Madog, who drank to his ruin
   With his foes in all the tongues.
Door of a fort he was, companion shield,
Buckler on battlefield, and in brave deeds:
A tumult like flame blazing through heather,
Router of enemies, his shield stopped their way;
Lord sung by a myriad, hope of minstrels,
Crimson, irresistible, unswerving companion.

They called Madog 'The Snare', before he died,
Snare of his foul and predatory foes.
Generous to me, he fulfilled my hopes,
Gave clothing and well-managed Gascon mounts.
His the red spear of Brân ap Llŷr Llediaith,
Loaded his plunder made easy his praise,
Nor ever shunned he a pillaging host.

His favour was constant, good friend to hostages,
Blade that caused terror in combat, in slaughter,
Blade that loved blood, battling in concert;
Under a shield streaked with lime, his hand was prompt,
The helm of all Powys, a land now forlorn.

He claimed his man's right, wanted no child's play,
Keen was his mettle, shield of four tongues,
Of a line of kings iron-armed in old time,
Generous Madog, jealous of his own:
Since he is dead, we are dead of his dying,
Since he's in earth, friendship is lost.

He loved the poets, the pure idiom of song;
Was a strong anchor in the deep, barren sea;
His welcome was long, he was generous and friendly,
Loudly the blood spoke of his doings;
Was a mansion of meadhorns, prop of the blood-right,
Was a gold lion, from warrior stock;
Was, without fault, strong companion of chieftains,
Was a man armed with iron, with iron was crowned.

Now that he's dead, may he find at last
All his wrongs righted, though great their effects,
In the light of saints, in the bright journey,
The brilliance of grace, find perfect forgiveness!

Stanzas
to the Lord Rhys ap Gruffudd, Prince of Deheubarth

This is a *dadolwch*, or plea to the poet's patron to be reconciled with him.
The cause of Cynddelw's quarrel with the powerful Lord Rhys is
unknown, but it may have concerned his support for Rhys's rival, Owain
Gwynedd.

I call down God's protection – sure your gifts,
    And I your gifted one –
    On your warriors, war-eagle,
    On your land, lord of the South.

I call down, I beseech a great boon from the Creator
    Who made heaven and earth,
    Aid from your anger, friend of songs,
    On your gates, on your gateman.

CYNDDELW BRYDYDD MAWR

I, that they call 'The Suppliant', call down and supplicate
    True, constant protection
  On your doors, swayer of battle,
  On your doorman, dawn of the land.

I call down your protection, hide not your help,
    Repentance befits me.
  Court-silencers, cry Silence!
  Silence, bards – a poet speaks!

I invoke protection, Deheubarth's quick bounty,
    That true stay of minstrels,
  Your tumult of shield-bearers,
  Your hosts, and your royal sons.

I invoke protection, quick bounty and bastion,
    No king withstands you,
  On your hosts, pillar of battle,
  On your war-band, worth their mead.

King falcons of Britain, your chief song I fashion,
    Your chief praises I bear;
  I'll act as your bard, your judge,
  Your support, it befits me.

That my song may make answer, lord, I sing –
    Since I've come, O hear me!
  Lord of Lleision, lion of war,
  Ease your wrath – I am your poet.

EINION AP GWALCHMAI
*fl.*1203-23

Elegy
for Nest, daughter of Hywel, of Tywyn, Merionethshire
(Extracts)

May, and the day's long, time to give freely:
Trees are no prison, fine colour of grove.
Vociferous birds, but ocean is placid,
Hoarse is the wave's shout, wind dying down.
Gifts are weapons, purpose of prayer.
Her hiding is quiet, but I'll not be still.

I have listened to waves that beat on the land
By the great shore of the sons of Beli:*
Fierce inroads made the inflowing sea,
And her lament for Dylan was strong.*
Her rule made none but gentle demands,
Cold and bitter her tears, surging of brine...

A song I sang Nest, before she died,
A hundred sang praise to her, as to Elifri.
Now, with a bitter thought for her, I sing
The song of her elegy, pity is great.
St Cadfan's candle, veiled in fine silk.

---

*All the leading Welsh dynasties claimed descent from the legendary Beli Mawr; here the name is used as a kenning for Britain. The whole poem is full of reference to Welsh legend.

*Dylan, in *Math fab Mathonwy*, as soon as he was born, took to the sea like a fish. What the poet means by Nest's lament for him is not clear to me. Neither is the later comparison to Elifri – Arthur's chief groom in the story of *Geraint*.

EINION AP GWALCHMAI

Brilliant to see her nearby Disynni,
Fair gentle virgin, dealing true wisdom,
A wife I'd love from, and yet no treason –
Red earth covers her, now she is silent.

O wretched need, stone grave for her tomb,
To cover Nest was an open grief:
Eyes of a pedigree proud forceful falcon,
Gossamer-white, and her gift of goodness.
Honour of Gwynedd, we had great need of her,
No mere good fortune made virtue her custom.
Gold coins, once, paid those that praised her.
Never a fuller measure of pain
Was given in penance than mine without her!...

Secret below is a veil that pains me,
It hinders her, bright as frost on Eryri.
I ask of my Lord, the master of heaven,
No vanity surely, this that I ask him...
That through the faithful pleading of Dewi
And ten times as many saints at Brefi,*
A maiden under a new dispensation
In the choice kinship of the prophets
(Wise her election into God's kingdom)
In the company of Mary and the martyrs,
For her sake this prayer I offer,
For her who gave me passion to pain me:
As none was so dear to me as she was,
May she not know pain, may Peter protect her!
It will not seem good to God to deprive her –
May Nest not want, may she find heaven!

---

*Dewi Sant (St David) preached to the assembly of Brefi, and the
ground lifted beneath his feet.

ELIDIR SAIS

*c.*1195-1246

It Must Someday Be Answered

Breaking the commandments, upholding thieves,
    Oppressing the poor, I know does not prosper.
Tribulation, at last, ends treacherous wrong,
    Pride of riches and unjust presumption.
Think, wicked man, because it is laid down
    That with God there is no disputing –
Only truth, and gentle peace,
    And such true mercy as befits Him:
Before you go to your grave, look to your life,
    If you do wrong, do not then marvel
When before Jesus you must pay the price
    And the three hosts see what anguish it entails.
Woe to those that sin, putting their trust
    In a wretched and treacherous world that will vanish!
They do not consider what really they merit,
    Nor remember at all the course that they keep.
Though the pomps of this world may give pleasure,
    Where wonder is done, it is prayer makes the feast.

I have seen Llywelyn like Merfyn in his hosts,
    And all of Wales trooped around him.
I have seen chiefs of Gwynedd and the South,
    Columns of war, assembled together.
I have seen men in battle, and stallions restless,
    Wine and people and the field of pastime.
Multitudes I have seen, and all the time feasting,
    And the world thriving, the jarring of lords –
With a flick of the wrist, it has all gone by,
    Everyone leaves this transitory time.

To have long life the rich man manages
    No more than the ragged, who quarrel not at all.
With the fierce pain in mind, let man consider

While is yet time, what he wants, what he hates.
If he is blest, let him seek an unending feast,
  Quiet happiness, and faith that prospers,
And not, with false accusation, try treachery –
  That avails nothing, and heaven is so fair!
When one well meditates, in the penance of thought,
  The pain of Eve's false, empty lust,
And that no sin of his own brought heaven's Lord
  To suffer the wood, the arrogant will –
Woe the unfortunate-born, sinful in deeds,
  For them how hard, to see Him face to face!
He will show the scourges, and all his wounds,
  And the nails, and the blood, and the cross:
'I did all this – and you, what have you done?'
  Says Christ, king of heaven; then one would need
Purity prepared, made ready for the Trinity
  Against ravaging custom of wretched sin.
Alas for the misers, the men of deceitfulness,
  And those that think falsely and do not pray!
They'll see themselves set down for transgressions,
  Hidden in penance, in the pains of hell,
And see all of them that are found of good substance
  Enter into heaven, into their glory,
And find the happiness that shall never end,
  A company blest by the freedom of grace.

Y PRYDYDD BYCHAN
*fl.*1222-70

Elegy
for Rhys Gryg – Rhys the hoarse – d.1234

Many a tear flows on its way
Profusely for Rhys, fortress a grave,
Helm of Dinefwr, man of fine children,
Lion of combat, her rank and lord.

Y PRYDYDD BYCHAN

Lordly Rhys, king of a realm,
Raven-feeder, leader of battle,
Prime hawk of nimble hawks:
For a lost dragon, we are lost.

I'm lost to sorrow, a slave of grief,
A lord we've lost, red-bladed lion:
Spoiler of Rhos, Rhys is gone,
His end in Mynyw's a tomb of stone.

Near Mynyw a lord, a lion of Haverford,
I have seen Rhys, stormer of Rhos,
High prince in battle, of a great myriad,
Armed with iron, a prince was fair.

Fair court of Rhys, Rhos in thrall,
Chieftain, while he lived, of many,
Proud hoarse-talking, sword cruelly notched,
Passionate anger, harsh in battle.

Battle-wager, blade-plunging lion,
Quick fury had Rhys, red spear on slant,
Prince Gryg, of bright golden meadhorns –
A treasure was his hand to hosts!

DAFYDD BENFRAS
fl. 1220-57
From Exile

It's bright the icy foam as it flows,
It's fierce in January great sea tumult,
It's woe's me the language, long-wished-for speech
For the sake of tales, would be sweet to my ear.

DAFYDD BENFRAS

Ability in English I never had,
Neither knew phrases of passionate French:
A stranger and foolish, when I've asked questions
It turned out crooked – I spoke North Welsh!

On a wave may God's son grant us our wish
And out from amongst them readily bring us
To a Wales* made one, contented and fair,
To a prince throned, laden nobly with gifts,
To the lord of Dinorwig's bright citadel land,
To the country of Dafydd, where Welsh freely flows!

GRUFFUDD AB YR YNAD COCH
*fl.*1282

Lament
for Llywelyn ap Gruffudd, the Last Prince

Llywelyn ap Gruffudd, the last prince of independent Wales, was killed
in a skirmish near Irfon Bridge on 11 December 1282. He had with him
only a small party of men – traditionally eighteen – when he was
surprised by an English force. His head was struck off and shown round
Wales, and was finally put on a pole and exhibited in London. Aberffraw
(stressed on the second syllable) was the royal seat of the princes of
Gwynedd (North Wales) of whom Llywelyn ap Gruffudd was the last.

Cold heart under a breast of fear – grieved
For a king, oak door of Aberffraw,
Whose hand dealt gold new-minted,
Whom the gold diadem befitted.
Gold cups of a golden king bring me no joy –
Llywelyn is not free to robe me.
Woe for my lord, falcon unblemished,

gwladoedd - lit. countries; but presumably here the three ancient
countries of Wales: Gwynedd, Powys and Deheubarth. In the last
line, Dafydd is probably Dafydd ap Llywelyn; but it may also be
the poet himself.

GRUFFUDD AB YR YNAD COCH

Woe's me that foul misfortune felled him,
Woe's me his loss, woe for the destiny,
    Woe I should hear what wounds were on him!
A camp like Cadwaladr's, the sharp auger's pledge,
    He of the red spear, gold-handed ruler.

He dealt out riches, and every winter
    His own apparel put about me.
That lord, rich in cattle, does not profit our hands –
    Eternal life awaits him!
Mine now to rage against Saxons who've wronged me,
Mine for this death bitterly to mourn.
Mine, with good cause, to cry protest to God
    Who has left me without him.
Mine now his praise, without stint or silence,
Mine, henceforth, long to consider him.
Grief, for as long as I live, I shall have for him;
    As I am full with it, so I must weep.

I've lost a lord, long terror is on me,
A lord of a king's court a hand has killed.
O righteous Lord and true-minded, hear me –
    How high I mourn, alack such mourning!
    A lord of advantage, till eighteen were slain,
    A liberal lord – his estate is the grave.
Brave lord like a lion, directing the world:
    There is no rest from his destruction.
A lord all-triumphant, until he left Emrais –*
    No Saxon had dared to touch him.
A lord of Wales, there's a stone roof round him,
Prince of Aberffraw by right of his lineage.

    Lord Christ, how am I grieved for him,
    A true lord, freedom came from him:
O heavy swordstroke caused him to stumble!

*Snowdonia.

GRUFFUDD AB YR YNAD COCH

O long swords urged furious against him!
O wound to my prince, it makes me tremble
To hear of him prostrate, lord of Bodfaeo!
There indeed was a man, till a foreign hand killed him,
    All the privilege of his ancestry in him:
     Candle of kingship, strong lion of Gwynedd,
     Throned, there was no need of him, with honour!

    For the death of all Britain, protector of Cynllaith,
    Dead lion of Nancoel, breastplate of Nancaw,
Many a slippery tear scuds on the cheek,
    Many a flank gaping and crimson,
    Many a pool of blood round the feet,
    Many a widow crying aloud for him,
    Many a heavy thought goes errant,
    Many a fatherless child's abandoned,
Many a homestead flecked from the fire's path,
    And many a looted wilderness yonder,
Many a wretched cry, as once was at Camlan,
    Many a tear has run down the cheek:
Since the buttress is down, gold-handed chieftain,
Since Llywelyn is slain, my mortal wit fails me.

    The heart's gone cold, under a breast of fear;
    Lust shrivels like dried brushwood.
    See you not the way of the wind and the rain?
    See you not oaktrees buffet together?
See you not the sea stinging the land?
    See you not truth in travail?
See you not the sun hurtling through the sky,
    And that the stars are fallen?
Do you not believe God, demented mortals?
    Do you not see the whole world's danger?
Why, O my God, does the sea not cover the land?
    Why are we left to linger?
    There is no refuge from imprisoning fear,

And nowhere to bide – O such abiding!
I see no counsel, neither lock nor opening,
   No way to escape fear's sad counsel.
      Each retinue was rightly for him,
      All the warriors guarded round him:
      Not a man but swore by his hand,
      Not a land or ruler but was his.
Cantref and township, all are invaded,
Every lineage and clan slips under.
The weak and the strong were kept by his hand,
It is every cradled child that screams.
It did me no good, so to deceive me,
When his head was off, to leave me mine.

When that head fell, men welcomed terror,
When that head fell, it were better to stop.
Soldier head, head praised hereafter,
Head of a dragon, a hero's head on him,
Fair head of Llywelyn, a harsh fear to the world
   That an iron stake should rive it.
   Head of my lord, the pain of his downfall,
   Head of my soul, no name upon it,
A head that, once, nine hundred lands honoured,
   Nine hundred feasts gave homage.
   Head of a king, iron flew from his hand,
   Proud head of a king hawk, he breached the war-line,
   Head of a kingly and thrusting wolf –
   O high king of heaven, be refuge for him!
High lord and blest prince, support of the host,
   Ambitious even to Brittany,
   The true and regal king of Aberffraw,
   May heaven's white land now be his home!

BLEDDYN FARDD
*fl.*1255-85

Elegy
for Llywelyn ap Gruffudd, the Last Prince

Christ, great generous lord, I ask a grace,
Christ, pure son of God, consider me,
Christ righteous and bountiful, strongest of sureties,
 Whose image bore the hardest hurt:

It concerns a man, that which I speak of.
Whoever bears grief, let him be most calm.
Whoever by nature is highest in authority,
 Let his thought be most lowly.

Into the world came Christ, so that Adam
And his folk should not stay gaoled in hell,
But round the high Lord fill that space in heaven
 That the most blundering angel had lost.

Great Wales has lost her most manly of princes,
Manly his blade, quick, bright and most brave:
A manly leader is dead – what can I do now? –
 Manly and brave, generous, free with his gifts.

Man who was killed for us, who ruled over all,
Man who ruled Wales, boldly I'll name him,
Manly Llywelyn, bravest of Welshmen,
 Man not enamoured of too easy a way.

Man strong in attacking enemies on his border,
Man of green tents, maintainer of the camp,
Manly son of Gruffudd, most fertile for bounty
 In the high, lovely fashion of Mordaf and Nudd.

BLEDDYN FARDD

Man of the red spear, man grave as Priam,
Man fitly a king of the proudest host,
Famous his praise, man lavish in outlay,
  Far as the sun journeys furthest away.

That man's ruin was baleful, most courteous leader,
Man bitterly mourned, truest of kinsmen,
Man honest and wise and unsullied, choicest from Môn
  Far as Caerleon, fairest of places.

A man was Llywelyn, near the limits of the Taff,
King of his people, he dealt out apparel,
Man over all men, foremost of soldiers
  Far as Porth Wygyr, unruffled eagle.

May the Man who endured dire death and most anguished
For the world's five ages' sake, heaviest hurt,
May he take my prince, noblest in lineage,
  To share in the Mercy, great beyond greatness!

On his Death-bed

Receive me, my King, master of Christendom,
  Honoured by high saints by royal right,
You accepted and have now the praise of all souls
  For a death that the Devil dealt with nails.

You, from the bloody cross, received the Five Ages,
  Over yonder vast country supreme in sway:
To the flinty fire do not leave me, Lord Father,
  In the burning land, a hellish thing.

There is there great grief, and none intercede for it,
  There the great misery of a mortal soul,
There are the Antagonists, extollers of falsehood,
  There is the constant, violent pain.

BLEDDYN FARDD

Before I go forth from the dream of this world
   To the fine grave provided in the country of corpses,
Before the grave ends me, may I godly be shriven,
   Before it has caught me, may I learn prayer!

   Insofar as you suckled the kingly King,
   And all's done at your word, victorious Mary,
Remember and pray for me, for my peace,
   In the Ghostly Lord's Kingdom of Heaven.

GRUFFUDD AP MAREDUDD
fl.1350-80

Lament for Gwenhwyfar
(Extracts)

Gwynedd's sun, it's a grave, not living – a queen,
      We may not find her like;
   All admiration's ended;
   Bright moon, she sleeps cold tonight.

Cry troubles me sorely, was vileness – to dig down
      Her blackbird-coloured brows;
   Gold girl, she wore fine raiment,
   Bright sun face, bounteous with mead.

   Roof of stone has dressed her features,
   Pressure of loam after rich furs;
   Gentle two cheeks, bright as dawn –
   Obstinate, my long life after!

   A tomb was built, body of worth,
   My own soul, and marble round you;
   Your grieving memory has built
   In my heart such vexing wound.

GRUFFUDD AP MAREDUDD

Comes to this heart (bright as rapids from rock dell!)
    Ache of an anxious grief,
  For strong Geraint's descendant,
  Grief of mind more than measure.

It was surly work to confine (O fair Gwenhwyfar!)
    And a sore lamentation,
  This comeliest body under green earth,
  In churchfloor, ache, and frail, sweet life.

Fine lad I know died (O Mary!) from longing,
    Gold candle of Pentraeth is dead,
  Weak from her gossamer features,
  Grief's bane, where was wine and mead.

  Never was given, face of heartache,
  To harsh cold earth, gold moon beauty,
  After a hundred sighs still grieving,
  Conspicuous tears, so sweet an aspect.

Sadness my memories raise, crying and tears
    For the fairest in Môn,*
  Now she's gone to the Father of peace,
  Who hurt me, under heaven's care.

  Cold to prison the white moon last night,
  In a stone chest's sad ebbing of death;
  Many a face came close by woe
  For a wise one, gem of Dindaethwy.

  Many a man, overborne by longing,
  Colour of shallow white edges of foam,
  For the quiet, high-blooded maiden,
  By God's rape now is saddened.

*Literally *in three cantrefi* or districts; but presumably the three *cantrefi* into which Anglesey (Môn) was divided.

GRUFFUDD AP MAREDUDD

Where was fine fur and green, red cloth and blue,
    Is the ache of death's trouble;
  Where was gold round her two cheeks,
  And purple, now the chancel hides.

Winegiver sun is palled near the white shores of Cyrchell*
    In a strict, prisoning grave;
  Dire for him, to heaven she's gone,
  Who loved her, fierce the longing!

DAFYDD AP GWILYM
*fl.*1340-70

The Grey Friar

O that she who in a glade
Keeps court, my famous maid,
Had heard the fuss and blather
Of the mouse-coloured Brother
As I went to him this day
To shrive my sins away!
'I am,' thus I confessed,
'A poet like the rest,
And love, but always lack,
A girl whose eyebrow's black:
No profit, though near dead,
I've had of this white maid,
Save to love all entire
And languish with desire,
To praise her through the hills
Yet, solitary still,
To wish her at nightfall
Betwixt me and the wall.'

Quoth Brother in a trice,
'Hearken my good advice,

*A river in Anglesey.

And if you've loved till now
That white-as-paper brow,
Lessen the Doomsday pain.
Better the heart abstain
And poetry be still.
On prayers use your skill.
Not for a poet's ode
God ransomed man on rood,
Minstrel, for in your song
Mere vanities belong,
Incitings unto sin,
Falsehood, women and men!
The body's not praised well
If the soul's damned in hell.'

I answered to his face
Word for word, the friar's case:
'God's not so fierce, my friend,
As you old men pretend,
Nor would he damn the soul
For woman loved, or girl.
Three things are reckoned wealth:
A woman – sunshine – health –
And in the heaven's dower
(Save God) a maid's the flower.
To women all on earth,
Except three, owe their birth.
So how is it inhuman,
This love of maid or woman?
From heaven came every gladness.
It is from hell comes sadness.
Songs can make sadness fail
Young and old, sick and hale.
Here's needful trade for each –
I to rhyme, you to preach,
Neither of us does harm –

DAFYDD AP GWILYM

If I busk, you beg alms:
And hymn and sequence bode
No more than verse or ode.
What's in a psalm but singing
To holy Godhead ringing?
No one relish or food
Empties the bounty of God.
Time has been given to eat,
Time for devotion meet,
And time to preach amain,
And time to entertain;
Songs to amuse – at least
The young girls at the feast,
And also prayers, to search
For Paradise at Church.

'Drinking among his bards
True were Ystudfach's words:
"Glad features homes fill,
Sour looks come to ill."
Though sanctity some love,
Others more cheerful prove,
And few can sonnets say
While almost all can pray.
Thus, Brother, you're over-nice –
Song's hardly the greater vice!

'When each man feels as fair
With harping to sing prayer
As do this Gwynedd throng
To listen to gay song,
Then shall I sing no end
Of paternosters, friend;
Till then, Dafydd were wrong
Did he sing prayer, not song.'

DAFYDD AP GWILYM

The Seagull

A fine gull on the tideflow,
All one white with moon or snow,
Your beauty's immaculate,
Shard like the sun, brine's gauntlet.
Buoyant you're on the deep flood,
A proud swift bird of fishfood.
You'd ride at anchor with me,
Hand in hand there, sea lily.
Like a letter, a bright earnest,
A nun you're on the tide's crest.

Right fame and far my dear has –
Oh, fly round tower and fortress,
Look if you can't see, seagull,
One bright as Eigr on that wall.
Say all my words together.
Let her choose me. Go to her.
If she's alone – though profit
With so rare a girl needs wit –
Greet her then: her servant, say,
Must, without her, die straightway.

She guards my life so wholly -
Ah friends, none prettier than she
Taliesin or the flattering lip
Or Merlin loved in courtship:
Cypris courted 'neath copper,*
Loveliness too perfect-fair.

Seagull, if that cheek you see,
Christendom's purest beauty,
Bring to me back fair welcome
Or that girl must be my doom.

*An alchemical pun - see Glossary under 'Cypris'.

DAFYDD AP GWILYM

The Ladies of Llanbadarn

Plague take the women here –
I'm bent down with desire,
Yet not a single one
I've trysted with, or won,
Little girl, wife or crone,
Not one sweet wench my own!

What mischief is it, or spite,
That damns me in their sight?
What harm to a fine-browed maid
To have me in deep glade?
No shame for her 'twould be
In a lair of leaves to see me.

No time was, but I did love;
Never so fixed a spell did prove
That natures like old Garwy's knew –
Every day, one or two!
For all this, I can go
No nearer than a foe.
In Llanbadarn every Sunday
Was I, and (judge who may)
Towards chaste girls I faced,
My nape to a God rightly chaste,
And through my plumes gazed long
At that religious throng.
One gay bright girl says on
To t'other prudent-prospering one –

'That pale and flirt-faced lad
With hair from his sister's head –
Adulterous must be the gaze
Of a fellow with such ways.'
'Is he that sort?' demands

The girl on her right hand,
'Be damned to him, he'll stay
Unanswered till Judgement day!'

O sudden and mean reward
For dazed love the brightgirl's word!
Needs I must pack my gear,
Put paid to dreams and fear,
And manfully set out
Hermit, like rogue or lout.
But O, my glass doth show
With backward-looking woe
I'm finished, I'm too late,
Wry-necked, without a mate!

Trouble at a Tavern

I came to a choice city
With my fine squire behind me.
At gay cost I ordered food
(Proud I had been from childhood)
At a worthy enough hostel –
Liberally; and wine as well.

I spied a slim fair virgin
(My sweet spirit!) at that inn.
On that bright-as-dawn sweetheart
Soon I'd wholly set my heart.
A roast – not to boast! – and costly
Wine I bought for her and me.
Youth loves good cheer. I called her
(How shy she was!) to dinner,
And whispered – I dared the trick,
That's certain – two words of magic.
I made – love wasn't idle –
Tryst to come to the spry girl

DAFYDD AP GWILYM

As soon as all our muster
Slept; black the brows she'd on her.

When at last, wretched journey!
All did sleep, save her and me,
I to reach the lady's bed
Most skilfully attempted.
But I fell, noised it abroad,
Tumbled brutally forward.
It's easier to be clumsy.
Rising from such grief, than spry!

Nor was my leap unhurtful:
On a stupid and loud stool,
Ostler's work, to the chagrin
Of my leg, I barked my shin;
Came up, a sorry story,
And struck – may Welshmen love me!
Too great desire is evil,
Every step unlucky still! –
By blows in mad bout betrayed,
On a table-top my forehead,
Where, all the time, a pitcher
And a loud brass cauldron were.
Collapse of that stout table –
Two trestles downed – stools as well!
Cry that the cauldron uttered
Behind me, for miles was heard;
Pitcher shouted my folly,
And the dogs barked around me.
In a foul bed, at the wall,
Bothered for their packs, and fearful,
Three English lay in panic –
Hickin and Jenkin and Jack.
The young one spluttered a curse
And hissed forth to the others:

'There's a Welshman on the prowl!'
– O hot ferment of betrayal –
'He'll rob us, if we let him!
Look out you're not a victim!'

The ostler roused all the rest –
My plight was of the direst!
All round me they were angry
And searched for me all round me.
I stood, in the foul havoc
Of rage, silent in the dark;
Prayed, in no reckless fashion,
Hiding like a frightened man:
And such power has prayer for us,
Such the true grace of Jesus,
I found my own bed safe and sure
Though without sleep or treasure,
Thank the Saints, freed of distress.
I ask now God's forgiveness.

The Thrush

Music of a thrush, clearbright
Lovable language of light,
Heard I under a birchtree
Yesterday, all grace and glee –
Was ever so sweet a thing
Fine-plaited as his whistling?

Matins, he reads the lesson,
A chasuble of plumage on.
His cry from a grove, his brightshout
Over countrysides rings out,
Hill prophet, maker of moods,
Passion's bright bard of glenwoods.
Every voice of the brookside

DAFYDD AP GWILYM

Sings he, in his darling pride,
Every sweet-metred love-ode,
Every song and organ mode,
Competing for a truelove,
Every catch for woman's love.
Preacher and reader of lore,
Sweet and clear, inspired rapture,
Bard of Ovid's faultless rhyme,
Chief prelate mild of Springtime.

From his birch, where lovers throng,
Author of the wood's birdsong,
Merrily the glade re-echoes –
Rhymes and metres of love he knows.
He on hazel sings so well
Through cloistered trees (winged angel)
Hardly a bird of Eden
Had by rote remembered then
How to recite what headlong
Passion made him do with song.

*His Affliction**

Sweet Morfudd, Maytime's godchild,
Sprightly maid, has me beguiled.
She that I greet as truelove –
Sick I am this night from love –
Sowed in my breast (it will crack)
Seed of love, raging magic.
Such my woes, sorrow's harvest,
She, day-bright, won't let me rest.
Spellbinder, lovely goddess,
Speaks to my ears magic, no less.
She's careless how I chide her,
Slim odds I'll have her favour.

*In the original, every line begins with 'H'.

Sage I'd be, calm and learnèd,
Seek today my learnèd maid.
Sad outlaw, I've no ransom,
Shut out from her town and home.
She to her outlaw's bosom
Sent but longing, bitter doom.
Sea on the shore no longer
Stays than this outlaw in care.
So I'm bound with pain, shackled
Straitly, and my breast is nailed.
Scarcely, beneath her goldhead,
Shall I have my wise young maid.
Savage ills come upon me
Such that long life's unlikely.
Sprung from Ynyr, she's wellbred –
Soon, without her, I'll be dead.

The Wind

Masterly wind of the sky
Striding with mighty outcry –
Ah, what a man, unheeding
And harsh, without foot or wing
Given out from the pantry
Of the sky – how can it be?
How is your pace so nimble
Now, across the highest hill?
No need of horse for transport
Or, on river, bridge or boat –
You'll not drown, you've been promised!
Angleless, go where you list,
Take nest, strip leaves – there's no one
Arrests with accusation,
No posse, captain or corps,
Blue blade or flood or downpour.
Thresher of treetop plumage,

DAFYDD AP GWILYM

You nor king nor troop can cage,
Nor mother's son foully kill,
Fire burn, nor trick enfeeble.
Though none see you in your den,
Nest of rains, thousands harken,
Cloud-calligrapher, vaulter
Over nine lands wild and bare.

You're on the world God's favour,
High oaktops' tired-cracking roar;
Dry, for you tread prudently
The clouds in your great journey;
Archer of snow on highlands,
Useless chaff, swept into mounds –
Tell me where, constant credo,
Northwind of the vale, you go?
Tempest on the ocean, you're
A wanton lad on seashore,
Eloquent author, wizard,
Sower, and tilt at leaf horde,
Laughter on hills, you harry
Wild masts on white-breasted sea.

You fly the wide world over,
Weather of slopes, tonight there,
Man, go high to Uwch Aeron
With clarity, with clear tone.
Don't falter, frighted fellow,
For fear of the Little Bow,*
That querulously jealous man!
Her country is my prison.
Too grave a love I've given
To my gold girl, Morfudd, when
My own land's made my thraldom –
O speed high towards her home!

*The 'Little Bow' (*Y Bwa Bach*) was Dafydd's nickname for
Morfudd's husband.

Beat, till they loose the doorway,
Messenger, before the day:
Find her, if you can, and bring
My sighs to her, my mourning.
You of the glorious Zodiac,
Tell her bounty of my lack.
I'm her true lover always
While the quick life in me stays.
Without her, I go lovelorn –
If it's true she's not foresworn.
Go up, till she's in prospect
Under you, the sky's elect,
Find her, the slim gold damsel –
Good of the sky, come back hale!

The Ruin

'Punctured, broken hut, laid low
Between moorland and meadow,
Woe for us, who saw your prime
A residence of pastime,
And now see the house again,
The ribs of its roof broken;
And near your sprightly wall, once
Was the day, pain's remonstrance,
There – you'd more fun then, somewhere,
Old scabby-roof, then you've now! –
When I saw (bright praise I bore)
A fine one in your corner,
A maid, a gentle lady,
Lively as she lay with me,
And our arms, dear clasp of her,
Knotted around each other;
Her arm, as friable snow,
For good poet's ear a pillow,
And mine, a simple trickster,

Under the courtly maid's left ear! –
Oh, wanton was your heyday,
And today is not that day.'

'I moan, a refuge blighted,
For ways the wild wind has made.
Storm from the East, and downfall
Agonized my slender wall.
Sighing and angry journey
Of the South wind's unroofed me.'

'Was it wind made this riot?
It threshed well your roof last night.
Foully it broke house and home.
World's but a parlous phantom.
In that ingle, once had I
A bed, and not a pigsty.
Yesterday, a noble court
Was snug above my sweetheart.
It's clear, by Peter, today
You've neither door nor doorway.
Riddling folly, on and on –
Was this smashed hut delusion?'

'The family's time's long ended,
Dafydd. And their ways were good.'

LLYWELYN GOCH AP MEURIG HEN
fl. 1360-90
The Tit

Go now, bird, urbane and civil,
Tomtit with the piping bill,
From the South to my sweetheart –
That dear she that shared my heart.

LLYWELYN GOCH AP MEURIG HEN

To Merioneth run straightway,
Bright sound in the thorns of May,
Swift above bridges of copse,
Rider on the strong birchtops.
Plaintive grey beak, and tired wing,
Four colours to your tinting –
Green and blue, a lad who'd lief,
Black and white, tend on greenleaf.
You, companion of the young,
Though tiny, bard of woodsong,
Are spry, little grey-cheeked bird,
Adept at secret concord,
Rush like the wind, luck's courtier,
To Merioneth to my dear.
Work your wings, master of idiom,
Toil above the forests' gloom:
Light on that fair form, and say
Unto Dafydd's wife, Good-day!

For my sake (she was my dear)
Ask her in her gold chamber
(Merioneth's bright as billow)
Not by day or night to go,
My second soul, gold-plaited
Modest girl, to Eiddig's bed.
Also, proud squire and sportive,
Wildwood poet hawks let live,
Possessing in your heart's-ease
Two slim feet, farers in trees,
Now be bold, match my desire,
Be bold to my soul's sister!

Say, author, diligent bird,
In pain's hour, woodland wizard,
My brother, that I've sung forth
To greet her from Deheubarth

And sevenfold anguish suffer
And barbs of longing for her.

Because, near the shining towers,
I've not seen her bright features –
Plead, bird, my winning praises –
Strange I've lived, this thirty days!

IOLO GOCH
*c.*1320-1398

The Court of Owain Glyndŵr at Sycharth

Twice have I promised you this
A journey, a fair promise
(And man should not be backward,
If he can, to keep his word)
To go – so dear my purpose,
My pure vow and profit was –
On pilgrimage, a comfort
Full of faith, to Owain's court.
As is good, thither straightway
I shall go, and there shall stay
To have my life honoured where
He and I greet each other.

My lord of lineage sovran
Can well receive an old man.
Poets make common knowledge
He delights to gratify age.
To his court I hurry ahead,
Most splendid of two hundred,
Court of a baron, courteous home,
Where many a poet's welcome.
Lo, the form of it – a gold cirque
Of water held by earthwork;
A court with one gate and bridge

Where a hundred packs have passage.
There are rafters coupled there,
Joined two and two together.
It's French, this Patrick's belfry,
Westminster cloister, easy of key.
Corners match, are bound together,
A gold chancel, all entire.
There are joists upon the hillside
As in a vault, side by side,
And each one, in a tightknit
Pattern, to the next is knit.
Twice nine dwellings to look up
To a wood fort on a hilltop.
Next to heaven his court towers
On four marvellous pillars.
On each thick wooden pillar
A loft tops all, built with care,
With all four lofts for friendship
Joined as one, where minstrels sleep.
These four well-lighted lofts,
Fine nestful, make eight cocklofts.
The roof's tiled on each gable,
There's a chimney that draws well.
Nine halls in true proportion
And nine wardrobes in each one.
Elegant shops, comely inside,
And stocked as full as Cheapside.
A church cross, lovely limewhite
Chapels and the windows bright.*

*The description is impressionistic and not easy to piece together.
Sycharth was not a stone fortress, such as Conwy or Caernarfon, but
an old-fashioned motte and bailey, made of earthwork and timber.
A large, shallow mound, surrounded by a ditch, held the main
buildings of the castle: two rows of nine dwellings, the shops let into
an arcade, a hall and a chapel. High above this, the second mound,
smaller in area but considerably higher than the first, had four great
wooden pillars driven into it: on these pillars a second hall was

IOLO GOCH

Each part full, each house in the court,
Orchard, vineyard and whitefort.
The famed hero's rabbit park,
Ploughs and steeds of a monarch.
And in another, even more
Vivid park, the deer pasture.
Fresh grazing land and hayfields,
And corn growing in fenced fields.
A fine mill on strong water,
A stone dovecot on a tower.
A fishpond, walled and private,
Into which you cast your net
And (no question of it) bring
To land fine pike and whiting.*
A lawn with birds for food on,
Peacocks and sprightly heron.
Servants to get each job done,
Supplying all the region,
Bringing best Shrewsbury beer,
Bragget, and choicest liquor,
Every drink, white bread and wine,
Meat and fire for his kitchen.
Poets from everywhere gather
Everyday together there.
The best wife among women,

reared, with lofts where the minstrels slept. It is rather ironical that this poem to the future national leader of Wales should contain so many English terms – the point is necessarily obscured in translation – to describe his castle. The shops of Cheapside seem to have particularly impressed the Welsh. They occur as an image of opulence in several poems of the period.

Gwyniaid (plural of *gwyniad*) does mean salt-water whiting; but it is also used for salmon-like fish that live in Welsh lakes. (Cf. the Concise Oxford Dictionary under 'gwyniad' – the same word is used in English.) Probably Iolo means these; but I decided to translate the word as 'whiting' because most people know that this is a kind of fish, whereas 'gwyniad' is not generally comprehensible.

I'm blest by her mead and wine.
Daughter from knights descended,
Noble, generous, royally bred.
And his children come in pairs,
A fine nestful of rulers.

Lock or latch very seldom
Has been seen about his home.
No one need act as gateman,
Here are gifts for every one –
No hunger, disgrace or dearth,
Or ever thirst at Sycharth!'
Haply the best of Welshmen
Owns the land, of Pywer's kin;
It's a strong, lean warrior owns
This most lovable of mansions.

GRUFFUDD GRYG

fl. 1360-1400

The Yewtree

Over Dafydd ap Gwilym's grave in Strata Florida (Ystrad Fflur)

Near the wall of the abbey
Of Ystrad Fflur, grows this tree,
A yew tree – God's grace therewith –
As a house grown for Dafydd.
Before you grew from sorrow
David prophesied of you;
And Dafydd, now you're fullgrown,
Has with youth (was once his own)
Ordained your house of greenleaf,
House where every beam bears leaf,
A castle that hides the dead –
As birch once did – from blizzard.

GRUFFUDD GRYG

Beneath you, bound and silent,
Is a grave I did not want;
All the worlds' angels' beehive
In that grave, brave man alive,
Gifts of song one with wisdom
And Dyddgu's woe, now he's dumb.*

As long as he lived, he made
Green and rich grow her homestead:
Now you must right the record,
Chosen branches, with that lord.
Gently guard his tombstone yet,
Like an aunt, good yew trivet,
Nor move a step from over
The grave, yewtree, do not stir.
Goats shall not corrupt or tear
The webbed house of your father.
There'll not scorch you fire's greeting,
Joiner won't break, cobbler ring
Nor lover carve, in this age,
The cover of your cottage.
Churl or woodman, from the sting
Of terror of transgressing,
Shall not axe you, break and slump
Green burden on your treestump.
Roof of leaves your good place bears –
May God not shame your wonders!

*One of Dafydd's principal girl-friends.

ANONYMOUS
15th century

The Poet dies for Love

Like a lily, gleaming maid,
Under a gold web's your forehead.
I've loved you long and greatly –
Mother of God, where's hope for me?
You, as you fear your kinsfolk,
Punish love. I'll not strike back.
Bitter groans come from the wish
I nurse for you in anguish.
Silly girl, if with heartbreak,
Jewel, you kill me for their sake,
Relic of grace, you'll incur
The guilt: beware my murder.

In a copse of leaf amid
Wanton trees, I'll be buried
(My last rites from birch) below
The ash tree tops tomorrow.
Round me, for white shroud, I'll wear
Gay summer cloth of clover.
Solemnly my shrine shall stand
To win grace from the woodland.
For a veil, blossom of trees;
My bier shall be eight branches.

Gulls from the sea assemble,
Thousands come to bear my pall.
Fine trees (a layman swears it)
Escort me on that transit.
Under the hill, gentlest maid,
My church shall be the greenglade,
And to pray there, as you'd choose,
Two nightingales for statues.

There, by the wheat, an altar
Of branches, a mosaic floor,
A choir Jealousy won't guess,
A door not banged in rudeness,
And Grey Friars, who don't judge sin
Yet know the best of Latin –
Metrics and grammar of it,
Learnt from leaves – sweet their habit,
And a fine organ, and pealed
Bells frequent in the hayfield.

In Gwynedd, the grave's ready
Where the birch shall cover me.
High honour for a minstrel
In Llan Eos, warbler's dell.
There the cuckoo for my soul,
Organ-like, chants his beadroll,
His hours and paternosters,
His psalms in alternate verse.
Many a Mass and sweet greeting,
Visits of love, come with Spring.

May God keep the tryst, and set
In Paradise his poet!

The Nun

A pious, dark-eyed maiden
Has with loving made me pine.
If for another's profit
I've loved, God, I'm lacking wit!
Woman I love, what's all this –
You don't like gay Spring birches?
You, that eight stars go to tint,
Won't let your beads be silent?
A saint of a religious,

Kind to the choir, not to us?
Enough of bread and water
For God's sake, and cress abhor!
Mary! with these beads have done,
This monkish Rome religion!
Don't be a nun – Spring's at hand,
And cloister's worse than woodland.
Your faith, my fairest truelove,
Goes quite contrary to love.
Worthier is the ordaining
Of mantle, green robe, and ring.

Come to cathedral birch, to
Worship with trees and cuckoo
(There we shall not be chided)
To win heaven in the glade.
Remember the book of Ovid,
Cease from this excess of faith.
We'll obtain in the vinetrees
Round the hillside, the soul's peace.
God loves with blameless welcome,
With his saints, to pardon love.
Is it worse for a maiden
To win a soul in the glen
Than what we have done, to do
In Rome or Santiago?

Building for Love

Long I've loved a tall young maid
But never have we trysted.
And when I, who've known distress,
Was hoping for her gladness,
She that I courted, whispered
To me, to cut short my word –
'I'll not love a wandering man's
Ungentle lack of substance!'

ANONYMOUS

I thought I understood this
Answer of lively malice.
A house I made to love her
Under birch, no fool's venture.
I trimmed a noble clearing,
Plaited praise, built in a ring,
Where leaf and lithe twigs covered
Like tiles the thick bowl of wood.
In that dear habitation
Two good tenants sang as one,
Two thrushcocks, sounding sweetest,
Comely brown with speckled breast,
Two bright passionate chiefbards,
Pure and paradisal birds.
Every day in coupled lines.
Seven lyrics grace the woodbines,
And I'd reckon on the hillside
Sevenfold, their tunes of pride.

I want for a splendid sweetheart
In this dwelling to hold court.
Unless I have a fair maid
My own age in the birchglade,
Nevermore (I put this ban)
I'll build for love of woman.

ROBIN DDU
15th century

Invitation to Morfudd

Who under my ribs put pain,
Girl I've long loved in vain,
Your colour that God dight,
Your brow like a daisy bright.
You God gave the redgold,
Your hair like a tongue of gold,

ROBIN DDU

Your throat's upright growth,
Your breasts, full spheres both.
Two cheeks of pleasant red,
Eyebrows of black London thread,
Your eyes like two rings are bright,
Your nose, it's on a gentle wight,
As the five Joys your smile,
Sweet body that from faith can guile,
Whiteness like a niece of Ann,
A fair colour, a goodly plan.

You, under your top of hair so mild,
So fair, come with me to the wild.
Be our bed high on the breast
Of a birchwood green, an agelong rest
On a dingle's mattress of leaf
Fringed finely with bracken leaf,
And trees for a counterpane
To shelter us both from rain.

I'd lie down as David lay,
Brave prophet, until day –
A man that begetting Solomon
Made seven psalms before the dawn.
So, should you there not miss,
I'd make a psalm each kiss:
Seven kisses of a maid,
Seven birch over a grave,
Seven prayers and Masses said,
Seven sermons the thrush read,
Seven litanies in leaves,
Seven birds and seven sheaves,
Seven accents on great words,
Seven circlets, seven odes,
Seven odes to Morfudd more,
Supple-limbed, then seven score!
So, she shall not keep with key
My love's due locked from me.

SIÔN CENT
fl. 1400-30

Repentance

Now I turn my thoughts to prayer,
To God and to his Mother.
Like Saul, it's high time for me
To cut short worldly folly.

I've led life unamended,
My sins loaded on my head:
Pride, in the midst of many,
An ill life vilely led me.
Pride did my custom inspire
To flattery and satire.
The bad faith of Jealousy
Inhabited my body,
And Wrath, a wretched burden,
Where it could, would enter in.
Sloth was mine, rash and foolish,
Life of ease was all my wish.
God weed a man! – The worst thing
Was Greed, in avarice drowning.
Gluttony, Adultery too,
Strove, both of them, with virtue.

Three enemies come to man,
Give shape to his deception –
The Fiend, the base World, the Flesh
That reaps the crop of Judas.
Woe to man, I knew his sin,
Wanton, that cannot govern
His life as a man would wish
Before the grave, the finish,
Chastising reckless evil
And the body's plausible ill!
My pestilence I confess

To God, and ask forgiveness.
I shall try now to admit
Every tale, every secret.
Without death or end, headstrong
Pride ruled me when I was young.
Wrong ways in birch and bracken,
In green woods above the glen.
Wrong listening, wrong speaking,
Doings of love, the magic ring.
Wrong touch, in evident converse,
Seeking good, hating its source.
Wrong arrogance and envy,
Wrong looks at a lovely she.
Praising, without grace or check,
Beauty, and breaking wedlock.

Wantonness brings to manhood
Vengeance if it's long pursued,
Unless we make atonement
To God, ere our time be spent.
Let no one leave contrition
Till they're dead, and in hell's fen.
I call on Heaven for mercy,
Call on Mary ere I die,
For a sweet place to brighten
The need of my soul. Amen.

The Lying Muse
To Rhys Goch Eryri

A false, bad, bold criterion,
A fool's path Welshmen go on.
Why that old man's lovely word
And shaping of a chiefbard?
Two kinds of inspiration
In the world's bright path are known.

SIÔN CENT

One to the true way will bring
You, is of Christ's inspiring,
Full of grace, given always
To prophets, masters of praise,
Holy angels of Hebron –
There was faultless verse begun.
The other inspires an outcry,
Many trusting its foul lie,
This Muse of impudent wits,
The false pomp of Welsh poets.

If it sings to a soldier
Praise (to get clothes to wear)
The giftless craft is satire,
A poem of lies on hire,
Saying there's brave wine and bragget
Where thin whey is all you'll get;
Then at the gay board, we're told
Of French forts fiercely tumbled,
Like bold Arthur, or Roland,
Deeds done of his lion hand.
Their wranglings – Oh, that no-one
Knows them, or the ills they've done!
Adulates then a poor man
As greater in his cabin
Than an earl on a gold floor
And greater than great Caesar.
The fool loves being flattered,
Trusts it as a sacred word.
O my God, who has less wits –
Him, or his best of poets?
If a girl's praised with fondness,
Or a wife, by the true Cross,
In three countries not Mary,
Not the sun's so fair as she.

It's futile, mere burlesquing
That this muse-praise is a king.
He's a cur, belly and claw,
Wrinkled with scab and tatter.
Nothing alive howls so loudly,
Never a dog worse than he!

It's a poor claim that he has
To escape from Hell's furnace.
God's guardian spirit is good,
Sober, and tells no falsehood,
No wheedling fraud, or futile
Fiction falsely sung from guile.
Over ten shires spreads the word
Of truth's guard, Thomas Lombard:
Every lie to gain credit
(Though little) has sin in it.
Alysanna in his treatise
Strongly testifies to this;
And Durgry's sweet-named tractate,
Much sought – do but go to that!
But they go, these Jews, these bards,
To insult folk with falsehoods
And provoke angry people –
A threat of force fits them well!
If there's a Welsh bard here yet
(Or even some meaner poet)
If he know how to answer,
Let his lips make answer here!

RHYS GOCH ERYRI
fl. 1385-1448

Answer to Siôn Cent
(Extract)

It must be admitted that Rhys Goch did not rise to the occasion. Most of his reply, anyway, concerns the way Siôn Cent had slandered him (presumably in a lost poem) for keeping goats for his mother. But, in spite of his cheerful vituperation, he does have a point; and both for that, and for its exemplifying the general run of bardic exchanges, I thought the poem worth translating.

You say two alien muses
Are competitive to please.
One, in tune, God has given
In his angels' sight to men;
The other's no match for her,
A tuneless, foul deceiver
Whom every bard and poet
Of the bothered world can get.
Know then, you clamp of bias,
Feeble John, like sounding brass
Your poor text held in scansion –
Know, there is no Muse but one.
This to the tongue not seldom
From the Holy Ghost has come,
And then is sent from heaven,
Home of all gifts, to us men
So that God's praise we may sing
As bond for her obtaining.
Here's my thrust, I've hunted hard,
At cold, daft Thomas Lombard.
His book's like a cross pigeon
Sourly grumbling on and on.
Mere copper you are, you scab,
Siôn Cent, for all your hubbub.

LLYWELYN AP Y MOEL

*d.*1440

To the Greyrock Woods
(Coed y Graig Lwyd – his outlaw lair)

By God, you're a fine Wood, hillock
Of Grey slate, Llech Ysgar Rock,
Circle of leaf, Irish snare –
God's grace along your verdure!
Row on row, you're clustered round
A fort, a warrior's playground,
A bracken glade, a snug lair –
How strange would be the summer
(Love's herald, I would argue)
If I were left without you
Where the weft of your twigs knits
Your hills, your leafy turrets!
You're my lord, my heaven gate,
My honour saved, my helpmate,
My saint and my true warrant,
My great house, my settlement.
Faultless nurture, it's been good
To have you for my safeguard,
Sweet close and veil of refuge,
Strong and swiftly sheltering hedge,
Beneath me level greensward,
Green, kind earth, gem of a lord,
Trusses of sweet leaves crowded
Like a dark tent overhead:
My bed is snug in safety,
Your branches overhead me
Are no turf-topped villein's den –
Fine, with the porridge eaten!
Better than bardic travel
For one anxious to do well
Is to strip a Saxon's harness
Off him in this pleasant place,

LLYWELYN AP Y MOEL

To scare with din and mischief,
And (you teach us) to break leaf
And hear from a fair castle,
In pure tune, the nightingale.
They've trailed me round the hilltop
Many a time; you give me hope
On snow ways, dark and trackless,
Where at night no English pass.

Wide circle above our den,
To Owain's men you're London.★
Meanwhile, England's state is marred –
God grant our fight goes forward!
To our side all good fortune,
All reward to Owain's men!

GUTO'R GLYN
*fl.*1450-90

To Hywel ab Ifan Fychan

On the nape of the rock, he
With a smile shares out bounty.
Long life to you, Hywel, there
In Tâl-y-Lan strewing silver!
Your ardency of nature
Throws us gold, tireless and sure.
Your heart won't cease its purpose –
That's how Ifan Fychan was.
Stag-natured, in your household –
God reward such generous gold! –
To give's your office always.
Minstrels needs must sow your praise.
Holding estate more than any,
And a name – God keep it free!

★Owain Glyndŵr, or, more probably, the awaited deliverer of the
Welsh, who was often called Owain in prophetic poetry.

GUTO'R GLYN

Men rightly call you Hywel
Who in bounty most excel.
They call you 'Roland' in Môn,
Generous king, great law-lion.
The further you walk, the more
Men reverence you with honour.
Number the seven seers of Rome:
You have their state and wisdom.
Your presents worked in redgold,
You are the eighth, tongued of gold!

A poet I am always
Of sweet language in your praise.
Deep umbrage feel these others
That for them I don't gild verse.
I'm a poet needs inspiring –
Difficult, unless love sing.
Praise everywhere's haphazard
Save on you, my art's gold lord.
Though half the world scowls at me
With the scruples of envy,
Hard for me not to, Hywel –
I do right, I'll not be still.

I've long been here, I've winnowed
On your floor many an ode.
Your cherishing and comfort
Will not let me leave your court.
A marriage-gift was honoured:
God has joined us evermore.
Unlike, because not jealous,
A lad's marriage to his lass.
It was no English friar spoke
The free banns of our wedlock.
After two stag lifetimes, God
You to your poet wedded.

To witness two banns were spoken,
I call my three odes and ten.
You shall have for a dowry
(While I live) keen song from me.
Although, with yonder abbot,★
I have sworn I'll leave him not,
Yet with priests, spouse or truelove
Counts no more than strumpet-love.
There are two knots of kinship
Between us, that shall not slip.
No divorce, bounteous nature,
Generous squire, will God endure.
God's bond will not be broken,
Nor the Father's grace undone;
No stranger may inhibit,
No impediment defeat;
No vicar may break this lock,
Or friar, not knowing wedlock;
No bishop, named and chosen,
Not the Pope, save Mary's son.

In his Old Age and Blindness
To Dafydd ab Ieuan, Abbot of Valle Crucis

Where are the old men? Dead, at last?
I tonight am left the oldest.
I was given more than my share
Of old age and bad temper –
A talkative man, and often
Rambling on about old men,
Like the all-too-eloquent tongue,
All summer, of Rhys Bwtlwng.
What babbles is the burden
Of my lack of these good men.

★The Abbot of Valle Crucis. Cf. *In His Old Age and Blindness*.

GUTO'R GLYN

It's tiresome, like prentice wit,
That old fools won't be quiet,
But more so, the blind man's plight,
If not dumb, kept from daylight.

This household has asserted
That I call out from my bed.
I must (it is my office)
Call my lord. My nature's this.
Some saint every feast is named with –
I name and call Lord Dafydd,
And won't be still, though hateful
Is my office to their Rule,
But in great love, and ruddy
With mead, name who succours me.

It's his bright wine and good cheer
Makes me sound such a babbler.
Like a father – may Mary
Preserve him! – he's nurtured me.
Like a mother, God's temple
Gives me his goods, here to dwell.
I, who chose it, go to his cellar,
Visit, too, his buttery store.
I go to heaven, to Dafydd
In fair Yale, bountiful Nudd.*
Thousands (I praise him more) got
Food from this kindly abbot.
The good lord of this belfry
Valle Crucis holds in fee.
He gives the weak asylum,
Across Yale he's made a home.
A stone web is his cuirass,

*Yale (Iâl) is the district of Powys, near Llangollen, in which Valle
Crucis stands. Nudd was one of the three generous ones of Britain,
often used as a kenning for a patron.

GUTO'R GLYN

Mansion hemmed with lead and glass.
One I wandered Môn, for mead
And gold's sake, Gwent to Gwynedd;
Now nearer I find gold ready
Here in Yale, for I cannot see.

No, I'll not mourn the ravage
Or the feebleness of age.
With but this abbot constant
And the two Siôns, I'll not want:*
Siôn Trefor, that saint, who is
Seal upon all of Powys;
Siôn Edwart, who makes me welcome –
Two earls I would not change for him!
And the happy trip to end with,
Here in Yale, home to Dafydd.
May these three, like a mainstream,
More and more grow in esteem,
Three chieftains thriving likewise,
And the One that sanctifies,
The One God, into heaven
Welcome them, the Three and One!

DAFYDD NANMOR
*fl.*1450-80

Praise of Rhys ap Maredudd

Companies to Tywyn valley – hosting men
    To the mansions of Rhys;
    May not a night's privation
    Through all ages stain his house!

*The two Siôns – Siôn Trefor Hen of Bryncunallt and Siôn Edward o'r Waun – were local noblemen, whom Guto still visited.

DAFYDD NANMOR

An age long on his land, like an oaktree – to Rhys,
    An age without ending
    Until each star be numbered,
    Or dust of the wood, or flowers.

As flowers of the earth in each kind – as snow,
    As birds on a wheatfield,
    As the rain comes, and the dew,
    So on one man my blessing.

Numbered as dew on each valley – blessings
    To Rhys by the Tywyn,
    So long as heaven stays, or rock,
    Or good loam in the hillside.

He buys the drink from the vineyards – rich
    Over the South waters,
    Eighteen loads, and there's still eight,
    Eighteen ships full with winecasks.

Winecasks there must be, and swords – surely
    Both for Rhys Amhredudd,
    Arms and men numbered as trees
    Swell roads about his journey.

To two hosts, countless as trees – he gives gold,
    To three hosts his silver;
    There take five hosts his payment,
    Thousands yet his mead and wine.

One host, yea two, march at his bidding;
Given his wool thousands go liveried;
    Whole swarms, to his praise, write songs – like
Honey of bees, a thousand sing them.

Many as snowflakes over Rhydodyn,
Many as leaves on saplings of ash,

DAFYDD NANMOR

As the sown seed all previous Mays – did Rhys
Sow riches, counted them out to us.

Courts by the hundred were his, did he ask it,
Every valley its men, its acres each hill,
    Hundreds of clanland, pulled he – towards him,
Hundreds of farms, hundreds of homesteads.

Every year he has nine score stallions,
Nine score breastplates buys against treason,
    Nine score of thin spears he finds – his homeland,
Nine score lands in his own safekeeping.

Never Italian has lived, or Scotsman,
Never from Calais his equal in strength;
    No one from Wales on a wide-nosed – white charger,
None from all England, fears less than he.

Under green holly, eye hath not seen
Neither tongue told where such muster was made;
    To the uttermost Llŷn, no throng has heard – one
That dealt better his meat or his mead.

Never so swift was a white-shanked steed,
Stag of the ford, nor roebuck from bracken,
    Never swam silver-white salmon – at ebb,
Swift as revellers ride into Tywyn.

Never star circled so far, nor bird,
Sunlight nor moon, nor salt sea nor lake,
    Nor the wide coasts of air, far as since – he first came,
Fame of him travels from shore of the Glyn.

DAFYDD NANMOR

Exhortation
To Rhys ap Rhydderch ap Rhys ap Maredudd of Tywyn

Rhys, rose of the summer moor,
Rhys' grandson, no mean nature:
You're rich of all Deheubarth
By the lineage of your birth;
House and homestead of our kin,
The land's right foot of Tywyn.

Growing you are, like ash trees,
From a cluster of princes.
Cobs do not crown the cornshoot
On summer wheat, where's no root;
But harvest from root to tip
Springs òn the stem of kingship.
Stags roam, and summer sunshine
Is good for wheat and for vine;
And for one so bred, 'tis good
To have off chiefs his manhood.
Never a page but was pure
Did St John write in Scripture;
But in your book of lineage
Even less disfigures the page.

New horn the stag is growing,
It's good blood that breeds a king;
Lineage, as to a cherished heir,
Gives nobility nurture.
Two rivers down the valley
Flood into the lake we see;
Father left estate and home,
His lineage gives you chiefdom.

Ice did never yet remain
In July on a fountain;
Nor man nor rabble's fury

DAFYDD NANMOR

Has forced you yet bend your knee.
No snow comes, if the day's fine,
On a slope bright with sunshine;
And none dare, save in friendship,
The land's right arm overstep.
He that best swims a river
Above the waves holds his hair;
You've come where they never went,
You're on shore, past the torrent.
It's slow going to the hilltop,
Burdened up a bitter slope;
Harder borne, your bitter word
When you were young and wayward.

Up the blue streams young salmon
In their fathers' wake will run;
Higher is your father's state
Than the Alps' tallest summit.
Of the deer thronging the slope
The strongest gains the hilltop;
Now climb it like a redstag
Where Maredudd breached the crag.
The hunter climbs on his course,
The hawk rises to windforce;
Summer stag, brindled lion,
Fain would stride the topmost run.
Flower and shoot crown the tree,
Eagle's foot crowns the oaktree;
But you, as upon the shore
The sea, Rhys, crown all honour.

Lordship came upon you there,
You'll thrive now like your father.
May you have, as the beard greys,
A lifetime long as Moses!

DAFYDD AB EDMWND

*fl.*1450-80

A Girl's Hair

Shall I have the girl I love,
The grove of light, my truelove,
With her silk top like a star
And her head's golden pillar?
Dragon fire lights a doorway,
Three chains, like the Milky Way.
A heaven of hair she'll set fire
In one bush, like a bonfire.
Broom or great birchtree's sweetness,
Maelor's yellow-headed lass,
An angel host, a legion,
Breastplate many links are on,
Pennon of peacock feather,
Tall bush like a golden door,
All this lively-looking hair,
Virtue's sun, maiden's fetter,
Were she a goldsmith, we'd guess
Who owned its splendid brightness.
There's something round her head then
Like summer on Rhiw Felen.
Round her, growing raiment springs,
Tent of thesun, like harpstrings,
Rush peelings, tips of harvest,
Fur upon a pinemart's chest,
Peahen that wears, from custom,
Head to foot, the hair of broom,
Tough amber, like a twig-chain,
All inwoven, golden grain.
As tall as trees are those locks,
A crown of twigs, new beeswax.
Labour of bees brought ripeness,
Shoots of sunshine from her flesh,
Saffron on herbs of eye-bright,

– 208 –

DAFYDD AB EDMWND

Gold cherries, stars of the night.
Good was the growing harvest,
Water grasses, golden-tressed.
Pure herbs, with the lye rinsed wet,
Yellow hammer, silk thicket.
Mass of Mary Maudlen's broom
Round her head, golden besom,
And ruddy, if it's loosened,
Like a gold gown she has donned.
Her two breasts are overall
Roofed in gold, each a marvel.
Her skull is weighed with tresses,
Flax upon the yellow trees,
And if it's left unravelled
Was there ever a bush so gold?

That the mark on her be patent
Of faith's chrism from the font
And this bush hold life's sunshine,
No bush under sun's so fine.

LEWIS GLYN COTHI
fl. 1447-86

The Death of Siôn y Glyn
(His son)

I'd a gem in that son there –
By Dwynwen, woe's his father!
Now is a great affection
Left to ache without my son.
Dead is my dice, my bobbin,
My·sides bleed for Siôn y Glyn;
I mourn again and again
A Mabinogi chieftain.

LEWIS GLYN COTHI

A sweet apple and a bird
The lad loved, and white pebbles;
A bow cut from a thorn-twig,
A frail enough sword of wood.
He feared a pipe, a scarecrow,
Begged his mother for a ball.
He'd sing through all the gamut,
Singing Oo-oh for a nut.
He'd cajole and coax me, then
Pretend he'd gone all sullen:
A dice restored our friendship
– He loved that! – or a wood chip.

O that the sweet innocent could
Like Lazarus be rescued!
St Beuno once changed seven
From heaven to life again:
Misery's my heart's dictate,
That Siôn's soul did not make eight.
O Mary, it hurts my bosom,
He lies down, he's in his tomb.
Siôn's death is a sharp despond,
In each breast like a stabwound.
My son, child of my fireside,
My one intent till I died,
My wise bard, my dream nightlong,
My breast, my own heart, my song.
My candle he was, my trinket,
My sweet soul, my one deceit;
My Iseult's gem, my kissing,
My chick that I'd teach to sing,
My strength, and alas 'tis hard,
My skylark, my fine wizard,
My arrow, my bow, my mood,
My suppliant, my childhood.

LEWIS GLYN COTHI

Love and the barb of longing
To his father did Siôn bring.
Farewell, the smile on my face,
Farewell to laughter's solace,
To pastime and to comfort,
To entreaties for a nut,
To the ball, at last, farewell,
To singing and loud revel,
And farewell to gay affection,
Whilst I'm alive. Siôn my son!

GUTUN OWAIN
*fl.*1460-1500

Asking a Stallion
From Siôn ap Rhisiart, Abbot of Valle Crucis, on behalf of his
nephew, Maredudd ap Gruffudd

Siôn, the companion of saints,
Free-giver, lord of presents,
Son of Richard, having liege
And mastery of knowledge:
Edwin you are, whose feast is
In goodly Valle Crucis;
Like Derfel, in Rhiwfelen
The old Cross yet hallows men:
Your courtiers in heaven share,
A blest host by the river,
While, to your feast, the Godhead
Mercy's complement hath led.
St Martin's grace is yours, Siôn,
Your breed is of Rhiwabon;
Your wine, a freer giving
Than of barons or of king!

And I who am your nephew,
Share that ancestry with you.

GUTUN OWAIN

Meredith, son of Griffith –
Through our sires we're kin and kith –
Ednyfed's stock, and Ierwerth's,
Flowering out of Nannau's worth.

Lord of Yale, I crave a boon,
Ask, without fear, this stallion:
A strong, thin-maned beast is he,
That turns a wolf when angry;
White upon his mouth, foam spills,
His head askew, closed nostrils,
Eyes of wild ox in his head,
Gleam of glass, and mouse-coated;
Gown that's on his breast would be
As fine-edged as I'd fancy;
To the reins, like a great bear's,
Or ox yoked, work his withers:
A hedge the height of a man
He'll clear, if swift the horseman;
He'll leap, to ride an errand,
Every stride an acre of land;
A wild roebuck up the slopes,
A stag to skim the hedgetops;
Clods the full breadth of his shoe
He punches from a meadow –
Four turfs tossed behind his head
As though a boar stampeded.
If, like Samuel, he rides fast,
With fire his road is broadcast:
From nails along the highway
Sparks as from an anvil play:
About him, the flames glisten
Like a steel-hearth in Milan.

Like Taliesin, my lord Siôn,
I've come to ask your stallion.

GUTUN OWAIN

Lord of three fearless tenures,
Maelor, Chirk and Yale are yours.
Your warrior on a warhorse
I'll be, if I get this horse.
Three lives and more may you have,
For this horse, in St Asaph.*

WILIAM LLŶN
d.1580

*Elegy for Syr Owain ap Gwilym**

Heavy to plod snow and ice,
Heavier to break a promise.
What in a glade you'd promised
Was to me like a girl's tryst.

Chief songwright, star of poetry,
Syr Owain, you have wronged me.
Alas, do you not remember
The three vows we plighted there –
To walk mid good gold and mead,
To sing to the girls of Gwynedd,
We two, to Tywyn from Llŷn,
And to the South from Tywyn?

To seek you out, I've ridden
To your home at Tal-y-llyn.
The sorrow you did not come
Pierced like a spear my bosom.
With harsh cry, son of Gwilym,
I called you. No answer came.
O grove of inspiration,

*i.e. promoted to be bishop.

*Syr, English 'Sir', was used in addressing a cleric. Since this usage
can mislead in English, I preserve the Welsh form.

– 213 –

WILIAM LLŶN

Spear of language, where've you gone –
Southwards, to places of mead,
Angel of gifts, or Gwynedd?
Like betrothal was that tryst;
You failed it, I can witness.
Poet, tell me, whose household
Charmed you with so fond a hold?

' That foe of all things mortal,
Strict dark death, has caught in thrall
My feet and two hands also –
There, by God, I may not go.
The good crops of the white flesh
In the earth blacken and perish.
Lips that were knotters of praise
In sand are silent always.'

Syr Owain, you wrong me, master
Of language, if you be there.
If for proud goods, hawk of wine,
You're gaoled, O wise Augustine,
Ask of the good God what sum
He'll take to grant you freedom.

'No, that I'll not do, nor yet
Ask my God. Best to be quiet.
Worldly goods cannot lengthen
For one hour the lives of men.
The fool counts on his lifespan –
It is God doles life to man.'

Yes, it is true, you strange one,
Woe's me, I know it's certain.
Now, if you may – O summit
Of three tongues! – the long grave quit.
If not, for three lives of an oak
Farewell fine sport and music!

WILIAM LLŶN

No more we'll hunt the stag then,
No more dogs, hawks or huntsmen,
Making love, trust in greeting,
No girls laugh, nor praises ring.
Henceforth no green spreading tree
Foliage will need to carry.
The abode of love has toppled,
Companionship's hall is felled.

By sad error God bore home
A strong stag, wise and winsome.
Court and hearth have lost their sight,
Song's handtools, haft and mallet.
Never was laid to rest so rare
A shaft-ox at his altar.

If friendship seeks its nonesuch,
No live man was loved so much.
If two regions should dispute
Which one owns music's tribute,
Minted more than snow they'd bring
Gold coins to have you living.
Above the team, in song's yoke,
Strongly you rhymed rich music:
The yoke, the team, the goldchain,
Now you lie at rest, are vain.
Brow of the road's cold and frozen,
Colder my breast now you've gone.

Farewell body, bright and fine!
It's time for me, Syr Owain,
Unremedied to say adieu –
Bitter it is to leave you.
Poet, if you wait down there
Under the earth for ever,
In the grave, then, wisdom stays
(Sad to admit it!) always.

ANONYMOUS
16th century

O the Jewels

Fine-spun brows, twice-graceful as flowers,
Gentle her frolics, revel and play –
　O the jewels, jewels are gay!

Had to have jewels, jewels my bright one,
No village could buy them, shepherding sheep –
　O my soul, my soul must weep!

The girl my soul is, down at the glenside,
Fills me with love, greeting me there –
　O that greeting, greeting me there!

Her poet greets her, Merlin's lady,
Since my heart, my tune is new –
　O when two days, two days are through,

I shall venture (look I'm ailing)
And if she fails me, I must die –
　O I sing, I sing and sigh!

I'll sing a satire to my bright maiden,
Her grief is so gentle in our debate –
　O the pining, early and late!

Continually pining for her fair features,
And my cheeks growing pale, loving her long –
　O the loving, loving her long!

Loving a slender one, happy of feature,
That's what has made me what you now see –
　Ah, down-dilly, down-dilly fa lee!

ANONYMOUS

The Shirt of a Lad

As I did the washing one day
Under the bridge at Aberteifi,
And a golden stick to drub it,
And my sweetheart's shirt beneath it –
A knight came by upon a charger,
Proud and swift and broad of shoulder,
And he asked if I would sell
The shirt of the lad that I loved well.

No, I said, I will not trade –
Not if a hundred pounds were paid;
Not if two hillsides I could keep
Full with wethers and white sheep;
Not if two fields full of oxen
Under yoke were in the bargain;
Not if the herbs of all Llanddewi,
Trodden and pressed, were offered to me –
Not for the likes of that, I'd sell
The shirt of the lad that I love well.

SALBRI POWEL
16th century

The Lover's Hope

I'm but an ailing poet,
I cannot keep it secret:
My voice grows faint for her fair face
Who's gone chase flibbertigibbet.

And now, no lad's so simple
Or lusty cheery damsel
But's glad enough to joke and pick
And hand me a stick of hazel.

SALBRI POWEL

In Gwaun y Plu I'll gather
    And plant each stick together;
If you can trust an old wive's tale
    The twigs can't fail to prosper.

And when the nuts shall ripen
    And the birds sing their burden,
Fairer than fair she'll come therein
    Like a linnet in my garden.

And there, there'll be no coupling
    Of art in my new dwelling –
Only the birdsong, sweet on the bud,
    And gentle greenwood growing.

And there I'll be desiring
    A bed, in shelter hiding,
To have, O lovely form, with her
    A skilful, tender loving.

SIÔN GRUFFUDD
16th century

Longing for Caernarfon

I am one that, by God's will,
    Lives exiled from his nation,
And full of care am I – why so?
    With longing for Caernarfon.

Wretched was Adam, pure of old,
    Cast out from pleasant Eden;
I'm likewise sad as all may see –
    A paradise was Caernarfon.

Joseph I am – God pay the cost! –
    And worlds away from kinsmen,

SIÔN GRUFFUDD

Forgetting what it is to live,
  So distant is Caernarfon.

I dearly love to speak its name
  With countless salutation:
Dear it was, and will again
  Be dearly loved Caernarfon.

The men so gifted, the life so free,
  Good habits and tradition –
Flanders perhaps is as good a land;
  There's more grace in Caernarfon.

Can it be strange that I should sigh
  So much, with such good reason?
My father and mother I must respect
  Remembering Caernarfon.

And for my brothers sorrow comes
  And makes my heart grief's prison,
And for my sisters this long age
  That tarry in Caernarfon.

From Llandwrog my wound is great
  And footpaths of Glynllifon;
There I would often wish to be –
  Yours be the praise, Caernarfon!

My kinsmen and sweet lineage
  And many a companion,
A fellowship of a thousand saints
  You go to adorn Caernarfon.

For want of a better, from afar
  Receive this salutation;
A string of pearls I'd give to you,
  Did I own one, dear Caernarfon!

SIÔN GRUFFUDD

John Gruffudd in each place of cheer
  I'm well known, there's no question;
Especially am I noted in
  Every parish of Caernarfon.

One from that land I stand in prayer
  To Christ of our salvation
To give of his gifts in every form
  And his blessing on Caernarfon.

Good health go with you, one and all,
  Till at last my joy's in season
And by the mercy of God's Son
  I see the land of Caernarfon.

Farewell, farewell, once more farewell,
  And tears must weep and glisten,
To great and small a hundred times
  And again, farewell, Caernarfon!

SIÔN TUDUR
d. 1602

Warning to the Poets

Alas for our art, scandal
Is rampant about us all!
Credit of our calling's gone,
Prized once without aspersion
First, we praised God; for mostways
Melts away unworthy praise.
Praised then a breed of strong men,
Princes, and rapid horsemen;
Lords redolent of learning,
Bishops in our midst we'd sing;
Earls to fulfil our blessings,
Barons of the blood of kings;

SIÔN TUDUR

Fine-tempered chiefs and fruitful,
From an old stock sprouting tall;
Faith's elders, priests and worthies,
Prelates, fortunate their sees.
Because they'd learning, these men
Were called to rule, were chosen;
Right was respect for learning,
Honouring God, learning's spring.
Right too for a bard to pour
His praise upon a warrior
Insofar's a wretch would not
Hazard his life in combat.

But base-born ploughman, now, we
Poets turn into gentry,
Give pedigrees to blazon
Jack with praise the same as John.
Every turncoat filches bits
From verses of good poets
To flatter some low fellow.
This painful bribe paints the crow.
Plumage from each brilliant bird
Makes even a crow be-glittered.
A bare churl, a false rascal –
Crowns make conquerors of all!
If we're paid by a tinsmith
He gets pedigree forthwith.
If he's preferred to office,
With ease, nobility's his.
These two signs, prudently won
Through usury and extortion:
A mansion of great splendour,
And a barred and bolted door.
It's easier, where he's hidden,
And his bailiff guards the den,
To break your neck than breakfast

Or cure hunger at his feast.
Without pride, he'll skimp and stint
To heap gold like a skinflint.
Hard of hearing, reared on bare
Buttermilk, bread and water,
Though he'd not feed a beggar
Or proffer alms to the poor
– Even to elude the scaffold –
Yet for lineage he'll give gold.
No lack, but what's ancestral,
Pains or troubles him at all.
Furtive the gift he granted,
A gold piece to patch his breed,
A chart by a poet written –
Poets' hands do many a sin,
Take pedigrees in dozens
Off the well-born for the dunce.
It's tiresome, to the uplands
Boosting his crest, line and lands:
A scab-patch of a satchel
Holds the dusty lineage-roll.
A shovel of dung, in earnest,
His good father had for crest –
We gave him (if truth were known)
A more dubious escutcheon.
Over the round earth, these men
From base estate have risen:
They risk a speedy downfall,
Who from lewdness grow too tall.
Soareth beetle over street –
He's back in dung by sunset!

Every ruffian would hire us –
Let's stop, confess our trespass:
Our reputation's forfeit
If we'll not forgo deceit.

God forfend that we waste craft
On men not fit for songcraft!
From our famed seat, let's always
Sing to those that merit praise,
Studying how to praise aright
Men worshipful and upright.
Let's leave (as that's what's lawful)
A wretched churl still a churl:
A chieftain is yet a chieftain
And chieftain he shall remain;
Ninth grade will be the eagle
And the crow no grade at all;
Generous the hawk shall stay
But a kite's a kite alway!
Whoever else does commerce,
No more churl's gold find Siôn's purse.

MORGAN LLWYD
1619-59

God and His Church

'My God, kiss my lips with thine,
Sweeter is thy love than wine,
   Beloved of my soul art thou.
A fragrant oil anoints thy head,
Thy name quickeneth the dead,
   The true virgins love thee now.

'Where may I look to find thee, say,
Feeding thy flock in heaven's day?
   Till I have had thee, all is rue.
Why dost thou toss me from my rest?
My soul yearns only for thy breast;
   Though I'm not worthy, yet I'm true.'

MORGAN LLWYD

God in Christ answered: 'O be glad,
My beloved, arise, be not sad;
    Black winter and the rains are past.
Flowers grow in every sward;
Listen, the turtle's voice is heard;
    Come now, hand in hand at last.

'My pure Church, my bride, my love,
My sister and my gentle dove,
    Hid where the cleft of rock allows,
Thy face, thy voice discover thee,
Welcome thou art to be with me,
    Who am the Lamb, and thou the Spouse.'

WILLIAM PHYLIP

d. 1670

A Leave-Taking
of Hendre Fechan, his home

Goodbye, the secret of the song, the brilliant right-order,
    Goodbye, Hendre Fechan,
  And the song-books, bright pure song,
  To you, goodbye now also.

I'd a house to sleep, to live I'd shelter,
    Food and drink sufficed me;
  I'd a home till I were dead,
  And a fire (thank God!) kept burning.

In place of my old homestead, and the woe
    Here, of an earthly life,
  In heaven God will give me now
  A home where's no returning.

WILLIAM PHYLIP

Green woods, farewell, where the small birds sang
    A choice, correct, sweet song;
  Farewell, all the song-chained groves,
  Each path where song would wander.

HUW MORUS
1622-1709

Praise of a Girl

My heart every day
Speeds on its way
   Glad fancy to a tansy top, faithful and gay;
As sweet is your pose
As a riverbank rose
   Or a posy where lily or lavender blows;
Like honey musk is
Your unconcealed kiss,
   The kernel of your lips I cannot dismiss;
There's more state and fame
In clasping your frame
   Than if I'd the wealth of a king to my name.

The goods of the earth
And trusting their worth
   To men and to women are all void and dearth;
Great love maketh sure
A wealth will endure
   Where houses and lands vanish years before.
Much love will you see,
And my heart and its key,
   My dear, if you say you will come with me;
But if you draw back
'Tis a perilous lack –
   My life is so wounded, there's no return track.

So that people don't swear
For my death from despair –
   'Let her who was asked and refused him, beware!'
Give a kiss and good grace
And pardon to trace,
   And purity too, in your faultless face;
Give a heart that's alight
With kindly delight,
   Gentleness, faithfulness, and we'll do right;
Listen now, give me,
Bright foam of the sea,
   Give mercy and home, friend Mary, to me.

OWEN GRUFFYDD
1643-1730

The Men That Once Were
(Extracts)

   Old, old
To live on, wretched to behold,
My hair is white, my smile is cold,
   All inspiration slack:
My two hands miss dexterity,
Their strength is twisted out of me,
To work exact and skilfully –
   Though bounty feed me, still they lack
And worsen in their shape and plight
Until they disappear from sight
   And I to brittle dust go back.

   Harsh stroke
To the old when the cold weather broke!
His poor fiddle's a shrivelled oak
   That no one now will play;
Longing a dull ache in my side
For the kind chieftains that have died,

OWEN GRUFFYDD

God's gracious works, who now must hide,
   Many a face I know, in clay;
I'm cold for all those generous men,
I'm doubting if I'll find again
   Such lords as in my memory stay.

    Hard pain
That they have gone, makes me complain
For their love and true respect again
   And bounty of their weal –
Alas, the breakdown of that race
Of generous power and famous grace,
My pure support in many a place
   Bestowed with love's good-humoured zeal!
Today my frozen cheek lacks cheer,
I don't see any that call me near,
   Nor banquet, nor profit, nor a full meal.

    It pays
Ill to have office nowadays,
Unthieving givers are gone, and my ways
   Are heavy and cold and long;
And as I go, not a house I've seen
Ready for praise, as it once had been –
Serious song has gone from the scene,
   There wants to hear me not one of the throng!
Pure Welsh they do not willingly use:
Twice better than the cywydd's muse
   Is the pampered note of the English tongue.

    Betrayed
To wander the world in search of aid,
I have to keep my poet's trade
   Hidden in my despair.
Alas for the broken strength of the earth,
True profit for the Muse of worth!

To follow her now means fear and dearth,
   Every hour a life of care.
To tedious dust I'll soon belong:
Farewell, dear Welsh and kindly song –
   I may not take you with me there!

TRADITIONAL
16th-17th century

Stanzas for the Harp

1

Went to the garden to pick a posy,
Passed the lavender, passed the lily,
Passed the pinks and roses red –
Picked a nettle sting instead.

2

I'll go to the church next Sunday
And beneath the bellrope sit me,
And my eyes will be avoiding
Who is sitting next my darling.

3

Upon a flat stone by the shore
I told my love one word – no more;
Over it now thyme is growing.
And a few sprigs of rosemary blowing.

4

Only earth now, shroud and coffin,
Come betwixt me and my darling;
Oft I've gone a longer journey –
Never felt my heart so heavy.

5

I imagined when I married
Dance and song as much as I wanted.
All I got when I did marry –
A cradle to shake and lullaby baby.

6

Once on marriage I put good silver,
Now not a farthing would I offer,
But I'd give a lot to anybody
If I could get my feet and hands free.

LEWIS MORRIS
1701-65

Poem of the Frost and Snow

Ere I freeze, to sing bravely
By Mary, is best for me;
I will make a new canto
To the terrible mist and snow,
Steel ground, grass short and withered,
The black month, the shiver-stirred.
I'm not hale here, nor wisely
Sing nor well, alas for me!
Better the awkward Muse might
Run in May or June's sunlight,
When a sweet bird in the thick
Of leaves charms with its music,
And under a birch like heaven
A fool enjoys hugging Gwen,
And his voice in a greenhall
Is found, and a poem's soul.
But not like this, I dare swear,
Does winter stay forever.

LEWIS MORRIS

How old it looks, white snowdrift
Hiding every slope and rift,
Everywhere cold, white each tree,
And no stream in the valley.
Water locked, no genial day,
Black frost along the footway;
Birds of the world, sad deadlock –
God's put their food under lock:
The key let Him take home then
Rightly to be kept in heaven!

EVAN THOMAS
c.1710-c.1770

To the Noble Woman of Llanarth Hall
(Who shut the Author's goat in a house for two days, its crime being that it gre
too near the Mansion)

O black-maned, horse-haired, unworthy one,
   What did you do to the goat, your sister?
She'd your father's horns, your mother's beard –
   Why did you put her falsely in prison?

WILLIAM WILLIAMS PANTYCELYN
1717-91

The Love of God

Always across the distant hills
I'm looking for you yet;
Come, my beloved, it grows late
And my sun has almost set.

Each and every love I had
Turned unfaithful to me at length;
But a sweet sickness has taken me
Of a love of mightier strength.

A love the worldly don't recognise
For its virtue or its grace,
But it sucks my liking and desire
From every creature's face.

O make me faithful while I live,
And aimed level at thy praise,
Let no object under the sky
Take away my gaze!

But pull my affections totally
From falsities away
To the one object that keeps faith
And shall for ever stay.

Nothing under the blue air now
Would make me want to live
But only that I'll know the joys
That the courts of God can give.

Relish and appetite have died
For the flowers of the world that fall:
Only a vanity without ebb
Is running through it all.

Pilgrim

Pilgrim I am in a desert land,
  Wandering far and late,
In expectation, every hour,
  I near my Father's gate.

In front of me I think I hear
  Sounds of a multitude –
They that have conquered and gone through
  Fire and tempestuous flood.

Come, Holy Spirit, a fire by night,
  A pillar of cloud by day, –
I will not venture half a step
  Unless you lead the way.

This way or that I miss the path
  And fall to either side –
Oh, to that paradise, step by step,
  Go before me, God my guide!

I've longing on me for that land
  Where the unnumbered throng
Anthem the death on Calvary
  Even as their lives are long.

Fair Weather

I see that the black clouds
  Now almost disappear,
The north wind that was loud
  Begins slowly to veer,
And after high tempest soon shall roll
Fair weather to my fainting soul.

The black night shall not toss
  Nor for long the storm rage,
No man to carry the cross
  Is dealt too long an age;
Delightful is yon rising dawn
Promising soon a glorious morn.

I look across the hills
  Of my Father's house, and see
The sunlight on the ground
  Whose grace sets me free:

That in Life's book my name is writ
And no man blots or cancels it.

And though in the desert night
   I've wandered many a year
And often had to drink
   Of the bitter cup, despair;
The yoke I suffered was my gain
And not for nothing came that pain.

The burden on my back
   Pulled heaven down to earth,
It sanctified for me
   All woe and grievous dearth:
The wheel turned to my fervent prayer,
The bitterest bile was sweetened there.

The chastenings of heaven,
   Lashed by the Father's thong,
Are sweet like honeycombs
   With healing blithe and long:
By cross and grief, by tempest driven,
The saints are ripened into heaven.

GORONWY OWEN
1723-69
The Wish

Could I have what I begged for from heaven,
What I'd ask would be after this fashion,
Not an idle favour of fortune – no
   This upright choice would be my ambition:

Alert good sense, unpampered body,
To have from health a heart that's healthy,
And to leave then the unruly, officious
   World, over-distressed and filthy.

GORONWY OWEN

I'd go back to my father's country,
Live respected, not lavish nor meagrely,
In sunlit Môn, a land most lovely, with
Cheerful men in it, full of ability.

A fair tithe, a parish that's orderly,
Home under hill, and books in plenty,
And a row of cattle in my dairy, cared for
By the brisk wife Elin, fair and kindly.

For me, I'd wish for most, a garden,
A bower sheltered to suit the season,
Whilst I'd read the elegant diction of poets,
Seed of Druids, a deft recitation.

And over my head, amid the branches,
A paradise of sweet, pure voices,
Treble of finches, echoing verses, chirps
Of songful blithe birds' vowelled speeches.

And while the birds were at their singing,
Lestthe bower incline me to sleeping,
Against the treble choir competing – my song,
Worthily versified, gay and diverting.

Myself, with my two boys around me,
I'd listen to Robyn rhyming gaily
To the apt strings of Goronwy – if two hands
On the harp he'll learn to delight me.

Let the Englishman have what he's after,
A wild-running brookful of crystal water
Through some dear glen – he's welcome rather – if I
Have Môn: for foremost I name her.

Grandiloquent she'll not make my praises,
Remembering gems, priceless prodigies,

Seas, land, mountain, leaf-laid copses, treasure
  Of far-off India's golden fringes.

The Pope loves Rome, a fine-built bastion;
Paris towers are gracious to Frenchmen;
The English has no need to mention London's
  Splendour of men: but Môn's my dear one.

A just return there, may God grant me,
And an unplagued age that will not irk me,
And children to cherish deftly their language,
  And a noble muse to give them glory!

An Invitation

To William Parry, Deputy-Comptroller of the Mint in the Tower of London, to visit Northolt

Friend most of all I value,
Parry – the Lord has loved you –
A man of such mild mettle,
Truly mild, that I love well:
Dear man, with you in London,
What's the point of loving on?
Maybe so sharp is exile,
Not to love were more worth while.

Is this your choice? – Not to stir
From town to Northolt yonder
And hear songs (what more sweet then?)
As you stroll the bard's garden?
But all year in the hubbub
Of the White Tower is your job,
Where cut and minted coin rings,
Small halfpennies and shillings.
Dear Gwilym, be no skinflint,
A whole month off give the Mint,

GORONWY OWEN

And come, for God's sake, and lief
Leave the town's smoke and mischief!

Though coins have such worth, yet come –
A song will be your welcome,
Water to drink, come what may,
Clean, fresh air, an ode straightway,
And (what better feast?) the heart
That greets you true and stalwart.
Why won't you come? I promise,
Dear fellow, much more than this:
You'll drink beer of a chief bard,
Conversing in my orchard,
And from vantage note in chief
God's miracles in greenleaf:
And every flower, as it were,
Indicates like a finger
Vast depths of mighty purpose
Of the God that made it thus.
Flowers, like hundreds of gold gems,
Splendid and shining emblems:
Silver is but a shadow
Of these lilies, tint of snow;
Solomon and his riches –
That wise silkworm! – weren't as these.

Look, if we'd heed it, faultless
The lesson it would teach us:
Man's empty joy deflated
By the flower's drooping head.
Like a flower, we have our store
Of the world's short-lived vigour.
Today's delicate bloom, though,
Will wither and die tomorrow:
To this end comes the blossom,
To this, also, man must come.

GORONWY OWEN

Gardens with wasting summer
Fade, no matter they be fair.
Come, before the year changes
And flowers, grown old, cease to please.
Two harvests gone! – for all that,
It is still summer's climate,
And the garden is quite fine,
Old age succumbs to sunshine,
And still, though soon it won't be,
The greenleaf's fresh and lovely.
Roses at the cold yearside
Wither, with all summer's pride;
Roses, they were old straightway,
But we too must waste away.

Yet, till the grave, here's my prayer
(And 'amen' you must answer):
Without distress may we live,
Though full of years, still active,
And return to our old nurture
– Ere we die – on Mona's shore.
May all our days be halcyon
And we two be bonded one;
And that day (God grant it fair!)
That ends our trek together,
Christ bring us home to heaven –
A blest world, may it be then!

IEUAN BRYDYDD HIR
1733-88

*The Hall of Ifor Hael**

A poor sight the hall of Ifor Hael – mounds
    In a swamp are lying,
  Thorn and blasted thistle own it,
  Bramble where was greatness.

No inspiration comes there now – poets
    Nor festive tables,
  No gold within its walls,
  Nor gift, nor man to give it.

For Dafydd, the skilled in song – cold grief
    Gave Ifor into gravel;
  Much more vile that his fine court
  Should now be a place for owls.

Though the brief glory of lords had fame – their walls
    And greatness perish;
  It's a strange place for proud ones,
  These houses built on sand.

ANN GRIFFITHS
1776-1805

Expecting the Lord

  Being myself so corrupted
  With the forsaking life I lead,
  To be on your holy mountain
  Is high privilege indeed;
  There the veils are rent, and coverings

*Patron of Dafydd ap Gwilym.

Destroyed from that time forth,
And there is your excelling glory
On the transient things of earth.

O to keep at that high drinking
Where the streams of great salvation flow,
Till I'm utterly disthirsted
For the transient things below!
To live, and my Lord always expected!
To be, when he comes, up and awake!
Quick as a flash to open for him!
Enjoy him without stint or break!

Rose of Sharon

Look, between the myrtles standing
A true object of my thought –
Though I know only in part now
He surpasses the wordly sort,
        Yet, come morning,
I shall see him as he is.

His name is the Rose of Sharon;
He's white and ruddy, fair of worth;
He excels above ten thousand
Of the chief objects of earth;
        Friend to a sinner,
He's the pilot on the sea.

Why should I go any longer
To the poor idols at my feet?
None of their company, I swear it,
With my great Jesus can compete –
        Oh, if only
All my life stayed in his love!

ANN GRIFFITHS

Full of Wonder

Full of wonder, full of wonder for angels,
Faith can see great wonder in this –
Giver of being, abundant sustainer,
Governor of all that is,
In the manger a swaddled baby
Without a home to lay him in,
And still the bright hosts of glory
Are even now adoring him.

When Sinai's altogether smoking
And at its loudest the trumpet's cry,
Past the divide I can go feasting
In Christ the Word, and not die.
There in him dwells every fullness
To fill what man's perdition unmade;
He on the breach between the two parties
Offering himself, quittance paid.

He hung between thieves, who is Redemption,
Suffered death in anguish and loss;
Himself made strong the arms of hangmen
There to nail him on the cross;
Paying the debt of brands from the burning
He exalts justice (his father's law),
Forgives in terms of the free atonement
And justice, blazing, shines the more.

O my soul, look! Chief of kings, author
Of peace, he lay in that room,
The creation in him moving
And he a dead man in the tomb!
Song and life of the lost! Most wonder
Of all to angels and seraphim –
God in flesh, they see him and worship,
Choirs of them shouting, "Be unto Him!"

ANN GRIFFITHS

Thanks, ten thousand times I thank him,
Thank him while I've breath and tongue,
For being what he is, to worship
And for ever be theme of song!
In this my nature he's been tempted
Like the least man that ever trod –
A small child, he was weak, was feeble,
Was infinite, true and living God.

To carry no more corruption's body,
Co-penetrate with the choirs above
Fiery into unending wonders
Of Calvary's redeeming love;
Live to behold him, the Invisible
Who died and now lives flesh and blood
In never-to-be-broken union
And co-union with my God.

I may exalt there the Name that Godhead
Put as atonement over the whole,
Nor shall veil or imagination
Block his true image from my soul.
In the fellowship of the mystery
Opened in the wound he bore,
To kiss the Son to everlasting
And turn my back on him no more!

IEUAN GLAN GEIRIONYDD
1795-1855

The Free School-house, Llanrwst

World of my morning's playground,
  My boyhood walked this plot
Made dear to me by many
  A familiar knot:
Where's the muttering and hubbub

IEUAN GLAN GEIRIONYDD

Your walls once confined,
The children round you playing
    And their echo in the wind?

On all sides you've about you
    So grave and sad an air,
As if you kept a vigil
    Solitary and bare;
Once as a saint you were comely,
    Today you look far more
A widow mourning her children,
    Destitute and poor.

Sound of the bell is silent,
    No multitude leaves the town,
The bolts of your strong doors,
    Unused, are rusted brown;
Weaving their way of an evening
    Bats fly with silent beat,
Where rang the poems of Homer
    And Virgil, elegant-sweet.

Over large patches of gravel
    The unnurturing grass is tall,
The lawn where we sent rolling
    In their turn hoop and ball;
May the hand that struck you be withered
    And plagued with the plague it breeds,
He that unchilded you be childless
    And barren as your weeds!

And now, where are they scattered,
    The muster that were here,
Playing and learning together –
    Such conferences dear?
Some in graves are sleeping,
    And some to the world away,

IEUAN GLAN GEIRIONYDD

There is no bell can call them
  Together again today.

O wise and vigilant watcher,
  If you should chance to meet
Some of my fellow-scholars,
  My playmates at your feet,
Pay them my dearest service,
  And say, though many a wave
Swept over me, my bosom
  Still keeps their memory brave.

FOLKSONGS

My Darling's a Venus

My darling's a Venus,
    She's slender of form,
My darling is prettier
    Than blossom on thorn:
My darling's the purest,
    The fairest to view,
I'm not here to flatter,
    I speak what is true.

My dear one's a fine girl,
    She's loveliest of all,
Her cheeks are so rosy,
    Her teeth they are small;
Her eyes are so merry
    And dainty her brow,
My heart, how I'd love her
    If she'd but allow.

FOLK SONGS

Rew di ranno

A bird's so fine and careless,
She neither sows nor harvests:
 Not a trouble does she fear
But sings all year regardless.
  Dummily dummily dummily dummily
  Dummily dummily dummily dummily
  Dummily dummily dummily dummily
   Rew di rew di ranno
   Rew di rew di ranno
 Not a trouble does she fear
But sings all year regardless.

Tonight she'll eat her supper,
But where's tomorrow's dinner?
 That's her way to bed and board –
She lets the Lord provide her.
  Dummily dummily dummily dummily
  Dummily dummily dummily dummily
  Dummily dummily dummily dummily
   Rew di rew di ranno
   Rew di rew di ranno
 That's her way to bed and board –
She lets the Lord provide her.

Hunting the Hare

It's the hare that we go hunting
On a fine and bracing day.
From the furze she's just been started –
Dogs and puss are both away.
Like the wind, or maybe faster,
After hare and hounds we go,
Dodging through the upland sheeptracks
Such a clever to and fro.

Running for her life by hedges
Skirts the edges of the groves;
Greyhound looks as if he's flying,
Hare is just beyond his nose!
Long may hunting be our pastime,
Wine and feasting, songs and tales –
Stories of the ninefold huntings
Ringing round the land of Wales.

Bittern he took a bundle

Bittern he took a bundle
Leisurely to ramble –
He fell over then on his head, on his head,
    Boom, boom, boom, boom,
Into a load of apples.

Bittern he rose and hasty
Did all the apples carry
Over the hills to Chester fair, Chester fair,
    Boom, boom, boom, boom,
And sold them there intently.

Apples he unloaded,
Yellow fruit a myriad –
The children shrieking for more and more, more and more,
    Boom, boom, boom, boom,
A ha'pence for a hundred.

Bittern back home was hasting,
Over the hilltops walking,
Shouted, 'Missis, O look what a lot, look what a lot,
    Boom, boom, boom, boom,
I've got at apple-selling!'

FOLK SONGS

There's my darling

There's my darling down there in the orchard,
    Too rum di ro, rum di raddle iddle al.
How I wish that there I wandered,
    Too rum di ro, rum di raddle iddle al.
There's the farmhouse, there's the shippen,
There's a door that starts to open.
      Fal di raddle iddle al, fal di raddle iddle al,
      Too rum di ro, rum di raddle iddle al.

There's a splendid, branching oaktree –
    Too rum di ro, rum di raddle iddle al.
Sight of it's entirely lovely.
    Too rum di ro, rum di raddle iddle al.
I shall wait where it can shade me
Till my darling comes to meet me.
      Fal di raddle iddle al, fal di raddle iddle al,
      Too rum di ro, rum di raddle iddle al.

Here's a harp,and strings to string it –
    Too rum di ro, rum di raddle iddle al.
What's the good if no one plays it?
    Too rum di ro, rum di raddle iddle al.
Here's a girl alert and proper –
What's the use if she won't answer?
      Fal di raddle iddle al, fal di raddle iddle al,
      Too rum di ro, rum di raddle iddle al.

The Holly

    Come friends, together let us raise
        Λ song of praise for the greentree,
    Lovely wood and worth its fame –
        The name of it's the holly.
          Fal di roo di lam tam

FOLK SONGS

Trooli riddle ee
Trala-lamtam talam tani
Lovely wood and worth its fame –
The name of it's the holly.

And where shall the like of it be found –
In boxtree bush or yewtree
Or in some rich palace hall? –
But finest of all's the holly.
Fal di roo di lam tam
Trooli riddle ee
Trala-lamtam talam tani
Or in some rich palace hall? –
But finest of all's the holly.

Whether rain pours down, or snow,
I can still be happy:
Even if worse weather break,
It would not penetrate holly.
Fal di roo di lam tam
Trooli riddle ee
Trala-lamtam talam tani
Even if worse weather break,
It would not penetrate holly.

The sparrow's home its branches rock,
The blackbird cock so dainty –
Here's my sweetheart sits beneath
The shady leaf of the holly.
Fal di roo di lam tam
Trooli riddle ee
Trala-lamtam talam tani
Here's my sweetheart sits beneath
The shady leaf of the holly.

FOLK SONGS

Idle Robin

I have a neat little scrap of a house,
    A scrap of a house, a scrap of a house,
I have a neat little scrap of a house,
      A windy door in the morning.
        Hey di ho, di hey di hey di ho
      A windy door in the morning.

A fraction open the door ajar,
    The door ajar, the door ajar,
A fraction open the door ajar,
      You'll see the rolling ocean.
        Hey di ho, di hey di hey di ho
      You'll see the rolling ocean.

I went last night to my father's house,
    My father's house, my father's house,
I went last night to my father's house
      To get for free my welcome.
        Hey di ho, di hey di hey di ho
      To get for free my welcome.

My mam she arose to give me some food,
    Dear flesh and blood, to give me some food,
My mam she arose to give me some food,
      Dear flesh and blood, my own one.
        Hey di ho, di hey di hey di ho
      Dear flesh and blood, my own one.

My father arose, he stood on the floor,
    A stick he bore, he stood on the floor,
My father arose, he stood on the floor,
      A great big stick he was holding.
        Hey di ho, di hey di hey di ho
      A great big stick he was holding.

When I'd been trounced in a scrap of a house,
   A scrap of a house, a scrap of a house,
When I'd been trounced in a scrap of a house,
    A windy door in the morning.
      Hey di ho, do hey di hey di ho
    A windy door in the morning.

ALUN

1797-1840

Song to the Nightingale

When our dear earth is hid by night
   Under its black wing,
The woodland choir is mute, but you
   Then gently sing,
And if against your heart a thorn
   Throbs beneath your breast,
You, till generous day should break,
   Will but sing, and leave the rest.

And like you is this gentle girl,
   Partner more than rubies dear,
At sunset, though across the land
   A thousand clouds appear,
When all day's comforters are dumb
   Her fidelity's complete;
In the night's anguish and dismay
   Never sounded voice so sweet.

Though the worry almost numbs her heart
   She'll not complain
Nor tire her dear ones with distress –
   Her smile hides her pain;
Nor ends her song the long night through
   Until bright hope shall dawn,
Shining like an eye of gold
   Through the clear lids of morn.

EBEN FARDD
1802-63

From *Jerusalem Destroyed*

Sound of disquiet is in the great halls.
To the sad breast, what profit in palaces?
Grief penetrates into each splendid corner
    Of the houses of the great, howe'er wide their walls.

The van of the soldiery, O, as they shout,
The heights and the rocks there split asunder;
Wretchedly these others weep for the agony,
Their breath they lose, their strength and life;
In pain, I know, there'll live hardly a hundred; though
    Scores of them wail, death breaks their glory.

Soldiers in savagery waging warfare
Capture and fire Antonia's castle;
Very soon will fall God's glorious Temple, soon
    Will be shattered that gem bright as snow.

Through the dark gloom, see, the spears flame out,
    An unnatural rumbling sound like thunder.
The comely temple of Moriah in flames turns to ashes;
    The uproar, hear it! the rafters snap.

Now is the fabric reduced to poverty,
As though skill did it, in every quarter;
Piercing embers of flame go through it;
It vomits from its bosom timber and stones.
It was mighty on high, now it is scattered; to dust
    It is turning, sad sight to see it.

Flames in vehement conflagration
Consume the Temple, the holy splendour;
Golden doors melt, and with them the silver,

The decorative flowers, and all the rest.
Vain dwelling of dishonour, with shouting and noise
   Battered by thousands, where once was praise.

   Slippery the smooth white pavements,
   On the white marble a sea of blood.

WILLIAM THOMAS (ISLWYN)
1832-78

From *The Storm*

I

Everything is sacred, all these mountains
Have in them heavenly music. I had here
(If such quick love of country be allowed me)
Many a kinsman, forefather dear to me,
Whose names and honour are by no man known,
Mere quieted ghosts of the lost age that bore them
Among these mountains, where they sang or mourned
Many a noonday, as experience brought
Good luck or ill. And we must, even as they,
Leave legacy of sweet remembered things,
An inspiration, an astonished thought
For the gentle breeze ever to cherish, or
To fade forever in the mists above.
Who talks of Jacob's well? One greater than Jacob
Is imaged through the world in every stream.
Over this river did my fathers go,
And every breeze of heaven, many a time,
The moon, the many stars divinely dawning,
The sun, and claps of thunder. All the world
Is sacred, not a mountain but doth bear
A cherub on it, and eternal song.
And even the remote Aegean shores –
Those headlands of the eternal dawn of Greece

WILLIAM THOMAS (ISLWYN)

Rising for ever from the seas of time
And on each rock the light of many ages –
They're but small parts of the poetic world.
No, Homer never sang of yonder hills,
He never saw them! What would Snowdon be
Could she have shadowed that man in his cradle?
A yet more splendid Ida in his song,
As the dawn of the gods breaks on her peak.

2

Sweet sadness of memory is mankind's bliss.
The soul, as it remembers, can enjoy
Greater than what the very world can give.
It can supply from its own workings all
It lacks, and evermore create the whole
Lovely and great and perfect, like itself.

   From memory's height,
It seizes on the rude events of being
And raises on them a great edifice
Of lofty things. It is the power, indeed
The divine faculty in the soul, desiring
The pure unbounded, perfect and eternal.
Out of the chaos of remembered things
It orders law, unknown almost to itself,
And, as it ponders what has been, to what
It wishes it to be the whole is raised.
And thus doth the soul imagine it once saw
Such paradises, for so fit are they,
So proper to it. Yes, the day was sweet
That crowned Time's rising, but far fairer that
Which dawns above the mountains in the soul,
And in its forefront, memory, the star
Of morning. Pleasant is the blossom culled
On life's tempestuous bank; – but find the roses
Of memory's high gardens, *they* are divine.

WILLIAM THOMAS (ISLWYN)

And life has times, minutes of heaven, when
The soul forsakes the present for a while
And searches the eternal places, for
The dear sweet things that were; when today's sun,
From all our noise and weariness, has set,
And the divine sobriety of Being,
Like an excelling night, on the free soul
Descends, and all God's ages are like stars
Eternal.

What is today? The soul claims
Eternity as really its today,
Day proper to it, divinely without hours.
Tomorrow? Yesterday? All that has ended.
In itself the soul has risen to the height
Where the everlasting sun is on the shore
And it is infinite day; whence every milestone
Along the road of man's unbounded life,
All measurement of being, is but part
Of the defilements of Time, a mere phantom
Divorced from the inseparable, a shadow
Of frail branches on the eternal flood.
Even the mountains of death upon its way
Are only an hour's postponement, or a moment's –
A brief glitter till the floods sweep it on
Into eternity; there, the chiming voice
Of the hours is lost, and with it a myriad
Of the discords of harsh time; there, no more
A shadow traces the hour on the cold dial.

JOHN CEIRIOG HUGHES
1832-87

A Bushel of Chaff

When I was a young lad, no pleasure was higher
Than whittling and chipping before my dad's fire,
While sister sat knitting and Mam evermore
Was spinning, was spinning upon the stone floor.
    Come what may come now,
    Man that I am now,
    Eagerly I'm flying
    On the wings of longing
      Back once more
  To the cosy, unassuming old homestead that I knew.

When I was a shepherd at Hafod y Rhyd
At hayfield and cornfield my sheep came to feed.
In shade of an oaktree by collie I'd lie
And dozing and drowsy how happy was I.
    Look as I may now,
    Where I may stray now,
    There are my affections
   With my recollection
      Of those fields
  Enjoying the meadows all summer's livelong day.

The swallow must wander from home in the eaves
But next Spring returns to the nest it now leaves;
And we too must wander, again and again
Remembering the old home that nurtured us then.
    Troubles are heavy,
    Bitter life's story –
    But let who'll be bitter,
   Sweet yet to remember
      My white home
  In the glow of inspiration that is smiling on me still.

JOHN CEIRIOG HUGHES

A Pothersome Pair

Once a sleepy wife there was
   In Llan Mathafarn dwelling:
Would not for her husband wake
   Though he was hoarse with yelling.
'Heigh ho,' she spake, laid like a pancake,
   And he cried in his sorrow,
'If you're not ill, rise with a will
   Or lie there till tomorrow.'

Ten o'clock, and kids let out
   A blaring row that second:
When she'd calmed them with a shout,
   Said she, but half-awakened,
'Illness or such, you don't know much!'
   But he said, 'Damn your scorning!
Yawning's the taint of your complaint
   And has been every morning!'

But the husband, all too soon,
   Contracted his wife's ailment:
Now the household sleeps till noon
   And all without curtailment.
Gander nor goose flies down from roost,
   Make breakfast or fire kindle,
And on my life, husband and wife
   In equal slumber mingle.

What Passes and Endures

Still do the great mountains stay,
   And the winds above them roar;
There is heard at break of day
   Songs of shepherds as before.
Daisies as before yet grow

Round the foot of hill and rock;
Over these old mountains, though,
A new shepherd drives his flock.

To the customs of old Wales
Changes come from year to year;
Every generation fails,
One has gone, the next is here.
After a lifetime tempest-tossed
Alun Mabon is no more,
But the language is not lost
And the old songs yet endure.

JOHN MORRIS-JONES
1864-1929

The Wind's Lament

Sooner tears than sleep this midnight
Come into my eyes.
On my window the complaining
Tempest groans and sighs.

Grows the noise now of its weeping,
Sobbing to and fro –
On the glass the tears come hurtling
Of some wildest woe.

Why, O wind against my window,
Come you grief to prove?
Can it be your heart's gone grieving
For its own lost love?

JOHN MORRIS-JONES

The North Star

There wanders many a lighted star
  That in the high vault burns,
And every star an orbit hath
  And in that orbit turns.

There's one white star, of all the rounds
  That wheel high overhead,
And it is hung on heaven's pole
  And will not rise nor bed.

So too with me: my firmament
  Its own white star reveals,
And every sphere my heaven holds
  Round her fixed axis wheels.

THOMAS GWYNN JONES
1871-1949

From *Arthur's Passing*

[The poem tells more or less the same story as Tennyson's *Morte D'Arthur*.
After Bedwyr has thrown Arthur's sword into the lake – reluctantly, for
what will protect his people now? – the boat full of noble maidens arrives
to take the wounded king to the island otherworld of Afallon.]

Then Bedwyr carried the Lord of the land,
Bravely he bore him over the stones;
And they minded over him, the noble maidens,
Their breasts, too, throbbed with the bruise of it.

Arms clearer than the cambric or brocade
To the gold chair were there to lift him;
White hands were attentive to the King,
They gave him wine to assuage his pain.

"Sooth, if you would," said Bedwyr, "to me
He has been so dear – I will not part from him!
Together we fought in battle – together
To go in the moment of death would be right."

Said one of those pure maidens:
"Arthur does not go to the grave.
Wise as he is, for your part, go,
Be a man, suffer the waiting!"

Bedwyr the while stood silent,
Watching, looking where they went.

He, in his anxiety
There, the message of Arthur
Heard: "Be brave, be impeccable!
Endure challenge, be cheerful!
I go to the summer world
Of Afallon, to recover.
But I'll come back to my land
Once more, bring her victorious
When her time is come, the day
She's honoured among nations
Though now she's wounded and sick,
Yet of her tale shall poets
In the chief tongues of the world
Speak, and great ones sing sweetly.
But every change, come what may,
Shall before long be over:
All our custom pass from mind
And our truth, too, forgotten;
Our land know treason, and foes
Make desolate her honour;
Ignoble the world, and worse,
Captivity long and vicious.
But from the pain of it, world
Shall shout again for gladness,

THOMAS GWYNN JONES

Shall come back, back for ever
To the holy Age of Youth.
When the Day at last cometh,
My bell sounds, I'll grip my sword,
And a second time bring honour
To our nation and our tongue."

The boat sailed. Bedwyr was left
In astonishment, yonder.

The fine sails were spread like slanted wings;
He heard from the shining rim of air
A dulcimer on the evening breeze, sweet waves
Striking its enchantment on every sense.

So gently it dropped, as small
Rain through the sunlight in May,
That Bedwyr was enchanted,
All his desire satisfied;
Kindly, a miracle of evening,
It was this praise filled the air:

"Over the waves there's a gracious country,
Nor in that land lingers lamentation;
Whoever comes there, no old age or pestilence
Strikes down, for the clean breeze of freedom
Keeps every heart of us nimble and merry,
As the Isle of Afallon itself is so.

"Old dreams are in that country of blessedness
That have eased the terror of countless ages;
All ancient hopes are alive for ever;
In that spot high purposes make progress;
No loss of faith comes there to scorch it,
Neither time of shame, nor breaking heart.

"There's fire in every singing inspiration!
Strength, confidence, relish to every endeavour!
Energy for those who'd change things the better,
And a basis always for wanting to hope!
We do not grow old while that protects us – right custom
It is, breath of life to the nation."

In the distance, as a sweet
Breathing, scarcely a whisper,
The voice ended: from the winding
Desolate lake, a grey mist spread:
Slowly it widened, slowly,
Till it fused the boat under it
And hid it. Into the mist
Like a phantom it vanished.

Bedwyr, sadly, silently,
To the battle turned again.

Argoed

I

Argoed, Argoed of the secret places...
Your hills, your sunken glades, where were they,
Your winding glooms and quiet towns?

Ah, quiet then, till doom was dealt you,
But after it, nothing save a black desert
Of ashes was seen of wide-wooded Argoed.

Argoed, wide-wooded... Though you have vanished,
Yet from the unremembering depths, for a moment,
Is it there, your whispering ghost, when we listen –

THOMAS GWYNN JONES

Listen in silence to the wordless speech
Where the wave of yearning clings to your name,
Argoed, Argoed of the secret places?

2

Away in Gaul, 'mid its splendour and famed
Riches, were the secret solitudes of Argoed;
There, there was inspiration and adventure,
And words, for truth's sake, chosen by the wise;
The heart of her people kept faith; richness
Of her history never lapsed to oblivion,
And sweet there and pure the old tongue continued
And custom as old as her earliest dawn.

Mystery, in that place, kept its repose
Under sleep lingering in her dark shades;
Her oaks and maples, the silent might of ages,
Sunlight, and warmth, and the crystal rain,
World-wonder, the wheel, the miracle of seasons,
Labouring green through innumerable veins;
Old history feeling its way out of them
(As it were) in perfumes and great mounds of colour
And many a murmur, till, being fused,
They became soul and quick of every inspiration,
A force, momentum of dreams half-remembered,
That to the thought of a poet gives form
When tumultuous senses have for long lodged it.

When Winter had fled the country of Gaul
And it was Spring there, come once more,
In the quiet, mysterious forests of Argoed
The old, irresistible miracle quickened;
Under the beating of its wing, slowly,
The countryside over, opened the eyes
Of buds innumerable: life broke forth

THOMAS GWYNN JONES

In a flood of colour, diversity of kinds,
Till the vigour of it raced in the blood of the beasts
And it rolled like fire through the hearts of men;
Which new vigour and virtue of Nature,
Despite bias of lethargy, grew in strength,
Withering, growing old, and yet renewing –
That inextinguishable flame that was given
To conquer anguish and the power of death.

Yet lovely also was Argoed when, over the trees,
Spread all the magic of autumnal pomp,
Colours innumerable, and sleepy hours,
Hours rounded in unruffled plenty,
Hours untroubled, as if the berries were ripe
On Time's branches, and the splendours of it,
Its sleep, its peace, had all been pressed into them
As the Summer gives to the juicy fruit of the vine
Its virtue and sparkle, and reckless power.
There, in the midst of her knotted oaks
And privet, was a stretch of open ground,
And webs of bright gossamer with dew upon it
Whether in Summer or Springtime, or Winter,
And under the dawn the uncountable dew
Was as if each drop were an opening eye
That glinted an instant, presently closing
As the yellow-gold sunlight rose before it
Like seaspray that dies even as it splashes,
Or sparks of a smithy, fading as they fly;
And on that open ground, a town at the wood's end,
Time out of mind the Children of Arofan
Had sustained their state purely, and never forsaken
The life of blessedness their fathers had known –
Hunting or herding, as there was need of it,
Living and suffering, as life required them,
Fearing no weakness, craving no luxuries,
Nor sought to oppress, nor feared the oppressor;

THOMAS GWYNN JONES

In such tranquillity, generation to generation,
They raised strong sons and lovely daughters;
Recited their tales of courage of old times,
Attentive to hear, to know the true sentence
Of words of wisdom of men that were good men
And all the mysteries hidden in musecraft;
They listened to the secret learning of Druids,
Men with the gods themselves acquainted,
Who kept in the mind, generation to generation,
A wisdom of wonder-lore, not proper to be graved
On stone or wood, or preserved in writing.

Oh then, how joyous were the days
In the quiet, mysterious forests of Argoed!
But she, in her ancient piety, knew not
Gaul was pulled down, under heel of her enemies,
And already the fame of her cities had dwindled
With coming of trickery, foreigner's ways,
To tame her energy, waste an old language
And custom as old as her earliest dawn.

Argoed, Argoed of the secret places...
Oh then, was not a poet born in that land,
One inspired to sing her old glory,
Turning the tales of courage of old times,
Words of wisdom of men that were good men,
And all the custom hidden in musecraft,
To fit a new song, whence glory grew
Of his country and its past, and praise of its language?

And Argoed was proud that her poet was gone
To the courts of Gaul and seats of her splendour,
Reciting there of the might and valour
And manners of men, heroes of old times,
Glory and legendary past of his nation
And the gods themselves walking the world.

Argoed, Argoed, of the secret places,
How great would be the day of his homecoming
Back to them, bearing his fill
Of the gifts and honour that rightly rewarded
The new song he had fashioned his nation
In the quiet, mysterious forests of Argoed,
Argoed, Argoed of the secret places!

3

One night, from a court of Alesia city –
A citadel that, in the day of her might,
Had held back the pomp of Roman soldiers
Nor stooped to cherish the yoke of her enemies –
One night, from this court of Alesia city,
From the good cheer of the feasting within,
From the unthinking crowd's dull tumult,
Women half-naked and daintified boys
Of that famed city, that danced therein,
Their flesh and their smiles passionate with wine,
From that tight throng and its wantoning friendship
And many an eye wandering ardent in lust,
Into the air of the night, cold and dark,
A man stepped forth; he was nearing the wall,
His features weary, as if with the knowledge
He was disgraced there, instead of honoured.

In grievous pain he stood for a moment
With a weariness on him like despair,
For in his heart that night he knew
His nation's valour and ancient glory
Was lost for ever, gone from the world –
He, that had sung the chief of that glory,
Turning the tales of courage of old times,
Words of wisdom of men that were good men,
And all the custom hidden in musecraft,
To fit a new song, whence glory grew

Of his country and its past, and praise of its language –
And now, as last, vain was the labour,
For Gaul was pulled down under heel of her enemies
With coming of trickery, foreigner's ways,
To tame her vigour, waste an old language
And custom as old as her earliest dawn;
Now they could grasp neither metre nor meaning,
Nor would his singing earn him ought better
Than the sneer of a slave, awkwardly mocking him
In a patois malformed from wretched Latin –
Ah now, at last, how vain was his labour!
Slaves must be slaves, then? Ay, he that sells
Of his birthright, his be the shame of it...
And yet, despite that, in Argoed also
Would there be heard this broken-down Latin
On the lips of slaves, defiled and unworthy?
A generation come there not comprehending
The words of wisdom of men that were good men?
An end in that place of talent and nobleness
And all clean living, oppressed by her enemies?
This jabbering to oust a dignified language,
And vile dishonour, where men had been brave?

Then did the bright fire light in his eyes,
The blood in him boiled as that servile laughter
Again burst from within. He listened, head bent,
For a moment stayed hesitant. Then,
Like a man that can finally see before him
The day of his hopes ended for ever,
With a kind of sob, a catch in his breath,
Did he laugh also, striding on his journey,
His path soon hidden in the cold, wet gloom.

4

And tribute from Argoed was decreed, three times,
And then, three times, Argoed refused it,

For never had Argoed at all given honour
To a foreign might or brutal oppression;
The heart of her people kept faith; richness
Of her history had not lapsed to oblivion;
And none but the vilest among them would suffer
An enemy's yoke without wincing in shame,
Or bear, without blushing, its naked disgrace.

'We'll not give tribute, let forests be fired first,
Let the last of the Children of Arofan die,
Nor mock our past, nor forswear an old language,
Nor custom as old as our earliest dawn!'
To the bounds of Argoed quickly the word went,
Each of her citizens was constant and sure;
The doom was pronounced, without one to cross it,
The course was ventured, no man flinched from it;
For all his trickery, no foreigner had tribute,
Chattel nor booty, nor man to be beaten;
Nothing was found there, or only a wasteland,
Desolation of ashes, where once were wild woods.

5

Argoed, Argoed of the secret places,
Your hills, your sunken glades, where were they,
Your winding glooms and quiet towns?

Ah, quiet then, till doom was dealt you,
But after it, nothing save a black desert
Of ashes was seen of wide-wooded Argoed.

Argoed, wide-wooded... Though you have vanished,
Yet from the unremembering depths, for a moment,
Are you there, unconquerable soul, when we listen –

Listen in silence to the wordless speech
Where the wave of yearning clings to your name,
Argoed, Argoed of the secret places?

WILLIAM CRWYS WILLIAMS
b.1875-1968

Gathering Leaves

All night autumn winds were howling,
Rattling in our eaves,
So this morning an old man comes
Sweeping leaves.

Over his brush stooping and weary,
His faint footsteps pace
Like a dead leaf to a dead leaf
Giving chase.

One heap done: he pauses a moment
And his force retrieves;
The next Fall, though, he'll be surely
One with the leaves.

ISAAC DANIEL HOOSON
1880-1948

The Flame

A red caravan, a greyhound bitch,
A lame mare sheltering under a hedge,
A girl dancing to a tune debonair,
As her sweetheart's fiddle glints to the fire.

Up and up the white flames float
Like an arm about a black cauldron's throat;
A tall gipsy seals a lover's oath,
On honey lips pledges troth.

And the moon climbs above the hill –
Like her, the fire's now dead and chill;
Flame's every gust and passion's fire,
In their turn, to ash expire.

WILLIAM JOHN GRUFFYDD
1881-1954

This Poor Man

Because there was disquiet in the wind
    And sound of old griefs in the beating rain,
Sad echo of erstwhile afflicted rhymes
    Turning their tunes unceasing through his soul;
Because the far sea's roar on a quiet night
    Related virtue of the lost generations,
        And because trilling streams
    Awoke the entire anguish of their passion –
Like one mute he went to a phantom silence,
    And one by one all his companions fled,
Leaving him rapt in his mysterious secret,
    To the strange voices listening alone.

Where his companions had invoked God's anger
    On an unclean world, he saw its beauty,
Refused their path to heaven, took instead
    The insubstantial echo of magic pipes,
The murmuring bees of Arawn from the vineyards
    Heavy with honeydew from down the vale,
        The nectar of hidden dwellings,
    Caer Siddi's gold enclosure on the hill.
Before he died, banquets were his to sit at,
    He listened entranced to the unseen choir –
The birds of Rhiannon in the porches of pearl
    That open on the old forgetful sea.

ROBERT WILLIAMS PARRY
1884-1956

The Fox

A furlong from the crest, when the bells' cry
Of hillbreast churches called us villageward,
And the sun, bright and unsetting in July,
Invited to the summits – suddenly stood
By step unwitting and delicate mute tread
A rare wonder before us, a red fox.
We did not move, even our breath stopped dead,
Paralysed utterly. Like three cold rocks

We stood. Then, at a careless crest of his stride,
He too froze dead, stunned for a moment there.
Above his poised foot, two flames, unflickering wide,
Gleamed of his eyes. Then, without haste or fear,
His dry red pelt slipped over the rock scar,
And was; and was not – like some shooting star.

The Geese

December through the high
Trees made a wretched cry
   Like waves breaking.

Below in a bit of field,
Heedless their fate was sealed,
   Geese were grazing.

Leaves were a feather-stack,
Blood-colour, pied and black
   On the green ground.

I explained to the daft geese
This moral of the trees –
   Death's sight and sound.

"Therefore, do not stay!
Fly on wide wings away
    Before, hark it,

The Goodwife takes her cheese,
Her butter and her geese
    To the Great Market!"

But fie on such falsehood!
Geese waddle under the wood
    In scornful order,

Unanimous in each
Frivolous and jeering screech
    Over and over.

The Strangeness of Dawn

Strange to reach Paradise without crossing Jordan,
    In a moment, all unwarned, to step into lovely day –
Hear the cuckoo's mountain voice in the trees of the garden,
    See the pigeon to the ash grove slip on her way;
Strange to meet a hedgehog across the peacock's lawn,
    And find rabbits nibbling the breadth of a field from their
        tunnels,
The carefree young hare in mid-meadow, without shelter or form,
    The incredible heron stark in the estuary channels.

Yet stranger still, O sun on the otherside slope,
    Did you stay where you were, and man in his houses impound,
And lest timely smoke rise again from his chimneys, stop
    Till the crowbars of grass topple them to ground –
Man rid of his woe, and earth of his respect and savour,
Ere steeds be in harness again, and skies travelled over.

ROBERT WILLIAMS PARRY

The Propaganda of the Poet

To green Nature, not the world, the poet belongs;
    He has no truck with it: to make his mark
Does not climb pulpits singing fashionable songs
    Nor stands his box in the grass of Hothead Park.
Wasn't he born of a hag inhuman and unreclaimed
    Whose show of stars and sunset pomps amaze
Till the sick heart melts, till the healthy are tamed,
    Though she's not herself concerned in our shrunk days –

Save when her thunder's loose, and the word's there
    That frightens from our fatal weaving the matter-of-fact,
Brings ghost to feast and phantom to the fair,
    And shows the worm in the wood, and the creation cracked:
Thunder that drives brave men to mosque and mascot,
Cloudbursts extinguishing sun on the roads to Ascot.

The Old Boatman

There were assembled, so the papers say,
    Seven and four score motorcars in conclave
To the solemn task, the day before yesterday,
    Of running someone dead towards his grave.
Though flashy's the paint on each fat, pampered cur,
    Yet at the funerals hereabouts, their guise
And conduct are as prim as if they were
    In God's Eisteddfod trying for a prize.

And when the body tires of the ferry road
    And the spirit its appointed end must meet,
Can we not quicker lay our brother's load
    In these luxurious vans than on two feet?
But on the flood that's shrouded from our dust,
Though boats be old and slow, Charon's not fussed.

ROBERT WILLIAMS PARRY

A Wish

Strange to be seeing waves of the sea
   Like dogs snarling around
Tooth to tooth with the rock, yet we
   Never to hear a sound,
But seeing them, as might
A deaf man's sharp sight.

And strange to listen at night for the cry
   Of some invisible host
When there may be wild geese in the sky
   Across the sounding coast,
And to listen them, the way
The blind listen the day.

If life would give me choice of a skill
   To practise till the grave,
I'd choose to know how to reap my fill
   Of two fields joyous and brave –
Glean them for all they find,
The wise deaf, and the blind.

T.H. PARRY-WILLIAMS
1887-1975

The East Wind

Winds are necessary. Times wouldn't be there
Without you had winds coming from somewhere.

It's they that turn with their round thrust
The wheel of the world and this living dust.

Transparent and colourless all of them toss
Save only the East Wind, the breath of loss.

T.H. PARRY-WILLIAMS

When those bright ones leave the welkin's crown
He comes with his red blackness down,

Flooring mortals that way and this
To show humanity what wind is.

From a Travel Diary

1. On Deck

A nun went past, and her girdle swung,
And I saw on the cross her Christ was hung –

A metal Christ on her rosary,
In anguish hanging on Calvary;

And like us all, the sea's Creator swayed
To an ocean swell Himself had made.

The Atlantic, Sunday, July 1925

2. Death in the Channel

Tonight an old man, around seven o'clock,
Found journey's end before reaching dock.

A service, a prayer, a splash as he sank,
And where he had lain, an empty plank.

The Ushant lighthouse flashed on the right
And the Evening Star to west of the night,

And between them the old man went to his Lord,
Wrapped in sackcloth, overboard.

The Channel, September 1925

T.H. PARRY-WILLIAMS

*Llyn y Gadair**

The jaunty traveller that comes to peer
Across its shallows to the scene beyond
Would almost not see it. Mountains here
Have far more beauty than this bit of pond
With one man fishing in a lonely boat
Whipping the water, rowing now and then
Like a poor errant wretch, condemned to float
The floods of nightmare never reaching land.

But there's some sorcerer's bedevilling art
That makes me see a heaven in its face,
Though glory in that aspect has no part
Nor on its shore is any excelling grace –
Nothing but peat bog, dead stumps brittle and brown,
Two crags, and a pair of quarries, both closed down.

SAUNDERS LEWIS
1893-1985

The Deluge, 1939

I

From Merthyr to Dowlais the tramway climbs,
A slug's slime-trail over the slag heaps.
What's nowadays a desert of cinemas,
Rain over disused tips, this once was Wales.
Pawnshops have closed their doors. Clerks
Of the labour exchange are the chiefs of this prairie.
All flesh has tainted its way on the face of the earth.

The same taint's in me, as I second proposals
In committee after committee, to bring the old land to life.
I'd maybe be better employed on a Tonypandy corner

*A lake near Rhyd-ddu

And my eyes meditating up the valley and down
On the human wreckage adrift in the mire of despond,
One function common to man and the standing slag.

Eyes have been changed to dust, we know not our death,
Were buried by our mothers, had Lethe milk to drink.
We cannot bleed, no, not as former men bled,
Our hands would resemble a hand, if they'd thumbs to go on
them.
If a fall shatters our feet, all we do is grovel to a clinic,
Touch our caps to a wooden leg, Mond pension and insurance:
Knowing neither language nor dialect, feeling no insult,
We gave our masterpiece to history in our country's M.P.s.

2

From empty docks the scourings rose
Over dry ropes and the rusted cranes.
Greasily civilized was the flood
Of the proletariat creeping to chipshops.
It crept like blood round policemen's feet.
The spittle of its silicosis spread like a lake
Through faceless valleys of the industry of the dole.

The rain poured down its diligent needles
On the soft palms of old colliery hands.
Hailstones spurted onto the leathern breasts
Of dry mothers and their wrinkled babies.
Even where girls' legs twisted with rickets,
They turned cow's milk into sticks of umbrellas.
They gave an old man's pension to the lads of the dole.

And still the moon was keeping her orbit;
Apollo still washed his hair in the dew
As he did when the wise counted their seasons
Centuries back, in the Sabine hills.
But Saturn and Jove, and the golden age of the Babe,

In their turn, are ended. Sorry destruction,
Ash in the chimneys and the pointless birth
Drown out the stars under the slime of the dole.

3

In the beginning, we did not see it like this:
We thought it was only the redeeming ebb and flow, the thrifty
    unsettling
That our masters blessed as part of the economic law,
The new scientific order, that threw over natural law
As Jove supplanted Saturn, in the undulating progress of being.

And we believed in our masters: we put on them priestly vestments,
Had them preach in plus-fours and tortoise-shell spectacles,
Preach the sanctity of the surplus of unemployed and the flexible
    providence of prices;
And one day in seven, not to break with a courteous custom,
We'd offer an hour to the pretty witchcraft of antiquity
And sing a psalm in the old Pantheons of our fathers.

Then, on Olympus, in Wall Street, Nineteen Hundred and
    Twenty-Nine,
At their infinitely scientific task of steering the profits of fortune,
The gods decided, with their feet in the Aubusson carpet
And their Hebrew nostrils in the quarterly statistics,
That the day had come to restrict credit over the cosmos of gold.

They did not know, these latter-day gods of earth,
That the world's last floodgates they'd thrown open;
They did not visualize the marching of men,
The fists closed, and the raised blustering arms,
Through the agonies of Vienna rank on rank,
Or the deaf fury raving in Munich,
Nor the dragging steps of the unemployed,
Those tortured somnambulists, twittering in processions.

But it came about, though, the mothers wailing,
The noise of men like a whimpering of dogs,
A myriad myriad, without hope, self-thrown
To the starless ditch, the anonymous quiet.
Here failed the wisdom of the governors of nations,
Dragon's teeth sown over Europe's acres;
And Bruening went out, from their seething rages,
From Basle's derision, foul with usurers,
Husks and dead shells of the hosts at Geneva,
Went to his long, mute fast and his exile.
And the fragile mob, the halfpenny populace,
Children of the dogs and the footballpool,
Surfeitedtheir bellies with lascivious pictures,
Chaff and dust of radio and press.

But the sky grew black over the districts of Ebro,
Blood became wine in the hunger of our passions,
And paralysis froze the defective will
Of the impotent rascals of Basle and Geneva.
We saw we were cheated. The fiendish disillusion
Festering our end, was the work of our gods:
Thrown down and raped was our peerless idol,
Reason's masterpiece, a man without fetters;
The planet-masters' magnificent creed,
Man's faith in man – that was extinguished:
We, poker-faced giants, measurers
        Of suns and of stars –
        Vain was that journey,
        Empty all laughter –
The deluge of hopelessness is our black haven.

And over the waves comes the sound of tanks gathering.

SAUNDERS LEWIS

Awdl

to his Grace, the Archbishop of Cardiff

The song that was sung for Non and Sant's son,*
    You – kind, witty father
In scorn's night, in fraud's season
Spitting at hurt of its Pope –

Do not hear. Our own Dewi! Woe for grace,
    For Welsh of Christ's poets!
Pangs of irreligion's war
Make sore the crown of Cardiff.

Day of odes of the Faith has fled. Teilo's land
    Reveres no archbishop.
God in the bread, well, heigh-ho!
After Freud and mass media

Who needs the Mass of the Lord? We're only
    Brute cinemals, trooping
Film to film, till in a trice
The frivolity ceases

There, in the city, in the kindly night –
    The Catholic family
As at a fair, hushed by the jerk
Of a bell, a strong man's summons.
Soul from that awesome sharing-out,
From illusion's vale awakens
Naked, latterwise, from the great defilement
    To a tomorrowless hour

Where the keen silence clings to the secret
    Torn Calvaries of Wales
And sweet power mindfully offers

*i.e. Dewi Sant – St David

A mediation made once and always.
There'll be worth in your sacrifice
At church, in the cup of Jesus,
One only intercession – Christ on high,
    And down here, under heaven.

Altar and door, it's you that give them, and
    Goodness bring to Cymru.
Clap, slam, trample at stoptap, buzz
Of waltz-noises, scold, fret and roar...
Under it all, heaven's treasure you bring,
Lamb of God unto his dwelling,
Patrick's breastplate to protect an old church
    And Mary's gift, to cleanse it.

Ascension Thursday

What's going on in the hills, this May morning?
Look at it all, the gold of the broom and laburnum,
The shoulders of the thorntree bright with its surplice,
The ready emerald of grass, the quiet calves;

The chestnut-trees have their candlesticks alight,
Hedgerows are kneeling, the birch is still as a nun,
The cuckoo's two notes over the hush of bright streams
And a ghost mist bending away from the meads' censer:

Before the rabbits scatter, O man, come forth
From your council houses, come and with the weasel
See the earth lift up an immaculate wafer
And the Father kiss the Son in the white dew.

DAVID GWENALLT JONES

1899-1968

Dartmoor

Once again looking between iron bars,
Hearing doors, double-locked, clang through the gaol,
And the strangely inept mutter of prisoners
As they sow, and reap, and lift the flail –
We see how August downs the heavy sun
Like blood of murder, in each ditch and mere;
How criminal, warped fogs are by November sown
Like a prison for the prison on the moor.

And the fiends and hobgoblins come crying at night,
In the rough marsh their chilly conventicle try;
From some valley or dip, ghost screams and sprite,
The guilt of ages that has failed to die;
And Tywi's blue thread, like old beatitudes, drawn
Winding through husbandry of hay and corn.

The Dead

With his fiftieth birthday behind him, a man sees with fair clarity
    The people and surroundings that made him what he is,
And the steel ropes that tether me strongest to these things
    In a village of the South, are the graves in two cemeteries.

I'd ride a bike pilfered from scrap, or with a pig's bladder
    Play rugby for Wales; and all that while,
Little thought I'd hear how two of my contemporaries
    Would spew into a bucket their lungs red and vile.

Our neighbours they were, a family from Merthyr Tydfil,
    The 'martyrs' we called them, by way of a pun,
And five of them by turns had a cough that crossed the fences
    To break up our chatter and darken all our fun.

DAVID GWENALLT JONES

We crept in the Bibled parlours, and peeped with awe
    At cinders of flesh in the coffin, and ashes of song,
And there we learnt, over lids screwed down before their time,
    Collects of red revolt and litanies of wrong.

Not the death that goes his natural rounds, like a gaol warder,
    Giving notice in the clink of his damp keys,
But the leopard of industry leaping sudden and sly
    That strikes from fire and water men to their knees.

The hootering death: the dusty, smokeful, drunken death,
    Death whose dreadful grey destiny was ours;
Explosion and flood changed us often into savages
    Fighting catastrophic and devilish powers.

Mute and brave women with a fistful of bloodmoney,
    With a bucketful of death, forever the rankling of loss,
Carrying coal, chopping wood for a fire, or setting the garden,
    And more and more reading the Passion of the Cross.

This Sunday of Flowers, as we place on their graves a bunch
    Of silicotic roses and lilies pale as gas,
Between the premature stones and the curb yet unripened,
    We gather the old blasphemings, curses of funerals past.

Our Utopia vanished from the top of Gellionnen,
    Our abstract humanity's classless, defrontiered reign,
And today nothing is left at the deep root of the mind
    Save family and neighbourhood, man's sacrifice and pain.

The Depression

    Above our cupped world no tall stack opens
        Its smoky umbrella handled with flame;
        Neither crane's running din nor screech of the hooters

Comes between us and the slow heights about us;
    The stars have all been scrubbed of stain.

No fog sinks down on the gardens near-by;
    On man's new Egypt, where locusts have been,
Ventures the green grass, the weed grows thick,
And the gipsy sheep more rarely come down to lick
    Buckets of tins of salmon and sardine.

Once more foam whitens on river and brook,
    And clears the scum from the speckled stone;
Easier to find are trout, in the oily waters shaping,
And eels to the edge of the stream are escaping
    The vitriol stink to tuck themselves home.

It is not heard, the morning alarum of feet,
    And, of an afternoon, round eyes laugh no more;
A stranger now, the little something in the pantry;
In each home the fare on the board's but scanty,
    The paint's grown shabby on windows and door.

Idleness a sour dog on every street corner,
    Workers tramp shadowless from place to place;
There has come to the town's Eldorado this finish:
Neighbourhood scuttled, and break-up of village,
    Roots of the South, a culture, a civilized grace.

Oberammergau

It was a privilege, my going to Bavaria, a pilgrim,
To see staged their Passion:
Under the Zugspitze and Köpfel,
Rambling by rail the way back to the mediaeval,
To the midst of a mountain and woodland people,
Craft-loving, Catholic folk –
For in that land there were no industrial resources

DAVID GWENALLT JONES

That an ass-eared Mammon might dig up
So establishing the modern culture of banks
On coaltips, scrapheaps and hovels.
Here there were forests and family farms,
And country crafts with centuries-old tradition behind them
And that tradition flexible, to meet every demand.
Incomparable clocks and knick-knacks they fashioned,
And at Mitwald violins famous the world over;
Our Lord's story they picture in wood, brass, cloth, bowls, soap,
And carve Calvary from a nut.

How could Catholics so guileless
Nurse enough hate for their drama to crucify him?
Over the border the Marxist Pharisees
Have the fervent brutality to flay him and hang him up;
Americans amongst them
Could act business men in the Temple exactly;
A Yank playing Judas
Had driven a harder deal with the High Priests:
But not in all Moscow or Wall Street
Could you find a Christ, Virgin Mary, Mary Magdalen or the
    Apostles.

"When will the next war come?"
The natives were asking –
War between Marx's barbarism and Mammon's.
If it should come, and atom bombs and rockets
Mow down every hairy top, and smash the Cross
On the peak of the Zugspitze and Köpfel;
The images of Mary and Child in the caves
And the screens on the side of streets;
Pictures of Nativity and Last Supper in the shops,
And the fountain of Christ in the village square:

Then they'd come, angels from Heaven,
To plant the Cross on top of the ruins
And set images of Mary in holes of the rubble

And Saints and Apostles in odd corners of debris;
And at the end of ten years, they'd clear a flat space
To act the Drama of His Passion on Calvary
In the midst of the Bavarian desert.

F.R. *Könecamp*

One has to die a martyr these days, to be an artist –
Live like a monk, or at least half a saint!
To Pembroke he came, to Pwll Gwaelod of all places,
With his high carelessness, wretched brushes, brave flashes of
     paint.

He didn't stoop to do dead portraits of worthies
Neither followed shibboleths dear to the academy,
But he lived in a zinc hut and held in his pictures
The unquiet, the miracle of the sun on earth and sea.

I watched his brush dance, the joy and the energy,
Every sinew and joint at work, a live spirit of a face;
With a monk's diligence, the knack of a mathematician,
In the depths of line and colour he set symbols in place.

Always his trees grow mighty with primal strength;
Intellectual swim his fish; birds sing in geometric motion;
His storms rush round in whorls of equi-weighted rages;
Over his canvas flood waves of the abstract ocean.

One picture he did, atomic energy as the heart of Nature,
Heart of world's fruitfulness, world's tragic woe;
Another one, Western Europe's saints and artists –
How like intercessions they swim – round an El Greco Christ how
     they flow!

Then he drew prisons – two rows of crooked doors
Meshed with barbed wire for a crown ply on ply;

And nothing they did, the petty-cash boys, the mini-politicians,
But stare at a banana moon in the vacancy of the sky.

His master is El Greco – artist of yellow holiness,
Painter drunk on Gethsemane, on nail, on thorn,
Of the twisted Christs and the attenuated martyrs
With their spirit like Toledo blades through the sheath torn.

He curses, remembering his fellow-artists over in Russia –
Monstrous as Nebuchadnezzar's the captivity they are in;
The totalitarian bear chaining the great light of the Steppes,
Withering brush and paint, murdering the freedom of the wind.

And what about Wales? – Yes, a country where the light's always
    changing
But eyes are dead, and religion's the ugliest there is;
Though your artists go prostituting their talents up in London,
On the doorstep there's art, a literature all images.

And your own country? – Yes, my Germany, skeleton of
    Germany,
The *Volksland*, metaphysical country, bravest under the sky;
The artists are painting the ribs and the bones of her
Because art's a necessity, like the flash of God's eye.

Rhydcymerau

Near Rhydcymerau,
On the land of Esgeir-ceir and the fields of Tir-bach,
They have planted the saplings
       to be trees of the third war.

I call to mind my grandmother at Esgeir-ceir
As she sat, pleating her apron, by the fireside,
The skin yellow and dry on her face
       like a manuscript of Peniarth,

And the Welsh on her old lips the Welsh of Pantycelyn.
A bit of the Puritan Wales she was of last century.
Although I never saw him, my grandfather
Was a 'character' – a brisk and twinkling little creature,
Fond of his pint;
He'd just strayed in from the eighteenth century.
They reared nine children,
Poets, deacons, and Sunday School teachers,
And each, locally, a man of authority.

My Uncle Dafydd used to farm Tir-bach,
And was, besides, a poet, the countryside's rhymester;
His song to the little cockerel was famous in those parts:
>   '*The little cock goes scratching*
>   *In the garden here and there.*'
It was to him I went for the summer holidays
To watch the sheep and fashion lines of *cynghanedd*,
Englynion, and eight-line stanzas
            of eight-seven measure.
He brought up eight children,
The eldest son a minister with the Calvinistic Methodists,
And he too wrote verses.
In our family we'd a real nestful of poets.

And by this time there's nothing there but trees.
Impertinent roots suck dry the old soil:
Trees where neighbourhood was,
And a forest that once was farmland.
Where was verse-writing and scripture
            is the South's bastardized English.
The fox barks where once cried lambs and children,
And there, in the dark midst,
Is the den of the English minotaur;
And on the trees, as if on crosses,
The bones of poets, deacons, ministers, and teachers of
            Sunday School
Bleach in the sun,
And the rain washes them, and the winds lick them dry.

EUROS BOWEN
b. 1904

The Swan

Today the art of our retreat
Is to see portents and mystery –
To see colour and sinew, the flash of white
As the bare hills of the age are visited from heaven:
His solitude swims in the quiet of the water,
A pilgrim acquainted with sedges,
And he washes the weather of the lake with his form
That (as it were) spotlights the passion
Of a soul's breath
At it goes its slow, bare way in the chill of March:
His neck became a vigil,
The immaculate arm of a hunter,
The poise there, the stance of his eye! –
And the flame of his beak plummeted down to the pool:
The mountains looked disquieted
As he resumed his glide, easing himself to the flood:
A shiver ran through his wings, then stopped,
And on a sharp beat he broke from the water:
Slowly he went, then up to the high air,
And the fire of his wings draws a soul from its cold.

Glint

This was no image that held me
With compelled response.

I saw no sorcery in the shape,
The pure of feature; this was no idol

But flesh and blood, mouth and hair,
Breasts, thighs – the stuff of clay

And feeble blood,
The lineage of the grass, the stirring corn,

All whose desire went
Quietly to earth,

Like seaweed in the drunken wave,
Like clouds in light.

– To see her, a luxury; a leaven
Everlastingly young, the glint of her.

WALDO WILLIAMS
1904-1971

The Moment

All mention of the Moment
Scholars must do without.
River suspends its flowing
And rock cries out
Witness to what
Our two eyes have no sight for
And our ears hear not.

Breeze among the breezes,
Sun from beyond the sun,
Truly our homeland's wonder
On earth is come
With inviolate power –
And we know by the Moment's coming
We are born for the Hour.

WALDO WILLIAMS

*In Two Fields**

Where did the sea of light roll from
Onto Flower Meadow Field and Flower Field?
After I'd searched for long in the dark land,
The one that was always, whence did he come?
Who, oh who was the marksman, the sudden enlightener?
The roller of the sea was the field's living hunter.
From above bright-billed whistlers, prudent scurry of lapwings,
The great quiet he brought me.

Excitement he gave me, where only
The sun's thought stirred to lyrics of warmth,
Crackle of gorse that was ripe on escarpments,
Hosting of rushes in their dream of blue sky.
When the imagination wakens, who calls
Rise up and walk, dance, look at the world?
Who is it hiding in the midst of the words
That were there on Flower Meadow Field and Flower Field?

And when the big clouds, the fugitive pilgrims,
Were red with the sunset of stormy November,
Down where the ashtrees and maples divided the fields,
The song of the wind was deep like deep silence.
Who, in the midst of the pomp, the super-abundance,
Stands there inviting, containing it all?
Each witness' witness, each memory's memory, life of each life,
Quiet calmer of the troubled self.

Till at last the whole world came into the stillness
And on the two fields his people walked,
And through, and between, and about them, goodwill widened
And rose out of hiding, to make them all one,
As when the few of us forrayed with pitchforks
Or from heavy meadows lugged thatching of rush,

Weun Parc y Blawd and *Parc y Blawd* – two fields in Pembrokeshire.

– 289 –

How close we came then, one to another –
The quiet huntsman so cast his net round us!

Ages of the blood on the grass and the light of grief,
Who whistled through them? Who heard but the heart?
The cheater of pride, and every trail's tracker,
Escaper from the armies, hey, there's his whistling –
Knowledge of us, knowledge, till at last we do know him!
Great was the leaping of hearts, after their ice age.
The fountains burst up towards heaven, till,
Falling back, their tears were like leaves of a tree.

Day broods on all this beneath sun and cloud,
And Night through the cells of her wide-branching brain –
How quiet they are, and she breathing freely
Over Flower Meadow Field and Flower Field –
Keeps a grip on their object, the fields full of folk.
Surely these things must come. What hour will it be
That the outlaw comes, the hunter, the claimant to the breach,
That the Exiled King cometh, and the rushes part in his way?

The Catholic Martyrs

(After the mute centuries)

I knot their praises, for long centuries mute.
The core of all faith is one, it is splendid to meet
With souls one with the quick at Being's root.

Over my head they are there, they are one with the light
Where through the expanse peace gathers. When night
Veils the sky, each is a shining gap to my sight.

John Roberts of Trawsfynydd, priest to the needy,
In the dread plague shared out the bread of the journey,
Knowing the powers of the dark had come, and would break his
     body.

WALDO WILLIAMS

John Owen the joiner, that many a servant concealed,
For the old communion his hand an unwearying shield,
Lest the plait be unravelled, and the beams of the great house
    yield.

Richard Gwyn smiled in their face at what they were at:
'I have sixpence towards your fine' – for he'd not
In the cause of his Master, price his life more than that.

They that ran light, I cannot reckon them all,
A company gathered together beyond the pits of hell:
Surely nothing can scatter them who paid the selfsame toll.

The last, quiet payment. World for world giving then,
For the Spirit to guide them giving that ultimate pain,
Giving a flower for his root, for his cradle a grain.

Torture did rack them, disembowelling rend,
Ere the sight where a ladder was given their souls to ascend
To the broad next morning of Golgotha, their blest Lord's world
    without end.

Welshmen, were you a nation, great would be the glory
These would have in your story.

ALUN LLYWELYN-WILLIAMS
b.1913

Star of Bethlehem

This was a star stood still;
   but it is the rule on high
that to live is never to rest,
   and to stand still is to die.

And how of this rebirth
   should a dead thing glitter aright?

ALUN LLYWELYN-WILLIAMS

Both poet and scientist probe
   into round creation's night,

and our wise men cast for a marvel
   nebulae that career,
at a gallop over being's horizon,
   and for dread void, leave here

all this negligible world.
   Even as their orbits last,
what lustre we see is old
   from an inconceivable past –

like a dawn of long-dead suns,
   like a memory that has been,
whose yesterday's ever changing
   to the now that'll yet be seen.

Though in the whirligig's hub,
   still stings mortality's mark:
when the stars are scattered and lost,
   and lonely our world, and dark,

and the balance shall hang empty,
   and time be all dispersed –
yet then, in the quiet, the creating
   spirit again will be nursed;

and this was a star that stood still.
   From an unhorizoned clime
the light of its quiet came
   that is no slave of time.

BOBI JONES

b.1929

To the Poetry Clubs of Wales

I often from America think of Clwb Gwerin Cefni,
The class at Talgarreg or the Bro Dyfi poets.
They are the impossible! It's daft, these days, to imagine
A people without freedom can preserve its heartwood...
But often, through a Quebec winter, seeing by morning how the
    frost
Grew up within the trees, reached the branches and ripened
A few white apples overnight – white, white are these nights. –
I cannot help thinking how craft and principle were handled
Into the small hours, in fruitful village halls, in the crannies
Of Wales; where men I laud to my friends, poets out of the belly
    of the land
Still honed the cutting edge of their ears, a folk unbelievable!
One comes from Llanddowror to them, and another from Bro
    Gynin   *
To relish their home-baked dainties. The trunk's still so solid
It's as though all the twigs can't help bubbling out with plums.
More than the springtime in Wales, I remember her poets.
They scratch at my hiraeth oftener than the hills. There isn't a river
Cutting its vale through my heart deeper than those that work
    poems –
White, white were those nights – on Dyfi bank or Cefni.
America doesn't know – no, nor any country of Europe – of that
    contention,
Why they have it, those farmers, postmen, garage hands, ministers.
Writing their names on the snow, I feel warm in their company
As if I carved their memory in time's icy wind – Bro Dyfi,
    Talgarreg and Cefni.

*Griffith Jones of Llanddowror, a great educationalist in the
eighteenth century, who founded the circulating schools in the
Welsh language; and Dafydd ap Gwilym, reputed to be from Bro
Gynin in Cardiganshire.

BOBI JONES

The South Shore (Aberystwyth)

Bones I can understand. One after another
It's peeled them, turned them white as soapsuds
In the mad muscles of its belly. And even
Stumps of rare driftwood: to gnaw the elasticity
Of their grip, in the teeth of some of these nights,
Would savour of vegetables. I can understand
What moves it to digest those, and then toss
The remains on the beach. But shoes! Dozens of them,
One after another, every form, size and make –
What quality was in them? Was it the sea
Or (horrors!) some apparition of the sea bottom
That wore these leathers, and lorded it there?
Oh what dancing! What a show of feet!
Or was there one wave – as a rule so shy –
In the midst of lobsters, the mob of crabs, and that crew,
A wave which showed the glint of her heels, that kicked
For gladness in the face of deep seaweed?
To think in this way of the great sea
Putting on such teeny shoes, venturing out
In the gloom to prance – it is a portent
Of a gaiety at the bottom of grief: in labyrinths
That flow with blue and so transparent tears,
You'd see shoes awkward, not in pairs, tap the floor.
But what did happen last night? For here, in a bucketful
Of stars, behind the brows of the moon, the water
Shook the shoes off its feet; and then barefoot
Bounced out, wholly sure of itself, striking the beach.
There was much chanting, there was stretching
And much shaking of locks. Among grey stones
Like a squirrel come into a graveyard, full-drunken
(And wasn't it around here that Cantre'r Gwaelod waltzed?)
It was a night of ecstasy, when were flung up
Among the tyres, tin cans and bones – these shoes.

GWYN THOMAS
b.1936

Leaf

The leaf from the tree is shed.
It hovers, it flies,
Holds onto the breeze,
Gently hangs,
Quietly swims,
Slides – a bright flash –
White-bellied or yellow
It clowns, whirling with colours,
Fantastic it flaunts
To mouse shortfooted, gurgling tints,
It wheels, it slants,
Bright it swings downward.
The leaf from the tree is shed –
And what's it do?
                    It dies.

Goggy

Thursday (you should understand) is the day of the 'goggy',
That is to say – by a linguistic development
Peculiarly non-indoeuropean –
'A lorry',
And furthermore, in this context,
'A dustcart lorry'.
Shortly after eight
Milord will be squirming
With delight,
In wide-eyed gasps
Of admiration,
A full cot of pleasure.

And behold, Behemoth
Coiled in its metals

Backward
Rolls, unhurried, through the streets.
It opens the terrible doors of its head
For the contents of bins.
In the strength of its throat it grates them,
In the might of its belly.
From its nostrils comes smoke,
From the steel wefts of its majesty.
And before it, the dark divides,
Morning hurries to put its feet into shoes
And light shines at the sneeze of it:
In a word, 'goggy'.

Connecting rod of its thighs, is it slack?
Do the mighty gears refuse to grip?
Back axle of its power, has it cracked?
No,
A puncture outside Woolworths
Stopped Behemoth's
Morning perambulation
One Thursday.
Its huge absence weighed
Unspeakably along the street,
And likewise
On the said owner of the cot.

Before the face of tears and shouting
It ain't all that easy to explain
Such a defect in the procession of the 'goggy'.
From a year and three months' innocence
I'd a frown turned on me. I don't find it easy
To explicate that frown in any way
Except: 'Where's that bloody lorry?'

GWYN THOMAS

And For Your Children

(See Luke 23, 29)

Children.
Little children playing –
John and Joanne;
And Andrew the baby,
The little baby with them.

Between them, between the three of them,
You could count ten years
And six weeks of life:
John and Joanne
And Andrew, the baby.

And those men
In the iron and glass and plastic of their car
Came carrying guns,
Bullets, fuse-wire,
Black powder
With their hands already red with death;
And they came to destroy children:
John and Joanne
And Andrew, the baby.

Back they went then
To the concrete and glass,
To the wounded city
To eat, to sleep, to live
As if there was in their hearts
No death of John, no death of Joanne,
No death of Andrew, the little baby;
Children.

And then above the grieving crowds,
Above the mourners

Bending over the dead,
They were there again
Waving the banners of their anger,
Those men who can eat,
Can sleep, can live
After murdering children.

Crossing A Shore

It was, that day,
September the second.
And here we were, as a family,
Deciding to go to the sea.

It was, that day,
Sunny though a bit windy.
Over the great, empty shore
The wind would shake
The brightnesses of the sun,
Would whistle its yellow across the sand
And sparkle the water on the tide's far ebb.

And here we were, starting to do the things
That people do on beaches –
Shovel sand;
Put the baby to sit in the salty
Marvel of it; build castles; kick a ball.
The boys even went bathing
As though they'd a duty to.
But it was, that day,
Too cold to stay long in the water.
I just stood watching.

They came glistening out of the sea, their teeth
Chattering, laughing and splashing,
And here they were then, running in front of me

GWYN THOMAS

Across the long beach
To their mam, to their sister,
To shelter and towels.

I just followed at a distance.
But as I crossed the beach, about halfway,
It struck me with a shock
That this happens only once.
What I was doing would never, never come back.
Even the moment just gone
Is gripped within eternity
Fast as the Iron Age.
That's what it means, our mortality.
And I felt a bit lost then –
This thing won't ever happen again.

But I kept on walking
And before long I came back
To the family,
To the palaver of drying and changing,
To the sound of the present.
And what with digging the sand
And crunching through a tomato sandwich
And trying to calm the baby
That sense of loss went by.

I had, as it happened,
My birthday that day.
I was forty-one.

There's an old Russian proverb which says,
'Life is not crossing a field.'
Correct: it is crossing a shore.

NESTA WYN JONES
b.1946

Voices

Yes, this is my voice –
Voice of deft speech
Responding to eyes' knot
And rhetoric of hands.
A chain of words spoken –
Voice that asserts
One thing or the other.
This is my voice.

But, in a silence
When my eyes go dark,
Another, more importunate
Voice I hear –
A voice torturing every wire in my brain,
Lipped like a hooter at midnight
To shatter the dark of my being.

It's a voice lonely
Beyond expression
Where a wolf moans for ever its grief
At the wilderness moon –
A voice that would pace up and down
The widowed cells of my memory
In utter lack of rest.

O then, how terrible to look up and notice
You did not hear this agony –
The voice that stains silence with its shriek:
My dumb voice.

NESTA WYN JONES

Poppies

August, in Brittany,
And in the breeze sways and pirouettes
A red ballerina.

Brittany
As if someone
Had thrown tiny pieces of red
Tissue paper
Over the hedges
And they'd all unfolded
Flaming
In the sun.

August
And my hand itched to gather them,
But I knew, if I did,
There'd only be the stain
Of red
On my fingers
When the dew lifted.

Twilight, August in Brittany.
Into the dark staring and staring
I see their purple bruises
In every corner
Quaking
To the rumpus of crickets.

Here,
There's a wreath of plastic in the rain...
It's not that flower that's plaited in it.

ENGLYNION

14th-20th century

The single *englyn* has been the most widely used of the Welsh poetic forms. Corresponding in many ways to the Greek epigram, it is fiendishly hard to translate: without its articulation of rhyme and *cynghanedd* (too delicate a tracery to stand the equi-distancing tension of English stresses) its poetry usually evaporates. *Englynion*, far more than other forms, seem to belong to the language itself; more so, in fact, than they belong to their authors. I am told that a good *englyn* is not so much composed as part of a poet's *oeuvre* as finds itself written in his mind: I am reminded of the way Japanese poets talk of their own tiny *hokku* of seventeen syllables. An *englyn* is not much longer, by the way, with thirty! It is usual in anthologies to collect the *englynion* as a kind of appendix; and with some misgivings, I decided to follow the convention here. I have even abandoned chronological order, the better to show these little pieces off, one against another.

The Happy Man

From sea and manor and nearby mountain,
  From depths in the rivers,
  God builds all the livelong day
  With blessing for the blesséd.

Anon.

My Love

Dear cheeks under gay blue eyes, and two brows
  Under curls of yellow lattice;
  Ah, they called up heaven's host
  To whittle gold as hair for her!

Dewi Havhesp

ENGLYNION

Heather

They grow so comely, a quiet host, fine gems
    Of the shire of sun and breeze,
   Bells hanging from high rock places,
   Flowers of the stone, phials of honey.

Eifion Wyn

Nightfall

Silence brought by the dark night: Eryri's
    Mountains veiled by mist:
   The sun in the bed of brine,
   The moon silvering the water.

Gwallter Mechain

Wild Duck

Ducks are like seed the dawn-sower scatters
    To the garden of still water;
   Nightfall on gravel provokes them,
   They rise, they flower from the lake.

Euros Bowen

Foam

The Sea-god, when he walked the beach, shared out
    The hems of his silk surplice
   To break as a thread of silver
   On the cold bed of the rocks.

Roland Jones

ENGLYNION

Eaves

Giving, while the rain lasts, soft noises
    Like a thousand being milked;
    When the roof's thick with ice,
    Under it, strange teats appear.

Ellis Jones

A Wife's Epitaph

Let the gentle be at rest, in cold March,
    In wintry blizzard;
    Let ice the white face cover,
    And tenderness be under snow.

R. Williams Parry

Epitaph for Father and Son

The sickly leaf, still green, had fallen
    Inertly to earth;
    The wind of the ancient storm
    Struck at the tree thereafter.

John Phillips (Tegidon)

Sheepdog

Smooth steps that are easy to urge to the crags
    And inaccessible places;
    Gathering and halving flocks
    Is his exploit in far glens.

Thomas Richards

ENGLYNION

Deer

Yesterday I saw a jointed stick of horn
    And on it nine branches:
    A proud man, harrow-headed,
    And a bald wife from the rock.

Dafydd ap Gwilym

Mercy

My God, keep in Thy sight me, Owen – on a poor
    Cobbler, Lord, have mercy,
    As I would, were I Heaven's Lord
    And Thou the likes of Owen.

Anon.

Christ before Pilate

Terrible to see him, for no fault of his own,
    In the hands of a Roman,
    Indicted by a vile worm,
    God before man in judgement!

Robert ab Gwilym Ddu

Horizon

Look, a mirage, like a round rim, a strange
    Wizard's masterpiece about us:
    An old line that's not there,
    A boundary that never ends.

David Emrys James

ENGLYNION

Going Home

The salmon's no traitor – from his adventure
    He goes back home;
  When you're tired of sampling towns
  It's pleasant to look homeward.

Llawdden

Attraction

Never for more than a year stay in England,
    A place bleak and wretched;
  Where the bird is first nurtured
  Is the place he'll always seek.

Anon.

Epitaph

She lied as much as she could, while she lived;
    Take care you don't revive her,
  Or (I do believe) she'd tell
  Everyone she'd been to heaven.

Ellis Owen

Epitaph

Poor I am now: if any should call me home
    I cannot answer:
  The black, cold, bare, damp earth
  Of Trawsfynydd's overhead me.

Dafydd Jones

ENGLYNION

Dylan Thomas

He had harvested the poem's familiar tips
    Till his two lips were red;
  Truth on the grapes till, drunken,
  He fell dead, widowed the wine.

Euros Bowen

Hope

Though many a time we must weep, and observe
    The vicious heart's treason,
  God would not want our journey
  To lead to a hopeless land.

Robert ab Gwilym Ddu

The Rose and The Heather

A crystal home the rose was given, its soft
    Gentility to pamper;
  For brave heather, rock suffices –
  The bare republic of the wild.

Pedrog

Nobility

Certain marks one can see, it's a fact,
    In the way the branch grows:
  A man shows pretty clearly
  At what level was his root.

Tudur Aled

ENGLYNION

Two-faced

Repute and dishonour confused, and, like enough,
    Beauty untruthful:
    Sooner your crow says cuckoo
    Than you spot a two-faced rogue.

Siôn Tudur

A Beauty

If, as they say, you're a fool
    And your purpose is false,
    Remarkable that God saw fit
    To fashion you so fairly.

Anon.

Morfudd

I'll not break with Morfudd, dear wings of love,
    Though Rome's Pope should ask it –
    Her two cheeks bright as sunrise –
    Until honey come from stone.

Dafydd ap Gwilym

An Only Child

I've questioned myself, wandering, crying – Oh,
    Long enough I've sought her!
    I search through all her chambers
    And search, and never will find.

Robert ab Gwilym Ddu

ENGLYNION

Weakness

Old age has taken my quality, my top grown grey
    And my limbs bent;
  Wasted is the verdant tree,
  On the hill its branches wither.

Anon.

Old Age

'Old age never comes alone' – it brings sighs
    With it, and complaining,
  And now a long lack of sleep,
  And, soon enough, long slumber.

John Morris-Jones

In Memoriam

In a strange, unclamorous host, the dead
    And the seaweed tangle;
  Pearl parlours, acres of fish
  Are tomb to learning's splendour.

R. Williams Parry

The Last Englyn

For the sake of the flowing bright wounds of Jesus,
    For the bruise of his breast,
  For blood from his every stab,
  May I not feel this pain long!

Tudur Aled

Appendix on Metres

Introduction

Welsh versification, because of the nature of the language and the professional status of the poets, admits of an unusually clear exposition of its rules. It has an enormous technical vocabulary: Tudur Aled is reported to have outsworn a fishwife by using his metrical terms as oaths. Metrical complexity was useful to Welsh poets. It allowed them to do what they wanted with words. It gave them professional standards of workmanship.

As long as the bardic order lasted the system evolved. It responded (as these things do) to changes – sometimes revolutionary changes – in the social structure and ideology of Welsh life. To discount everything except its final form in the fifteenth century masters is a fetish. In any case, the system did not die with the bardic order. The *englyn*, for example, has had a continuous existence ever since. Other forms have been more or less consciously revived, and still others have in turn evolved.

The Nature of Welsh as a Substrate

Welsh words have two kinds of accent. They are *stressed*, usually on the last syllable but one; and they also have a rising *tonic* accent, invariably on the last. That is, Welsh words go up in pitch at the end. The stress accent is not usually marked in writing, and the tonic never is. Since it is invariable and does not affect the meaning of the word, the tonic accent tends to be ignored by grammarians. It is a characteristic of other languages however – ancient Greek and modern Norwegian for example. Prosodically it is probably more important even than stress: rhyming in Welsh, for instance, is usually on the tonic, not on the stress accent. (In English rising tone is either syntactical – as in the question, "You going to London?" – or associated with stress. English people are often uncertain where to stress Welsh words. They hear the rise in pitch at the end of the word and think that is where the stress must be: "Bangor" is made to rhyme with Bangalore.) Sometimes, as in monosyllables or words of irregular stress, the two accents coincide. This is one of the ways a Welsh poet can vary the quality of his rhyming, for example in the *cywydd* metre where stressed has to rhyme with unstressed; but actually what makes it a rhyme at all is the high tone equally on both.★

Since long vowels are more or less confined to monosyllables, vowel music is not a metrical factor of much weight. Instead the articulation of Welsh depends on the strength of its consonants. Welsh vowels are crystal clear and have a beauty of their own; but by themselves they are if anything too clear to engage the ear of a poet for long. A line by Tennyson seems designed to give the vowels a setting in the best available consonants; but a typical line by Dafydd ap Gwilym sets its articulating consonants in a thin, though exquisite, balance of vowels.

Grammatically these consonants play elaborate games with each other according to the mutation system: 'pen' (a head) can become 'ben' or 'phen' or 'mhen' according to its position. A Welsh poet can use this system to make far more intricate patterns with his consonants than would be convenient in most other languages.

These factors between them mean that a Welsh poet has many options open to him. Because of the tonal pattern, neither the consonants nor the vowels are slaves of the stress, as they are in English. An English poet more or less has to articulate on the basis of equi-distancing of his stresses; he can use vowels or consonants to give subtlety to his rhythms, but if he forgets the pull of the stresses he is in trouble. The play of syllable, of vowel-music and alliteration always has to be geared to the over-riding tramp, tramp, tramp of stress. But in Welsh versification, the tonal pattern (as it were) contradicts the stress sufficiently to allow alliteration and rhyming to cut clean across it. The only fixed element is the syllable. Everything else can vary, each in its own sphere; and so everything else can be reduced to rules, because the rules do not hinder the poet's freedom, they merely give it form.

★The only important exception to this rule is the internal rhyming found in *cynghanedd lusg* where a final syllable rhymes with a stressed penultimate one.

APPENDIX ON METRES

The Three Kinds of Metre

In what follows it must be understood that we are dealing with the native, so-called 'strict' metres, not the native 'free' metres or the introduced forms, like the sonnet or blank verse, based on stress. The strict metres are the pride of Welsh poetry: even now they exert a fascination which is difficult for a foreigner to understand. For centuries poets have meditated on their perfections. The native 'free' metres are but poor relations, sharing something of their structure, without their magnificence or their poise. There is something about these free metres that very easily runs to seed. So there is a moral in them: in a language as filigree as Welsh rules are not mere vanity, extravagance of spirit or denial of nature for the sake of arid artifice. They are the birthright of poetry, a mode of being human, a sharpening of the mind. Prosody, in Welsh, to some extent took the place of the play of ideas in more intellectually orientated cultures. And if you find this shocking, may I suggest you go and watch the mind, not just the body, of a great ballerina at work in classical ballet, or a virtuoso playing Bach.

Apart from attempts to use *cynghanedd* in English song-metres or sonnets, the imported measures stand separate from the rest. They took three centuries to become dominant – the sonnet was not introduced until last century. Welsh is an obliging language where poetry is concerned, and the stress-forms are now completely at home in it. But they offer no special problems, as most of them will be familiar to English ears.

All Welsh poetry until quite recently was rhymed. There is no trace of the more primitive unrhymed verse, based on cadence, that is occasionally found in Old Irish; unless, indeed, the 'Song to the Child Dinogad' represents a transitional stage, using rhyme and cadence simultaneously, and without syllable-counting. If it does, it has its counterpart in Irish transitional forms. Presumably rhyme came in with the Romans; the linguistic change of Brythonic into Welsh swept away the older, cadenced poetry.

APPENDIX ON METRES

The Awdl

The Welsh strict metres are again divided into three families, with twenty-four metres in all. This is somewhat arbitrary. Some of the metres developed before the distinction between strict and free grew as rigid as it is today. Others more properly belong to the free, and look a bit self-conscious dressed up in their Sunday best. But it is a convenient classification, and has the merit of being traditional.

The first family is of metres which pertain to the *awdl*, a word usually translated 'ode', but really more like 'lay'. An *awdl* consists of one or more sections, each with one rhyme throughout, and anything from two to a hundred lines in each. Early poets like Taliesin often used short lines of four, five or six syllables; but it is an open question whether these are not really half lines, the full line being of eight to ten syllables. Certainly, as time went on, the *awdl*-line became essentially a long one, having from eight to nineteen syllables. The only metrical connection one line need have with its fellows is the end-rhyme: many poems do in fact keep to one line-length, and certain standard patterns – for example, two lines of eight syllables followed by one of sixteen – have been found pleasing and often recur; but this type of secondary formation is not essential. The poet can change his line from one minute to the next, if he wants to. What he must keep, however, is the main-rhyme of his section.

These long lines can be unwieldy, and so a line longer than ten syllables is always broken up into a definite number of sub-sections (depending on the metre chosen) which rhyme with one another and set up another kind of quasi-stanzaic secondary formation within the main *awdl*-rhythm. These 'stanza' forms are often highly successful metres in their own right. Goronwy Owen used one of them as a true stanza form in his *awdl* 'The Wish', which I have translated. He changes the rhyme nearly every four lines, just like a stanza-poet would do. But this is to deny the *awdl* its essence, while keeping its accidents. I should explain, however, that the longer types of line are hardly ever printed as such; nor does the *cynghanedd*, or internal rhyming and alliteration, reach further than about ten syllables at the most. For both these purposes the long lines are best divided to suit with convenience.

Another device to make the long line more interesting is to

divide it into two sections; the end of the first is then rhymed with a point halfway along the second. This is the basis of the *awdl gywydd*, used by Taliesin in his 'Elegy for Owain ab Urien': both by itself and in combination it was a favourite Elizabethan free metre for songs. This type of rhyming was of great importance in Irish metrics, where it was known as *aicill*: its presence in sixth century Welsh is therefore of some interest to students of comparative prosody. In other *awdl* measures it was combined with yet another technique: the first section of the line was again divided at a point one, two or three syllables from the end, and this was rhymed with the end of the whole line, the main rhyme of the *awdl*. Here is an example, with the rhymes in italics:

> Tra bwy'n darllain cain aceni*ad* – beirddi*on*.
> Hil Derwydd*on*, olau adroddi*ad*.

(The dash in Welsh poetry is usually a metrical marking, not punctuation.) This is the nearest thing to alternate rhyming found in the strict metres.

The *awdl*, clearly, is a quite primitive metre in essence, no matter how sophisticated the variations one can play upon it. But after the conquest of 1282, it suffered a sea-change, becoming a two-movement symphony. First came a string of *englynion*, often two kinds of *englyn* alternating; and a second, the *awdl* proper, but keeping strictly to one metre, usually in quatrains. This is the secondary formation taking over completely. The only thing that reminds one it is an *awdl*, and not a series of stanzas, is the main-rhyme; which feature is found elsewhere in mediaeval lyrics (for instance, in Provençal) indubitably stanzaic in make-up. In these circumstances, the main rhyme sounds more like a *tour de force* than an absolute necessity of measure.

In the fifteenth century the custom arose of writing "exemplary" *awdlau*, giving examples of all twenty-four measures. This led to the modern Eisteddfod *awdl*, which is a sequence of stanzas or *cywydd*-couplets in any of the twenty-four measures that the poet chooses to use, of roughly three hundred lines. The main-rhyme is not usually kept beyond the individual stanza or couplet. It is for poems in this form (or rather, lack of form) that the Chair, the highest prize in the National Eisteddfod, is awarded every year.

APPENDIX ON METRES

In my translations I have usually found it convenient to use the Anglo-Saxon four-stress line, with variations upon it, to render the *awdl* rhythm. Perhaps it gives the wrong impression, too Germanic for the context: but I am surprised how readily it seems to fit. In one case, the 'Deathbed Poem' of Meilyr, I tried to reproduce the original metre as far as I could, and to keep the main-rhyme right through to the end. I hoped this might give some idea of the sound these poets make.

Here now are some of the more usual *awdl* measures:

Rhupunt. A long line is divided into sections of four syllables each. The last section carries the main rhyme, the others rhyme with each other. For convenience, as here, the long line is divided in printing:

> Mab a'n rhodded,
> Mab mad aned dan ei freiniau,
> Mab gogoned,
> Mab i'n gwared, y mab gorau . . .

Cyhydedd fer. Eight-syllable lines normally in sequences of two lines or more:

> Pen pan las, ni bu gas gymraw;
> Pen pan las, oedd lesach peidiaw.
> Pen milwr, pen moliant rhag llaw,
> Pen dragon, pen draig oedd arnaw...

Toddaid byr. A couplet of ten and six syllables. The main rhyme occurs one, two or three syllables before the end of the first line and at the end of the second. The end of the first line rhymes or alliterates with the middle of the second. *Toddaid* is often combined with *cyhydedd fer* to form *byr a thoddaid*, as here:

> Pen f'arglwydd, poen dyngngwydd a'm daw;
> Pen f'enaid heb fanag arnaw.
> Pen a fu berchen ar barch naw – canwlad,
> A naw canwledd iddaw.

Cyhydedd naw ban. Nine-syllable lines normally in sequences of two lines or more:

> Pob cantref, pob tref ŷnt yn treiddiaw;
> Pob tylwyth, pob llwyth y sy'n llithraw;
> Pob gwan, pob cadarn cadwed o'i law;
> Pob mab yn ei grud y sy'n udaw.

Cyhydedd hir. A long line of nineteen syllables, divided into five, five, five and four. The first three sections rhyme together and the last carries the main rhyme:

> Gwae fi am arglwydd, gwalch diwaradwydd;
>   Gwae fi o'r aflwydd ei dramgwyddaw.
> Gwae fi o'r golled, gwae fi o'r dynged,
>   Gwae fi o'r clywed fod clwyf arnaw.

Toddaid. A couplet of ten and nine syllables. The main rhyme occurs one, two or three syllables before the end of the first line and at the end of the second. The end of the first line rhymes with a word in the middle of the second:

> Arglwydd canadlwydd, cyn adaw – Emrais
>   Ni lyfasai Sais ei ogleisiaw.
> Arglwydd, neud maendo ymandaw – Cymry,
>   O'r llin a ddyly ddaly Aberffraw.

Gwawdodyn. A stanza of four lines, comprising a couplet of nine-syllable lines (*cyhydedd naw ban*) with a *toddaid.*

> Deued i Sais yr hyn a geisio,
> Dwfr hoffredwyllt ofer, a ffrydio
> Drwy nant a chrisiant, (â chroeso) – o chaf
>   Fôn im, yn bennaf henwaf honno.

If more than one couplet precedes the *toddaid,* it is called *gwawdodyn hir.*

Hir a thoddaid. A stanza of ten-syllable lines, concluding with a *toddaid*:

Y pennaf lueddwyr, O! pan floeddiant,
Acw'r gelltydd a'r creigiau a holltant;
Eraill gan loesion yn waelion wylant,
Eu hanadl a'u gallu a'u hoedl gollant;
Gan boen a chur, gwn, byw ni chânt; – angau,
Er gwae ugeiniau, dyr eu gogoniant.

The Englyn

On the analogy of heroic poetry elsewhere in the world, it is likely that the *awdl* was sung to a kind of chant, with a cadence on the main-rhyme, the harp being used percussively to pick out the metrically important syllables. This musical form is all that is needed to explain its peculiarities. But there were occasions when the rhythmic sweep of a chanted *awdl*, nearly always reserved for ritual praise, was not required. A tune had to be sung, for example, or a tale told. One usage in particular required a kind of song quite different from the *awdl*: the story-teller's art had in Celtdom this peculiarity, that at certain points it required a character (or sometimes two characters, in dialogue) to sing in verse, to draw attention to the dramatic or magical nature of what was happening. Thus, in *The Mabinogion*, Gwydion is looking for Lleu Llaw Gyffes, who has been bewitched; and he finds a maggot-ridden eagle sitting in the top of a tree. The storyteller goes on:

And he realised that the eagle was Lleu, and sang an englyn –

Oak grows between lake and lake.
Sky and glen one darkness make.
Unless false is what I say,
Flowers did my Lleu unmake.

When he had done so, the eagle let itself down until it was in the middle of the tree. And Gwydion sang another englyn –

And so on, until he has the eagle in his lap.

Now, how was this performed? Phyllis Kinney ('Narrow-compass Tunes in Welsh Folksong', *Canu Gwerin*', 9/86; and in personal communication) has drawn my attention to the way Welsh folksongs, particularly those in traditional metres, are often narrowly pentachordal in range, with declamatory openings beginning on the dominant. It looks as though this declamatory style, starting high and drifting lower, is very ancient. So why not something like it for these *englynion?* The narrator had to let the music establish itself on the hearer's mind and he didn't have many words to sing. This sort of declamatory style would be one answer; a highly decorated slow air, such as is used by Gaelic singers in Connemara, would be another – but of that there is no trace in Welsh tradition.

The earliest *englynion* were typically three-line structures, with one rhyme. Sometimes each line has seven syllables; sometimes the pattern is 10, 6, 7, or some variant of that. In the latter case, the rhyme occurs in the first line one, two or three syllables from the end; and the remainder of the line is connected by internal rhyme or alliteration with the beginning of the next. As far as we know, the main function of the *englyn* was to provide songs in the stories; but it had other uses, which soon became more important. One early use was in gnomic verse. An *englyn* could be remembered and used in speech – that is, it lost its musical function. Very soon, in the twelfth century if not before, the four-line *englyn* began to be used as a humbler counterpart of the *awdl*, particularly when the poet was not so much concerned with the ritual praise of a king that was his main duty, as with lesser matters like congratulating the king's troops on a victory, or personal elegies to his friends. And here is the puzzle: during this very period when the *englyn* was extending its usefulness rapidly, the three-line forms of it went out of fashion as if they had never been, and the various four-line structures completely replaced them.

Why? In the sense that no one saw fit to pass the information on, we do not know. But there are clues. One clue is that in the *awdl* itself 'secondary formations' of four lines apiece occur with great frequency in the poems of Meilyr, Gwalchmai and Hywel ab Owain, poets of the court of Gwynedd during this very period: so much is this so, that one can feel these poets thinking in quatrains (or sometimes six-line units) as one can certainly not feel Aneirin (say) or the poet of 'The Praise of Tenby'. Another clue is that Irish poetry in the twelfth century had already attained its highest level of polish, of beauty, and (just as important) political usefulness. This strict poetry, the *dán díreach*, is decorated in what looks at first sight a similar fashion to Welsh strict poetry. However, the resemblance is probably due to parallel development from a common source a long way back: the type of decoration is in fact quite different to that of the Welsh poets, and scholars are very dubious about any direct connexion between the two. But we remember that Gruffudd ap Cynan, the founder of Gwynedd's greatness in the twelfth century, came from Ireland, from a Dublin where the Danish settlers were in process of becoming Irishmen, more Irish than the Irish; we remember that both he and his grandson, the poet Hywel ab Owain, had Irish mothers and intimate experience of Irish courts and political life; and that Irish legends, to judge from the *Mabinogion*, were widespread in Wales. Is it conceivable that there should have been no Irish influence on the poetic revival that Gruffudd ap Cynan is traditionally credited with, and that he and his descendants certainly fostered and encouraged as a matter of policy? We may not be able to pinpoint any direct influence on the *minutiae* of poetic technique; but one fact stands out, a very simple fact which has nothing to do with incidental complexities. The basic unit of practically all *dán díreach* poetry is the *rann* or stanza of four lines; and the nearest thing to a *rann* that exists in Welsh is the four-line *englyn*; and the next nearest thing is the four-line secondary formation within the *awdl*. The actual mechanism of the change may well have been musical: poets with an Irish tune in their heads coming back and fitting existing Welsh metres to it. We do not know. All we do know is the fact that the four-line *englyn* very quickly matured and achieved practically its present perfection during a period when Irish influence was probably stronger in Wales than at any time since the age of the Saints.

Here now are the four main types of *englynion*:

Englyn milwr – soldier's englyn. Three lines of seven syllables, rhyming together:

> Pen a borthaf a'm porthes.
> Neud adwen nad er fy lles.
> Gwae fy llaw, llym ddigones.

Englyn penfyr. Three lines of ten, six and seven syllables, with the rhyme in the first line coming one, two or three syllables before the end. In fact both these early forms show a fairly wide range of variation:

> Stafell Gynddylan, a'm erwan pob awr
> Gwedi mawr ymgyfrdan
> A welais ar dy bentan.

Englyn unodl union. This is what one usually means by an *englyn*. It combines a *toddaid byr* with a couplet of *cywydd deuair hirion.* Four lines of ten, six, seven and seven syllables, all with one rhyme. In the first line the rhyme occurs one, two or three syllables before the end. If the third line ends on an accented syllable, the fourth must end on an unaccented, and *vice versa*. The end of the first line must either rhyme or alliterate with the middle of the second. The main rhyme in the first and second lines must not both be on accented syllables:

> Paham y gweir cam â'r cymod – neu'r Iawn
> A'i rinwedd dros bechod?
> Dywedwch faint y Duwdod
> Yr un faint yw'r Iawn i fod.

If the *cywydd* couplet (called the *esgyll* or wings of an *englyn*) precedes the *toddaid byr* (called its *paladr* or shaft) then the form is called *englyn unodl crwca* or crooked englyn, having four lines of seven, seven, ten and six syllables respectively.

Englyn proest. Four lines of seven syllables each, using a peculiar kind of rhyming (called *proest*) in which the final vowels must differ (though not in quantity) while the final consonant remains the same: for example, *den, ton, fin* and *ran* form *proest*-rhyme in English. Short vowels rhyme with short, long with long and dipthongs with dipthongs:

> Yfory i'w dŷ a'i dud,
> A heddiw y'm gwahoddid,
> A thrennydd gwneuthur ynyd,
> A thrannoeth saethu'r unnod.

There are several different kinds of *englyn proest*, but the differences need not detain us.

APPENDIX ON METRES

Englyn cyrch. See the section on free metres.

In my translations of *englynion* I have usually done no more than try to suggest the rhythm as far as I could. To all intents and purposes I have used free verse. I cannot pretend I am satisfied with this procedure, except in series of *englynion* where the form has time to establish its own rhythm. For the single *englyn* it always has the feeling of a wilting flower about it. Perhaps some experiments along the lines of my *cywydd*-versions would have provided a better answer.

The Cywydd

The increasing sophistication of Welsh metrics during the twelfth and thirteenth centuries was almost certainly matched by a parallel evolution in Welsh music. It is likely, for instance, that the style of singing an *englyn* and the style of singing an *awdl* converged more and more during the twelfth century, because in the fourteenth (as we have said) the chain of *englynion* became *de rigeur* as an introductory movement to the *awdl*; and this would not have been possible had the *englyn* kept to a completely different music. Both the music for the string-player, harp or crwth (usually thought of as a primitive fiddle: surviving examples are late, but are strictly bowed lyres), and the music for the voice probably developed to a point where the *englyn*-type slow air and the *awdl*-type chant had each become a kind of melodic descant over a quite independent air on the harp.

This may be arguing in the dark, but at least we do know that such a descant was (and is) used by Welsh singers in a tradition at least as old as the eighteenth century. The question is, how old is this tradition, and is it of bardic or folk origin? When I first wrote this essay I asked:

> How authentically does it preserve bardic conventions?
> That it was bardic in origin is both vouched for by tradition
> and sanctioned by common-sense: for such a highly elabo-
> rate affair is most unfolk-like in the impression it makes. My
> own guess is that the present style of *penillion*-singing (as it is
> often called) is a watered-down version of a technique that
> was evolved in its fullness to serve the musical and poetic

tastes of the Welsh nobility in the fourteenth century; and that it was this method of performing poetry that finally fixed *cynghanedd* in the form we know it today, and, incidentally, allowed the *cywydd* to become the dominant expression of Welsh poetry for over four centuries.

I know more about folk music now than I did then. The way the *penillion*-singer starts after the harpist has begun the tune, and then sings to a rhythm that only meets the tune at cadences, one verse at a time, seems to me very like what happens in step or clog dancing, with the dancer's feet playing the part of a percussion instrument. There, as in *penillion*-singing, the harp starts an air. About a quarter of the way through, the dancer starts to step out a rhythm which may be that of the air, but often is a variation on it. The harp and the dancer finish on the cadence, as in *penillion*, and the whole thing starts again, with each repetition of the tune. So there is no doubt in my mind that *penillion*-singing is well within the inventive range of folk-music. Osian Ellis, the harper, has indicated that the earlier you go, the simpler does *penillion*-singing seem to have been, which would not have been the case had it been simply a watered-down version of an earlier complexity.

However, even if we accept the theory that *penillion*-singing, literally the singing of stanzas, was a folk invention probably of the seventeenth or eighteenth centuries, it does not necessarily mean that it did not contain memories of an earlier bardic style of performance. This would clearly not have been stanzaic, since the *cywydd* was in continuous couplets, but it may well have involved counterpoint and descant. Indeed, the internal evidence, the use of broken rhythms, the counterpoint of phrases, ideas and even whole sentences within the couplet-framework, strongly suggests that it did. There is a reference, for it's worth, to descant in Dafydd ab Edmwnd's elegy for Siôn Eos the harper.

Strictly speaking, there are four metres that are called *cywydd* by the poets; but if you use the word *cywydd*, even more than *englyn*, you are generally understood to mean only one thing by it – the *cywydd deuair hirion*, the long-lined couplet. Each line has seven syllables, and if the first line ends on an accented syllable, the second must end on an unaccented one, and *vice versa*. Here is an example from Dafydd ap Gwilym:

Tri phorphor, dygyfor dig,
Trafferth oedd, triphorth Eiddig,
Trefnwyd wynt i'm tra ofni,
Trwch fu'm gyfarfod â'r tri.

And so on, for sixty-four lines. Whereas the *awdl* proceeds line by line, and the *englyn* stanza by stanza, the *cywydd* proceeds couplet by couplet. In an *awdl* every line can differ from its neighbours; and in a sequence of *englynion* more than one stanza form may be employed; but in a *cywydd* it is necessary for every couplet to be metrically equivalent to every other – otherwise the poem would break down into a sequence of two-line stanzas or *englynion*. The change from the *awdl* to the *cywydd* has its counterpart in many other cultures – that from the hexameter to the elegiac couplet in Greek, or that from the long mono-rhymed or assonanced *lai* of the *Song of Roland* to the octosyllabic couplet of the French romances. In fact, one could generalise and say that the appearance of the couplet as a dominant form marks a fairly constant point in the history of any civilisation where it occurs. The couplet's flexibility, its neatness, its air of being equal to any occasion, and above all its sheer convenience give it a decided advantage over its more ponderous rivals. And, just as the hexameter became self-conscious and attempted to imitate the sophistication of the couplet in the narrow fields where it still had the advantage, so did the *awdl* in fourteenth and fifteenth century Wales. The *cywydd*'s range drove the *awdl*-poet more and more into a wonderfully ornate virtuosity, a grandeur that had less and less to do with the day-to-day feelings of mankind.

Where did the *cywydd* originate? Scholars have concluded that it was probably one of the 'free' metres used by inferior classes of poet whose works have been lost; and that it was taken up by Dafydd ap Gwilym and his school, made more regular in structure, and used as 'strict' metre, that is, with *cynghanedd*. There does in fact exist a free metre, called the *traethodl*, which is exactly a 'free' *cywydd* – that is, both *cynghanedd* and the odd accents on the rhymes are optional. What is more, three of Dafydd's poems are in this metre. What could be simpler than to postulate this kind of origin for the *cywydd*?

But in fact this answer poses as many problems as it solves. Why, for instance, did Dafydd not stick to the free-metre *traethodl*, if what he was after was convenience and flexibility? And if it be answered that the form wasn't strict enough to suit his sense of craftsmanship, why did he not keep to the old *awdl*, for that metre was as strict as his heart could desire? Here, once again, I feel that the answer lies in the music of the time, in the sort of union of poetic and musical effects that the poet wanted to produce.

The *traethodl*, as Dafydd himself shows, was a perfectly good instrument when what you wanted was to tell a story or present an argument in verse – much better than the *cywydd* in fact. But it not merely lacks metrical finesse, it also cannot compass the sense of counterpoint, one idea, one image, one voice playing against another, that is so marked a feature of fourteenth- century poetry. To sing a *traethodl* as a descant to a harp air would add nothing at all to its own kind of perfection: it would merely be a rather awkward way of setting it to music. But to descant a fourteenth-century *cywydd* might well be a revelation. Not merely could the descanting voice bring out the metrical chiming of consonant against consonant, stress against stress, it could also articulate the often interrupted constructions, the counterpoint of imagery and syntax, in a way that no other method of performance could hope to do. Changes in pitch, in timbre and in the tempo of the vocal line, controlled as they are by the constancy of the harpist's air, make possible a much greater range of syntactical exuberance in descant than in either the singing of words to a tune or even the declaiming of them in speech. Articulation and balance are the secret of all art: and in fourteenth-century Wales the dialogue of voice and harp demanded a like dialogue to take place in every facet of the poet's work. It has been all too readily assumed that the so-called 'filling-in' phrases and the constant breaks in construction that are found in these poets, were merely forgivable concessions to a difficult and hampering metre. On the contrary, I believe that they reveal, more perhaps than any other feature of the form, what the poets of the *cywydd* wanted their poetry to do.

The principle governing the *awdl* had been accumulation; and that of the *englyn* had been the play of contrasts within a stanza. Neither of these forms could hope to do justice to the counterpoint inherent in the type of descant they themselves had evolved. That is why the *cywydd* was so successful. It could and in fact often did, behave like an *awdl* and simply pile up iines, one on top of another. Or it could pretend to be a sequence of *englynion*, as in the last part of Dafydd ap Gwilym's poem on 'The Ruin'. Or it could argue in neat little couplets, like a *traethodl*, as in much of the work of Siôn Cent. Siôn Cent, possibly under the influence of the French *ballade*, sometimes composed a *cywydd* in stanzas of eight or ten lines, with a refrain: but this was perhaps going a bit far, and his example was not followed. But you could also weave a sentence in and out of as many couplets as you could manage, counterpointing it with extra-syntactical phrases, or even have two sentences running at once. This is perhaps the typical manner of a Dafydd ap Gwilym *cywydd* – a generalization every bit as nerve-racking as one on Shakespeare's blank verse! In the fifteenth-century the poet's freedom in this respect seems to have been drastically curtailed – perhaps because he began to think of his poem on the written page, rather than as a performed piece of descant. The *cywydd* from then on became a series of more or less end-stopped couplets. Even so, the counterpoint inherent in the form is quite clearly reflected in the movement of the poet's mind: as, for example, in the play of imagery throughout Dafydd Nanmor's 'Exhortation to Rhys ap Rhydderch of the Tywyn'.

Cynghanedd

I have suggested that the *cywydd* could only have come into being as a dominant form when the music had evolved to a point where harpist and singer could go as if independently of each other. There was, however, another prerequisite to its success, and that was the full evolution of *cynghanedd* to more or less the fashion it has now. *Cynghanedd* (harmony) is the name the Welsh give to metrical patterns that operate within the given line, like internal rhyming or cross-alliteration. It is the *cynghanedd* in every line that makes a strict metre strict, and its absence, or merely spasmodic occurrence, that makes a free metre free.

One would want to distinguish very carefully between archaic and modern *cynghanedd*. The two things have many features in common, but a sea-change has taken place. Both in essence and in function the two patterns are different.

Archaic Cynghanedd – Notwithstanding my remarks about tone, Welsh is a strongly stressed language, and early Welsh poetry was probably as much based on counting stresses as on syllables.

Certainly this is how Sir John Morris-Jones in his treatise on Welsh poetry, *Cerdd Dafod*, classified the various *awdl* measures. The *awdl*-line usually has four or six stresses, and the practice grew up from very early times of decorating and strengthening these stresses with a whole battery of metrical devices – rhyme, cross-alliteration and so on. Functionally these picked-out stresses give the listener points of interest to counter the over-whelming pull of the main rhyme towards the end of the line. They give weight to the middle. Here is an example of this art at its most elaborate in the work of Cynddelw (twelfth century):

> Dôr ysgor ysgwyd ganhymdaith.
> Tarian yn aerwan, yn eurwaith.
> Twrf grug yng ngoddug yng ngoddaith.
> Tarf esgar ysgwyd yn nylaith.
> Rhwyf myrdd cyrdd cerddorion obaith.
> Rhudd ddiludd ddileddf gydymdaith.

Much of the *cynghanedd* can be seen at a glance. In the first line, for instance, *ysgor* rhymes with *dôr* and alliterates with *ysgwyd*. What is not so obvious is that the *r* from the preceding words plays a part in the full alliteration: r-s-g r-s-g. The combination of rhyme and alliteration is very common in archaic *cynghanedd*; it is called *cynghanedd sain*, and in this extract only line four involves another kind of *cynghanedd*, based on cross-alliteration. Since *f* is not a strong consonant in Welsh, here again the *r* from the preceding words might have played a part:

> Tarf e*sgar* / *ysg*wyd yn nylaith

This is called *cynghanedd groes*. There is another type, similar to this, where there are consonants between the two alliterating groups that do not take part in the alliteration:

> Llawen y'u *car*wn, / cyny'm / *cer*ynt

This is *cynghanedd draws*. A fourth kind is based on internal rhyme alone, and is much rarer in the *awdl*-poets:

> Cefais chwech heb odech pechawd;
> Gwenglaer uwch gwengaer ydd y'm daerawd.

This pair of lines from Hywel ab Owain shows *cynghanedd lusg deirodl*. *Chwech* rhymes with *odech* which rhymes with the stressed penultimate syllable of *pechawd*; and similarly *gwenglaer* with *gwengaer* and *daerawd*. *Cynghanedd lusg* would normally only involve two rhymes: a word in the middle of the line rhymes with the stressed penultimate syllable of a more-than-one-syllable word.

Two things are clear. First, the main purpose of this archaic *cynghanedd*, like that of Anglo-Saxon alliteration, is to pick out some of the stressed words in a line. It is usually more complex than simple alliteration, but it does the same kind of job. These metrical emphases would be still further stressed in performance no doubt by the percussive use of the harp.

Secondly, we notice about Cynddelw's *cynghanedd* that it need not involve the main rhyming word of the line at all. In our extract above, in two cases it does but in the other four it does not. This is in spite of the fact that five out of six lines use *cynghanedd sain* with its division into three parts, one and two rhyming and two and three alliterating: the tendency to go to the end of the line to get the third part in must be quite strong. It follows that Cynddelw's *cynghanedd* is essentially centripetal. It gives each line weight in the middle and helps to cut the *awdl*-line away from its fellows.

Modern Cynghanedd – Here now is an extract from a *cywydd* by Tudor Aled (ca. 1500):

> Y *c*ei*r*w *m*awr/ y *c*ei*r* eu *m*edd
> *Sy* o'*r* u*n*/ *s*i*r* o Wy*n*edd;
> I*mp* Y*n*y*r* he*n*/ a'*m p*e*n rh*aith,
> A'*m ff*r*i*w, *d*êl /i W*mff*r*e da*l*aith;
> Ae*r* Hywe*l*, *b*u'*n*/ *rh*yw*l*io *b*yd,
> A*p S*ie*n*c*y*n,/ a'*n p*wys e*n*c*y*d.
> *M*o*r* w*ych g*w*aed,/ *m*a*rch*og ydwyd,
> Â *d*e*g* o iei*r*ll/ a *d*u*g* wyd;
> *N*a *ch*olle*r* hy*n*/ o'*ch ll*aw *r*hawg
> O *d*d*r*wg *g*y*n*go*r*,/ *d*de*r*w *c*a*ng*awg.

Every one of these lines is divided into two parts. If we ignore the final consonant of each part (which is never repeated in *cynghanedd* as it would interfere with the main rhyme, and therefore the form) we get a sequence of consonants in the first part exactly repeated in the second. Only in a minority of cases do these consonants pick out the stresses. For example in the first line,

Y ceirw mawr y ceir eu medd

all four stresses are picked out by alliteration, as in Cynddelw; but in the sixth line, none of them are:

Ap Siencyn a'n pwys encyd

If you were trained only to spot alliteration at the beginning of words, you could miss it entirely. (That sixth line is also an example of a license that the *cynghanedd* poets allow themselves: the letter *n* can be ignored if it comes at the beginning of a sequence in either part of a line. In line 10, two voiced *g*'s count as an unvoiced *c*.)

This example from Tudur Aled is exceptional in that it involves only varieties of *cynghanedd groes*. Not many of the poets of the nobility used it as exclusively as that. Nevertheless even in Dafydd ap Gwilym (maybe a hundred and fifty years earlier) *cynghanedd groes* and *draws* preponderate over *sain*. From now on, the norm of *cynghanedd* – the kind that explains what it's all about – will be the full *cynghanedd groes*. Tudur Aled represents the orthodoxy of *groes* as Cynddelw does of *sain*. What you must look for now is not simply words that answer each other, sound for sound; it is rather sequences of phonemes that are repeated. Within limits it does not matter what words these phonemes are in. In the line

Na choller hyn, o'ch llaw rhawg

the sequence n-ch-ll-r(h) is repeated despite the fact that no single word in the second half of the line begins or ends with the same consonants as those in the first – and the *n* that begins the repetition is actually the last letter of the first half which is 'borrowed' for the purpose by the second. This degree of abstraction is why modern *cynghanedd* is unique: the concentration is always on sequences of phonemes rather than on words answering words.

It is worth looking at a *cywydd* by Dafydd ap Gwilym. This is an

extract from the one I translate as 'Trouble at a Tavern'. I mark
the divisions with a slash and italicise the *cynghanedd*:

Wedi cysg*u*,/ *tru* / *tr*myn,	*sain*
O *b*awb/ eithr myfi a *b*un,	*draws*
Profais yn hyf*edr* / *f*edru	*lusg*
Ar we*ly'r f*erch; / *alar f*u.	*groes* (ignore the first *r*.)
Cef*ais*,/ pan s*oniais*/ yna,	*sain*
Gwy*mp d*ig,/ nid oedd *gamp*au *d*a;	*draws*
Haws cod*i*,/ *d*rygion*i*/*d*rud	*sain*
*Yn d*rwsgl / nog *yn d*ra e*s*gud.	*draws*
Trew*ais*,/ ni *n*eidi*ais*/ *yn* iach	*sain*
Y *g*rimog,/ a *g*wae'*r* omach,	*groes*
W*rth* ys*tl*ys,/ ar wai*th* os*tl*er	*groes*
Yst*ôl* / groch *ffôl*,/ goruw*ch ff*èr.	*sain*

When at last, wretched journey!
All did sleep, save her and me,
I to reach the lady's bed
Most skilfully attempted.
But I fell, noised it abroad,
Tumbled brutally forward.
It's easier to be clumsy
Rising from such grief, than spry!
Nor was my leap unhurtful:
On a stupid and loud stool,
Ostler's work, to the chagrin
Of my leg, I barked my shin ...

(I give my translation, not because it answers the phrasing
exactly, but to give an idea of what's happening.)

Dafydd uses *cynghanedd* to push the language around, to splinter
it for (in this case) dramatic effect. Notice how, as the panic and
chaos increases, so, in these lines, does the complexity of the
cynghanedd. The first four lines are relatively relaxed – almost prim
in a conceited sort of way. Then the phrases start to fly off at
tangents, the *cynghanedd* becomes tighter and more all-embracing,
draws and *lusg* give way to *groes*, ending up with the elaborate *sain*
of the last line in which a rhyme and seven consonants pattern all
but the first syllable. This sort of analysis can, I know, run away

with one; but it is important to realise that *cynghanedd* is a supremely expressive instrument, and that its combination of freedom with complexity is quite different to what one normally thinks of as metrical difficulty. It is more like the problem facing a chess player about to make his next move: he has to move according to the rules, but which particular rule he chooses to obey and what he does with it are entirely up to him.

With modern *cynghanedd* the poet weaves his pattern out of all the phonemes in a line, or as many of them as he requires. He doesn't just pick out the stressed words. Instead of the metre giving weight to the central parts of any line, here the only word that *must* be picked out, either by alliteration or concealed rhyme, is the one at the end of the line, the word which both carries the main rhyme of each line and, usually, leads into the next. This means that the balance between centripetal and centrifugal tendencies in the metrical framework of the line is held by the poet's judgment, and is not biased by the metre itself, as it was in the *awdl*.

The use of *cynghanedd* in a *cywydd* is thus the main reason for the freedom that fourteenth and fifteenth-century poets found in the metre. This modern *cynghanedd* thinks essentially in terms of the phrase, not of the stressed word: it articulates individual phrases into an overall pattern, ideally suited to the voice freely descant-ing to an air being played on the harp. Without it the counterpoint of the *cywydd* would not be possible at all. But the *awdl* never recovered from its introduction. I believe that this was because it essentially contradicts the long *awdl* line: partly because of the difficulty of sustaining so delicate a tracery to a distance of more than seven or eight syllables, but more particularly in that the new insistence on the end of the line disturbed the balance of the *awdl*'s structure. An *awdl* is an accumulation of lines, each ending with the same rhyme. When one has heard this rhyme ten or twenty times, one tends to get hypnotised by it. It is quite essential to have points within the line with enough metrical interest to offset this mesmerising pull towards the rhyme. The new *cynghanedd* can of course manage this, but only at the cost of denying its own true nature, which is that of a mediator between going on and staying put. To expect such a creature always to pull the mind back and never to urge it forward is to risk making a *tour de force* and not a poem. In the *englyn*, on the other hand, where the new *cynghanedd* perhaps first crystallised out, it has always worked marvellously well. There are enough points in an *englyn* where the mind must wait poised for the next thing to happen so that the formal demands shall be met, for the new *cynghanedd* to do its job very happily indeed.

Here is a brief summary of the main kinds of modern *cynghanedd*. It must be pointed out, though, that as a recipe-book for strict metre poetry it is woefully inadequate: one would need many pages just to state the rules, without even mentioning the exceptions. That said, I must not give the impression that they are simply dry and academic. To write down the rules of any practical skill iș a difficult and time-consuming occupation. A Welshman with any interest in *cynghanedd* knows immediately and as if by instinct whether a line is correct or not. He does not have to look it up in a book.

Cynghanedd groes and *draws*. The line is divided into two parts. Each part can end with a stress (a), end on an unstressed syllable (b), or the first part can end stressed and the second unstressed (c). (It is not permitted for the first to end unstressed and the second stressed: this sounds arbitrary, but when you think about it there is no way that the consonants could be distributed round the final stress without involving the main rhyme.)

Cynghanedd groes. The sequence of consonants in the second half, except for those ending the final syllable, is an exact repetition of the sequence in the first, except that in (a) and (b) the consonants ending the final syllable are excluded. In (a) the consonant before the final stressed vowel has to be the same in both parts; in (b) and (c) the consonant before and immediately following the final stressed vowel has to be the same in both; but otherwise there are no restrictions on what words or stresses the consonants shall fall, provided the sequence is exactly preserved.

a) Ae*r* Hywe*l*, *b*u'n / *r*hyw*l*io *b*yd r-l-b r-l-b
b) A*p Si*enc*y*n,/ a'n *p*wy*s* enc*y*d p-s-n-c (n)- p-s-n-c

(An initial n, and sometimes r or m, in either part can by convention be ignored.)

c) *M*o*r* wy*ch* *g*wae*d*,/ *m*a*r*ch*o*g y*d*wyd m-r-ch-g-d m-r-ch-g-d

Cynghanedd groes o gyswllt. This is a variation where the repetition of the sequence in the second part begins before the first part ends.

a) *N*a *choll*er hyn/ o'*ch ll*aw *r*hawg   n-ch-ll-r n-ch-ll-r
b) O*nd dr*ygwei*thr*ed/ *r*hyw *gythr*awl   (n)-d-r-g-th-r d-r-g-th-r
c) *G*air a *dr*ig/ ar y *dr*ygwaith   g-r-d-r-g- g-r-d-r-g

Cynghanedd draws. As in *cynganedd groes* except that before the repetition of the sequence of consonants there is a bridge passage of consonants that play no part in the repetition. This bridge passage belongs to the second part of the line. The rules for stress in the two parts are the same as for *cynghanedd groes.*

a) O *b*awb / eithr myfi a *b*un   b-   b-
b) *D*y*f*od,/ bu chwedl e*d*i*f*ar   d-f   d-f
c) *Bl*in yw,/ megis *bl*ae*n* awen   b-l-n b-l-n

Cynghanedd sain. The line is divided into three parts. Part two rhymes with part one and forms *cynghanedd groes* or *draws* with part three, except that a fourth form is allowed, in that the second part may end on an unstressed syllable and the third on a stressed.

a) Yst*ôl* / *groch ffôl,*/ goruw*ch ff*èr   -ôl -ôl *and* g-r-ch-ff g-r- ch-ff
b) Cc*fais*/ pan *soniais* / yna   -ais -ais *and* s-n s-n
c) Ni'th ladd mab m*am, gam gym*wyll -am -am *and* g-m g-m
d) Haws cod*i, dr*igio*i dr*ud   -i -i *and* d-r d-r

The alliteration in these forms is often less than strict *cynghanedd draws* requires:

e) Wedi cysg*u,*/ *tru* / *tr*emyn   -u -u *and* t-r- t-r-m

There is another form, *cynghanedd sain gadwynog,* in which the line is divided into four parts. The first and third parts rhyme and the second and fourth parts alliterate.

Mae Cymr*o,*/ *t*aer / gyffr*o* / *t*wyll   -o -o *and* t- t-

APPENDIX ON METRES

This form is common in Dafydd ap Gwilym, but became rare later. It was never formally proscribed, however.

Cynghanedd lusg. The line is divided into two parts, and the second must end on a trochee – i.e. the final syllable is unstressed. The end of the first part rhymes with the stressed penultimate syllable of the second. It is the only serious exception to the rule that in classical Welsh versification the tonic accent is essential to a rhyme.

Codi o'r ostl*er* / nif*er*oedd   -er -er

Cynghanedd lusg is generally felt to be a rather weak variety, and is normally not allowed in the second line of a couplet or the last line of an *englyn*.

The Native Free Metres

The native free metres are similar to the strict ones save that they lack *cynghanedd*. The syllabic count is not always strict and there is some tendency to let the accent fall into trochaic, iambic or dactyllic patterns. But the rhyming is usually on the tonal accent – that is, two-syllable rhymes are rare – just as in the strict metres. One of the free metres, the *traethodl*, we have already discussed in relation to the *cywydd*.

It is simply a couplet of seven-syllable lines with a new rhyme every couplet:

> Nid ar un bwyd ac enllyn
> Y mae Duw yn porthi dyn.
> Amser a rodded i fwyd
> Ac amser i olochwyd,
> Ac amser i bregethu,
> Ac amser i gyfanheddu.
> Cerdd a genir ymhob gwledd
> I ddiddanu rhianedd,
> A phader yn yr eglwys
> I geisio tir Paradwys.

Other typical free metres that have strict-metre equivalents are:

Awdl gywydd. A couplet of seven-syllable lines. The end of the first rhymed with a word at the pause in the middle of the second. The second line carried the main rhyme. It was often used two couplets at a time for four line stanzas:

> Athrist oedd hen Adda lwys
> O'i wlad Baradwys dirion;
> Unwedd athrist wyf ar goedd –
> Paradwys oedd Gaernarfon.

Englyn cyrch. A couplet of *cywydd deuair hirion* (if strict) or *traethodl* (if free) followed by one of *awdl gywydd* with the same rhyme. As a free metre stanza this was called the *triban* measure:

> Myfi ydyw'r prydydd afiach,
> Ni chela'i mo'm cyfrinach;
> 'Rwy'n wan fy llais am deg ei llun
> A aeth i galyn gelach.

Cywydd deuair fyrion or short couplet. A couplet of four-syllable lines. If it is used as a strict metre, it obeys the rules of rhyming of the *cywydd deuair hirion.*

> Edrych yn dda.
> Di a gei yna
> Yn lle'r ddwy gog
> Ddau gyffylog.
> O medri di
> Ddal y rheini,
> Hwynt-hwy a dalan'
> Geioniog fechan.

Perhaps the most typical form used in *penillion*-singing is a quatrain of eight-syllable lines rhyming in couplets:

> Mynd i'r ardd i dorri pwysi,
> Pasio'r lafant, pasio'r lili,
> Pasio'r pincs a'r rhosys cochion,
> Torri pwysi o ddanadl poethion.

This form is clearly trochaic in its rhythm, but the rhyming is still only on the final syllable, the tonic accent.

APPENDIX ON METRES

The Carol and other developments

After the decline of the bardic order in the sixteenth century, a new kind of strict metre, the *carol*, became popular. Its basic structure (which varied from poem to poem) was dictated by its tune. This led to complicated verse forms using *cynghanedd* but based on stress not syllable count. Had the poetry been more exciting, the *carol* might well have emerged as the dominant form of Welsh poetry and shaken off the antiquarian revival of the strict mediaeval metres in the eighteenth century. It has survived precariously as a folk form, but as a literary revolution it succumbed. Compare the situation in eighteenth-century Munster where their more thorough-going accentual measures banished the metres of *dán díreach* based on syllable count. But then, the Munster poets wrote great poetry. On the whole the poets of the Welsh *carol* were too easily satisfied with prettiness and purely verbal excitement. There is one *carol* in this collection (by Huw Morus), which I have translated more or less as a song.

In the twentieth century, writers such as T. Gwynn Jones and Euros Bowen have used *cynghanedd* with accentual metres and even with free verse. This is a logical development that the *carol* was too feeble to explore.

The main drive of Welsh poetry, however, was towards the use of English accentual metres without *cynghanedd*. This gained impetus from the hymns of William Williams of Pantycelyn and has since the early nineteenth century, at any rate, provided the medium of most of the poets translated in this book.

Principles of Translation

Poems in English metres, like the sonnet or blank verse, offer the translator from Welsh as much, but no more, difficulty as poetry from other European languages customarily does. I have in general tried to follow the metre exactly in such matters as line-length and rhyme-schemes. Sometimes I have allowed myself a freer rhythm than the original; and in some cases I have simplified the rhymes, and even abandoned rhyme altogether, when I felt that the meaning was being unnecessarily twisted. Thus 'This Poor Fellow' by W.J. Gruffydd is rhymed in the original like a Keats' ode.

Poems in the native 'free' metres are more difficult. Sometimes, as in Alun's 'Song to the Nightingale', I have abandoned the original metre altogether, and tried to find an English metre roughly equal to it in complexity and general feeling. Dafydd ap Gwilym's *traethodl*, 'The Grey Friar', is a special case: I translated it as part of my search for an English metre with which to render the *cywydd*. I used a three-stress iambic line, with English-type rhyming. This seems to me preferable to the octosyllabic couplet, but were I doing the same poem now I would certainly try to use the original rhythm. Elsewhere, in the free metres, I have followed the Welsh-schemes fairly closely.

The strict metres, unlike these other two types, cannot possibly be used in English for any length of time. I have already explained that for the *awdl* I have used the four-stress Anglo-Saxon line; and for the *englyn* I have used free verse, preserving as far as I judged proper the syllabic patterns of the original. My technique with the *cywydd* is likely to be more controversial: the hunt for a method to translate *cywyddau* has been in progress for well over a century, and everyone has his own idea of how it should be done. The earliest translators (as was natural) used the octosyllabic couplet. This was nearly the worst possible English metre for the purpose: its deadly fluency and plebeian nature are quite unlike the aristocratic poise of a good *cywydd*.

Sensing this, Sir Idris and David Bell, in their *Fifty Poems of Dafydd ap Gwilym*, took a leaf out of Hopkins and 'sprang' their octosyllabics. Their verses come close to doggerel, but do preserve some of Dafydd's gusto, if not his formal grace and sophistication. But used on the fifteenth century masters, the Bells' method seems to me almost uniformly awful. Other writers have abandoned rhyme altogether and used free verse. Gwyn Williams was not the first to do this, but he is easily the most prolific. The trouble with using free verse to translate short couplets is that it tends to get out of rhythm, and therefore monotonous. Gwyn Williams in *The Rent That's Due to Love* succeeded very well with the fifteenth century closed couplets of Siôn Cent and the love poets – he called them all Dafydd ap Gwilym, but that wasn't his fault. His later book, *The Burning Tree*, is both more ambitious and less successful. The poems fall apart, into a series of images. This is the trouble with free verse: it isolates the imagery too much, at the expense of the whole poem.

APPENDIX ON METRES

In my *Formal Poems* of 1960 I think I was the first to use the principle of syllabic equivalence for the treatment of Welsh metres. Thus, for the *cywydd* – the poem is not a translation, but merely an imitation –

> I know a royal birchgrove
> Satan himself could not find.
> See, there's the meadow-pipit
> That tells you, give way to love.
> God's will be done in birchwoods
> Altarwise in the rich Mass...

This principle I rejected for translating *cywyddau*, though not *englynion*, because it did not seem to me to give me enough control. It was used on a large scale by Joseph P. Clancy in his *Mediaeval Welsh Lyrics*, a book it would be churlish not to welcome. My objection to it as a medium, however, is that it is too mechanical; and also that I believe Professor Clancy failed sometimes to think out what he meant by a syllable, and what he meant by stress. I am quite sure that, in both categories, the Welsh poets would have rejected some of his examples.

I next tried a rhyming couplet of three-stress lines, as I have already explained. About ten *cywyddau* were already finished and my dissatisfaction was growing towards stalemate. The line was twisting translations out of shape. Every couplet had to be warped into something else before it would fit at all. It avoided the jogtrot of the octosyllabic, but not very convincingly; and it wasn't really long enough for paraphrasing the extreme concision of the Welsh. I was (so it seemed) putting myself out of the running. Only two *cywyddau* remain from this period of my work – the rest I re-translated completely.

My salvation came from Ireland. There is an Irish strict metre called *Deibhidhe* that at first sight seems unnervingly like the *cywydd*. It is written in couplets of seven-syllable lines, rhyming accented with unaccented syllables. I had always assumed that this type of rhyme was almost impossible in English, until I read Frank O'Connor's translation of the famous 'Scholar and his Cat'. In his note Mr O'Connor says:

> Robin Flower's well-known translation in the metre of

'Twinkle, twinkle, little star' ignores the slowness of the original, which approximates more to iambic pentameter.

I could pass over the last extraordinary clause, for here, in outline, was my problem. I read on –

> Each of us pursues his trade,
> I and Pangur my comrade,
> His whole fancy on the hunt,
> And mine for learning ardent.

You will observe that the rhyming is not quite accurate; and that at first the effect sounds awkward. But the first fault (if it is a fault) is unavoidable in English; and I found that much of the awkwardness disappeared as one got used to it. Here was my *cywydd* metre in English. It remained to see if I could use it in translation. I tried it first on the two eighteenth century *cywyddau* in this book, and found that it was extraordinarily difficult, but not impossible. The *cywydd* in a sense is rhythmically an easier problem than the *deibhidhe* because it can vary the order – accented unaccented or unaccented accented – whereas the Irish metre cannot. The total effect was (I thought) sufficiently like a *cywydd* to warrant continuing the experiment. It was possible both to translate reasonably literally and to bend the metre to the rhythms of poetry. The difficulty was, and remained, quite formidable. It often took a week to translate a single poem. But no other method seemed anywhere like as faithful.

This is not an English *cywydd*. The metre is a compromise. The rhymes vary from clear to almost non-existent. In a few cases I have not rhymed a couplet or two, because they seemed adequate lines without it. Mostly, I think, the effect is more like a kind of alliteration – at the end of a word, not the beginning – than a kind of rhyme. I confess it sometimes still sounds awkward, in spite of my efforts. But I believe this is endemic to translating *cywyddau*, and is possibly not wholly unfaithful even to the effect of the originals. Sometimes, in the fashion of the Welsh poets themselves, I had to use compound words beyond what is usually considered legitimate in English. For all this I can only plead my incompetence to do better.

As for *cynghanedd* I have generally avoided it in its full forms even when the opportunity presented itself of using it. Full Welsh *cynghanedd* sounds too much like a tongue-twister in English – even Hopkins rarely made it sound natural. But imperfect *cynghanedd* of various sorts I have used quite often, in lines like "He fell dead, widowed the wine." This seems to give more of the effect of Welsh poetry than jangles like "A friend, with a week-end wink" or the like.

Appendix on Names

In Welsh, a man was called by his Christian name: Gwalchmai, Dafydd, Ifor, etc. He might also have a nickname, like Llywelyn Goch, Llywelyn the Red. If one wanted to be more specific, one added one or more patronymics: Dafydd ap Gwilym (Dafydd son of Gwilym), Rhys ap Rhydderch ap Rhys ap Maredudd (Rhys son of Rhydderch son of Rhys son of Maredudd). Unless one was compiling a genealogical tree, one such patronymic was usually adequate. The father might be called by his nickname, as in Gruffudd ab yr Ynad Coch – Gruffudd son of the Red Judge. *Ap* (son of), or *ab* before a vowel, is a shortened form of *mab*, son, which corresponds to the Irish *Mac*.

Surnames did not really make much headway until the Tudors. Then patronymics were converted into surnames by rule of thumb. A man called Siôn ap Gwilym, for instance, was likely to be made John Williams. Jones or John arose from ap Siôn; Pritchard from ap Rhisiart; Bevan from ab Ifan; and so on. These surnames have been a colossal nuisance ever since. Jones is proverbially meaningless, but many of the others are equally so. Other surnames arose from nicknames: Lloyd comes from *llwyd*, grey, and Vaughan from *fychan*, a mutated form of *bychan*, little.

It is common practice in Wales to have three names: a Christian name (John or Siôn, David or Dafydd) which is used in everyday speech; a bardic name – rather like a pedigree name of a dog – something like Meirion or Cyfeiliog, the older the better; and a surname – Jones or Williams or Thomas, sometimes hyphenated with another – which you use with a Mr in front of it for formal occasions.

It is quite absurd to call a Welsh poet (or even an Anglo-Welsh poet like Dylan Thomas) by his surname alone. The only time that would be done would be if he was being tried in a police court, when it sounds like an insult. David Gwenallt Jones, for example, is quite unidentifiable if you call him Jones. He puts plain Gwenallt on the front of his books of poems. If a man hasn't got a bardic name, or doesn't like it, he can follow one of a number of conventions. Either he or his friends can find him a new bardic name, or a nickname. He can tie his Christian name to his surname, and use the whole lot together; or, like W.J. Gruffydd, he can make his initials into a magic cipher mystically united with his surname so that never the twain are sundered.

In this book, I have mostly avoided the English convention of writing poet's names, except where it is plain that the poets themselves preferred it. I have not, fairly obviously, been consistent even in this. But I prefer to call Ieuan Glan Geirionydd that, rather than the paltry Evan Evans he was christened.

Appendix on Pronunciation

The following simplified guide to Welsh pronunciation will be found useful. Welsh is written very nearly phonetically, so that if you know what its symbols represent, any word can be pronounced more or less by rule of thumb. There are, naturally, a few exceptions.

THE WELSH ALPHABET

a, b, c, ch, d, dd, e, f, ff, g, ng, h, i, j, l, ll, m, n, o, p, ph, r, rh, s, t, th, u, w, y.

Notes. 1. These letters all stand for different sounds, except *ph*, which stands for the same as *ff*.

2. In order to fit the Latin alphabet to the sounds of the Welsh language, certain double letters (e.g. *ch, dd*) are used. These, however, count but a single letter in Welsh (like our *w*) and represent a single sound.

CONSONANTS

The following consonants are pronounced as in English:

b, c, d, g, h, j, l, m, n, p, r, s, t.

Notes. 1. *c, g, s* are always given their English 'hard' value (as in *cap, gap, sap*), and are never soft (as in *lace, huge, lose*).

2. *r* is always trilled.

3. *j* is found only in borrowed words, like *jam* or *Jones*.

The other consonants are pronounced as follows:

ch ... as in Scottish *loch* or (in a few borrowed words like *China*) as in English.

dd ... a voiced *th*, as in English *the* or *loathe*.

f ... as English *v*, as in *love*. Cf. English *of*.

ff ... as English *f*, as in *if*. Cf. English *off*.

ng ... as in English *singing*. Occasionally (as in *Bangor*) it represents two sounds, as in English *finger*.

ll ... an unvoiced unilateral *l*, pronounced by putting the tongue in position to sound an *l*, and then hissing.

ph ... the same as *ff* or English *ph* in *philosophy*.

rh ... an unvoiced, aspirated *r*.

th ... unvoiced as in *thin* or *kith*; never as in *then* or *with*.

Note. The foreigner to Wales is often alarmed by seeing words like *nghath*, *mhen*, *ngardd*. There is no need to be. They result from initial mutation of *cath*, *pen* and *gardd* after certain other words, such as the preposition *yn* (or *ym*, or *yng*), in, and the possessive *fy*, my: *nghath* is not a meaningful word by itself, and is as unpronounceable to a Welshman as it is to you. The following examples may clarify the position:

fy nghath (my cat) ... pronounced *fy'ng hath*.

fy mhen (my head) ... pronounced *fy'm hen*.

yng ngardd Rhiannon (in Rhiannon's garden) ... pronounced *yng ardd*.

yng Nghaernarfon (in Caernarfon) ... pronounced *yng Haernarfon*.

VOWELS

a ... long, as in *father*; short, as in *cap*.

e ... long, as the *a* in *made*; short, as in *get*.

i ... long, as in *machine*; short, as in *pip*.

o ... long, as in *sore*; short as in *pop*.

u ... in north Wales has a different sound; but in south Wales, which is obviously the convention for a beginner to follow, pronounce as *i*.

w ... long, as in *fool*; short, as in *took* (Welsh *w* equals English *oo*).

y ... has two sounds. In final syllables and in monosyllables (except *y*, *yr*, *yn*, *yng*, *ym*, *fy*, *dy*, *syr*) it is pronounced like *u* – and therefore, in south Wales, like *i*. Everywhere else it sounds like the *o* of *honey*.

Notes. 1. The English equivalents of these vowels are only approximate. Welsh vowels are all pure, whereas English long vowels almost always are dipthongized.

2. *i* and *w*, besides being vowels, can also be semi-consonants. *i* is pronounced like the *y* in *yet*; and *w* as in *watch*.

3. *i* after *s* (particularly followed by another vowel) is usually pronounced like the *sh* in *Shanghai*. Thus, English *shop* becomes Welsh *siop*.

VOWEL LENGTH

All unaccented syllables are short. In monosyllabic words the following rules apply:

1. A vowel is short if followed by two or more consonants, or by *p, t, c, m, ng*.

2. A vowel is long if followed by *b, d, g, f, ff, dd, th, ch, s*.

3. If it is followed by *l, n, r* or *ll*, the vowel can be long or short; if it is long, it is often marked by a circumflex: *mân*, small. But many words are not so marked: *hen*, old, has a long vowel.

DIPHTHONGS

ae, ai, au ... as the *i* in *fine*.

aw ... as the *ow* in *cow*.

ei, eu ... pronounce the *o* of *honey* followed quickly by the *ee* of *feed*.

ew ... pronounce the *e* of *get* followed quickly by the *oo* of *took*.

oe, oi, ou. oy ... as the *oi* in *join*.

ow, yw (except in final syllables) ... more or less as *ow* in *cow*.

wy ... there are no sure rules. Either the *w* is a semi-consonant, when the *y* goes according to its own rules; or the *w* is a vowel and the consonantal element is represented by the *y*. If there is a circumflex on either, that's the vowel.

uw, iw, yw (in final positions) ... the first letter is more or less a semi-consonant, like the *y* in *yet*.

STRESS

Final syllables are stressed if they:

1. Begin with an h.

2. Are marked by a circumflex (long vowel) or acute accent (short vowel).

3. Are a result of contraction, as in *Cymraeg*, from *Cymrá-eg*.

Otherwise, words are always stressed on the last syllable but one, except for a class of personal pronouns (not often used), some words beginning with the suffixes *ys-*, *ym-*, *yng-* (but by no means all), and some borrowings from English which retain their English stress.

Glossary

ABERFFRAW. Royal seat of the princes of Gwynedd, in Anglesey.

AENEAS. Legendary hero of Virgil's *Aeneid*, a Trojan who settled in Italy and whose descendants founded Rome. His grandson, Brutus, was believed to be the founder of Britain.

ALUN MABON. The hero of Ceiriog's pastoral of that name.

ALYSANNA. An unknown medieval moralist.

ANN. The traditional name of Mary's mother, grandmother of Christ.

ARAWN. The king of Annwfn, the Celtic Otherworld, wrongly identified with Hell. See the First Branch of the *Mabinogion*.

ARGOED. An imaginary country in Gaul that T. Gwynn Jones invented.

ARGOED LLWYFAIN. A battlefield where Urien of Rheged defeated the Anglo-Saxons under Fflamddwyn.

ARFON. Cantref of Gwynedd, on the mainland facing Anglesey.

ARWYSTLI. A cantref of South Powys (mid-Wales).

ASAPH, ST. A cathedral town in Clwyd; one of the four bishoprics of Wales.

BELI MAWR. A legendary ruler of Britain from whom all the early Welsh dynasties claimed descent.

BELYN or BELEN OF LLŶN. A ruler of Llŷn (Gwynedd), who may have fought against Edwin of Northumbria (d. 633). His was one of the three famous war-bands of Welsh tradition.

BEUNO. An early Welsh saint.

BRÂN AP LLŶR LLEDIAITH. Brân the Blessed, a colossus figure, who is the ruler of the Island of the Mighty, or Britain, in the Second Branch of the *Mabinogion*.

CADFAN. An early Welsh Saint.

CADWALADR. King of Gwynedd and son of Cadwallon (*q.v.*) He came to be regarded as the promised deliverer who would return to champion the Welsh against the English.

CADWALLON. Seventh-century King of Gwynedd who, according to Bede, allied himself with the King of Mercia to meet the growing menace of Edwin of Northumbria, whom together they defeated and killed in 633; and thus the Welsh were reunited with their Cumbrian kinsfolk. This reunion, however, was finally broken at the fatal Winwaed Field (655).

CAERLEON. 'Fortress of the legions upon the Usk' – the Roman fort of Isca in Gwent. Connected with the Arthurian legend, after Geoffrey of Monmouth.

CAER SIDDI. One of the names of the Celtic Otherworld.

CAERWYS. A parish in Clwyd.

CAMLAN. The last disastrous battle of Arthur, perhaps *Camboglanna* or Birdoswald on Hadrian's Wall.

CANTREF. An administrative division of land, corresponding roughly to the English hundred. A *gwlad* like Gwynedd (north Wales) contained twelve or so *cantrefi*. Each cantref was then further divided into two or more *cymydau*.

CAROL. A song. In Welsh it often means a more specialized variety of song, popular from the sixteenth to the eighteenth centuries, in which the accentual metres borrowed from English songs were elaborately decorated with *cynghanedd*. The poems by Huw Morus and Owen Gruffydd in this anthology are *carolau* in the Welsh.

CATRAETH. (See the note prefacing Aneirin's *Gododdin*.) Catterick, in Yorkshire.

CWMWD. See *Cantref*.

CYNDRWYN. See *Cynddylan*.

CYNDDYLAN. Son of Cyndrwyn, lord of Pengwern, probably Shrewsbury. There is extant an elegy to him from the seventh century; but it is in the somewhat later saga-literature that he really achieves poetic fame.

CYNGHANEDD. A metrical system of multiple alliteration and rhyme within every line of the Welsh strict metres.

CYNLLAITH. A district of mid-Powys on the English border facing Oswestry, in which Owain Glyndŵr's castle of Sycharth stood.

CYPRIS. 'The Cyprian' – one of the names of Venus, the Goddess of Love. In alchemy, copper was her metal. This is my solution of a famous *crux* in Dafydd ap Gwilym's *Seagull – Siprys dyn giprys dan gopr*: no very likely explanation has been advanced of *Siprys*. It would, however, be the natural Welsh transliteration of *Cypris*, if one gives the *c* its medieval soft sound. The poet then compares his girl-friend to Venus, a girl who is sought beneath copper (hair), as is natural for a goddess of that metal. He is, in fact, making an alchemical pun. The form 'Cypris' or 'The Cyprian' is found quite often in alchemical literature, and also in the *Carmina Burana*, love-songs of the wandering scholars of Europe. Dafydd might have picked it up from one of these.

CYWYDD. One of the three divisions of the Welsh strict metres. Though there are in fact four kinds of *cywydd*, only one is usually meant – the *cywydd deuair hirion*, seven-syllable lines in couplets. This was the dominant metre of Welsh poetry from Dafydd ap Gwilym until the eighteenth century.

DEHEUBARTH. South Wales.

DERFEL. An early Welsh saint.

DEWI. St. David, patron saint of Wales.

DINDAETHWY. A *cwmwd*, the south-eastern part of Anglesey, after an early fort of that name near Menai Bridge.

DINORWIG. A township, near Snowdon, in Gwynedd.

DURGRYS. An unknown medieval moralist.

DWYNWEN. Early Welsh saint, patron of lovers. Her shrine was at Llanddwyn near Newborough, in Anglesey.

DYDDGU. A girl to whom Dafydd ap Gwilym wrote poems.

DYFED. The old Pembrokeshire, and surrounding districts.

DYGEN FREIDDIN. A stream known as Dygen flows by Craig Freiddin in Powys.

EDNYFED. Llywelyn the Great's chief minister, and ancestor of the Tudors. Died 1246.

EFYRNWY. The river Vyrnwy in mid-Wales.

EDWIN. Once a king of Tegeingl (Clwyd) and an ancestor of Siôn ap Rhisiart, Abbot of Valle Crucis.

EIDDIG. The conventional name for the Jealous Husband in Welsh love poetry.

EIGR. Arthur's mother, famous for her beauty.

ELPHIN. Son of Urien of Rheged. He was the patron of Taliesin in legend.

EMRAIS. Emrais apparently occurs as a name for Snowdonia. Dinas Emrys, in medieval orthography Dinas Emrais, is an early fort near Beddgelert.

ENGLYN. A verse of three or four lines in strict metre with one rhyme. There are several kinds, but since the thirteenth century nearly all *englynion* are of the variety called *unodl union*, with four lines.

EPYNT. A mountain in Powys.

ERYRI. Snowdonia, the hub of Gwynedd.

ERECHWYDD or **YRECHWYDD.** An unlocated area, or people, in sixth-century north Britain.

EWIAS or **EUAS.** A district in north Gwent, between Brecon and Hereford.

FFLAMDDWYN. The word means 'Flame-bearer' and was a Welsh nickname for the Anglo-Saxon leader who was defeated in the sixth century by Urien of Rheged at the battle of Argoed Llwyfain.

GARWY. A legendary Welsh lover.

GERAINT. A hero of SW. Britain who was brought into Welsh Arthurian traditions. See the romance of Geraint in the *Mabinogion.*

GODODDIN. A British tribe in NE. Britain. See the note preceding Aneirin's poem of the same name.

GODDAU. An unlocated area in sixth-century North Britain.

GRUFFUDD AP CYNAN. King of Gwynedd, 1081-1137. Half a Viking, he won his kingdom by conquest after previous unsuccessful attempts, and laid the foundations for Gwynedd's supremacy over the next two centuries. He was associated traditionally with a revival of Welsh poetry; his reign, and that of his son, Owain Gwynedd, mark the beginning of the period of the *Gogynfeirdd.* See the Introduction.

GWEN. Not really a name, but an epithet (fem. of *gwyn*) meaning 'white' 'fair' or 'blessed'. But, as in English eighteenth-century usage with 'fair', often used alone to indicate a girl.

GWENHWYFAR. Arthur's wife. Whether because of national sentiment or because of the vogue for Arthurian romance, it seems to have become a popular girl's name after the conquest in 1282.

GWENT. SE. Wales, roughly the old county of Monmouthshire.

GWYNEDD. NE. Wales, varying in extent, but including Anglesey and the old counties of Caernarfonshire, Merioneth and most of Denbighshire and Flintshire.

HELEDD. The daughter of Cynddylan (*q.v.*) in the saga-literature.

ISEULT'S GEM. Perhaps a better translation would be 'chaplet'. Iseult was Tristan's beloved. The phrase arose from the habit of exchanging gifts between lovers, and came to mean anything that was precious.

LOCHLYN. Scandinavia. The men of Lochlyn were the Norsemen.

LOMBARD, Thomas. A medieval moralist, probably Peter Lombard, 'the master of the sentences'.

LLAN EOS. Literally, Church, or enclosure, of the Nightingale. Probably an invented name.

LLIW. A river name, perhaps the Dee.

LLŶN or LLEYN. The cantref of Gwynedd that comprises the Caernarfonshire peninsula.

LLYWARCH HEN. See the note preceding the ninth-century saga-poetry.

LLYWELYN AB IORWERTH. Llywelyn the Great, King of Gwynedd, prince of Aberffraw and lord of Snowdon, 1187-1240. After an initial period of civil war, he became overlord of practically all of independent Wales. He tried to solve the political problem by establishing a quasi-feudal state on the Norman model. But tribal custom worked against this aim, and when he died, the future was still unsure.

LLYWELYN AP GRUFFUDD. Llywelyn the Last, grandson of the above, ruled from 1246 to Edward I's conquest in 1282. He continued his grandfather's policy, but a series of somewhat unwise moves against the English crown precipitated his downfall. He was the only Welsh ruler to have been granted the title 'Prince of Wales'.

MABINOGI. The word means 'Boyhood'; it was also used of the *Four Branches of the Mabinogi*, that we incorrectly call the *Mabinogion*, and hence of any tale.

MAELOR. The district of northern Powys in which Wrexham is situated.

MARTIN, ST. Bishop of Tours in the fourth century.

MEIRIONNYDD. The southernmost cantref of Gwynedd.

MENAI. The strait dividing Anglesey from the mainland.

MERFYN. King of Gwynedd, 825-844. Though not of the royal line of Gwynedd, he handed on to his son Rhodri Mawr a much strengthened land.

MERLIN or MYRDDIN. A poet, prophet and magician of a rather confused legend. He went mad and wandered the woodlands (like the Irish Suibhne) and was connected to a girl called Gwenddydd. Many poems of a prophetic nature were attributed to him.

MÔN or MONA. Anglesey.

MORDAF. One of the three generous ones of Britain, the other two being Rhydderch and Nudd.

MORFUDD. The wife of a man from Uwch Aeron, nicknamed Y Bwa Bach, the little Bow. Dafydd ap Gwilym wrote many poems to her; in other love-poems, perhaps, the name is a conventional name for a sweetheart.

MYNYDDAWG MWYNFAWR. Lord of Dineiddyn, leader of the Gododdin in the sixth century. See the note prefacing Aneirin's poem, *The Gododdin*.

MYNYW. St. David's, the principal shrine of Dewi Sant, and a cathedral in Pembrokeshire. One of the four bishoprics of Wales, the others being Llandaff, Bangor and St. Asaph.

NANNAU. A mansion near Dolgellau.

NUDD. One of the three generous ones of Britain, with Mordaf and Rhydderch.

OWAIN GLYNDŴR. Often called Owen Glendower. A nobleman of Powys who led a national revolt against England in 1400. By 1403 he was master of most of Wales, and engaged in the conspiracy of Mortimer and Percy against Henry IV. He set up a parliament at Machynlleth, four members from each *cwmwd* or district, and proposed far-reaching reforms in the Church, including the elevation of St. David's to an archbishopric and the setting up of two Welsh universities. He signed a treaty with France in 1404, but a French expedition failed to offset his waning fortunes. By 1409 the 'revolt' was practically over. Owain Glyndŵr is a mysterious figure, but his claim to be regarded as the first great Welsh Nationalist seems fairly substantial.

OWAIN GWYNEDD. Son of Gruffudd ap Cynan (*q.v.*), king of Gwynedd 1137-70. Under him, Gwynedd became stronger, literature flourished, and the power of England was contained. He survived two punitive expeditions by Henry II against him, and succeeded for a time in uniting the Welsh princes under his banner. But he left the political problem unsolved for his successors.

PANTYCELYN. The farmhouse home, in Carmarthenshire, of William Williams, the eighteenth-century Methodist and hymn-writer. Williams is usually known in Wales as Pantycelyn.

PENIARTH. A mansion in Gwynedd where an extensive library

of Welsh manuscripts, including an important early copy of the *Mabinogion*, was collected. The Peniarth collection is now in the National Library of Wales.

PORTH WYGYR. Cemais in Anglesey.

POWYS. The ancient kingdom of mid-Wales, comprising the counties of Montgomeryshire and south Denbighshire, together with parts of Shropshire, Merionethshire and Radnorshire. In the late twelfth century it split up into North and South, or Powys Fadog and Powys Wenwynwyn respectively.

PRIAM. King of Troy.

PYWER or PYWER LEW. An ancestor of Owain Glyndŵr.

RHEGED. The ancient British kingdom of SW. Scotland and Cumberland.

RHIANNON. In the First Branch of the *Mabinogion* Rhiannon is the wife of Pwyll, 'Head of Annwfn' and mother of Pryderi; she is wrongly punished on a charge of killing her son, who has been snatched by the powers of the other world. In the Third Branch she marries a second time, with Manawydan son of Llŷr, and is imprisoned in a magic fortress. Originally her name meant 'Great Queen'.

The singing of the birds of Rhiannon, according to Welsh tradition, gave sleep to the living and awoke the dead.

RHIWFELEN. Literally, 'Yellow Slope', to the north of Valle Crucis Abbey near Llangollen.

RHOS. The name of the two cantrefi, one in Gwynedd, the other in Dyfed. Rhys Grug captured the latter.

RHYDODYN. A mansion near Llansawel, Dyfed.

SANTIAGO. Next to Rome, the shrine of St. James of Compostella in Spain was the most popular in Europe.

SAUL. St. Paul before he was converted.

TALIESIN. A sixth-century poet: but also the hero of a folk-tale. A good deal of very obscure poems are foisted on to Taliesin in the manuscripts. They contain many references to Celtic myth, and also some early references to Arthur.

TÂL Y MOELFRE. A headland on Anglesey where the naval battle between Owain Gwynedd and Henry II was fought.

TRENN. A township in east Powys, perhaps in modern Shropshire.

TYWI. A river in south Wales.

TYWYN. A mansion in Dyfed, near the mouth of the river Teifi.

GLOSSARY

URIEN. A sixth-century king of Rheged, celebrated by Taliesin.

UWCH AERON. A cantref of Dyfed.

YALE or IÂL. A district of north Powys, near Llangollen.

YNYR. The ancestor of the noble family of Nannau (*q.v.*).

YSTUDFACH. A medieval poet of whom nothing is known.

Index of Poets

INDEX OF POETS